Introduction

'Miscellany' *noun* a miscellaneous collectio
or unrelated items.

The entries on the pages that follow are indeed mis[illegible] in that their topics and themes are diverse and seemingly unconnected. Of course, what ties them together is that each and every one is a celebration of the many different aspects of Sheffield, its people, culture, geography and history. Entries are alphabetical, with occasional narrative listings on a broader theme – for example 'disasters' and 'sport.'

I hope that your experience as you flick through this book will be similar to my own when researching and compiling it. I imagine that, like me, you will know Sheffield better than some and not as well as others. I enjoyed a fascinating voyage of discovery into a city that I thought I knew well. This journey took me down rabbit warrens of trivia and to new vantage points from which to view and take in everything that makes Sheffield what it is. I made new personal discoveries and came away with a more coherent understanding of how Sheffield 'fits together'.

Please do not take offence at the inclusion or omission of an entry on any particular topic. What is contained is, by definition, limited by the size of this publication and a need to stop and draw a line somewhere. Perhaps there will be an even more expansive compendium in the future, so please feel free to make suggestions as to what could be added.

I sincerely hope that this book gives you some *'Wow, I never knew that'* and *'That makes sense now'* moments, and that you too come away with an even greater appreciation of our great city.

John Coats

© John Coats 2020

Printed and published by:
ALD Design & Print
279 Sharrow Vale Road
Sheffield S11 8ZF

Telephone 0114 267 9402
E:mail alistair@aldprint.co.uk
ISBN 1-901587-93-7

First published November 2020

All rights reserved
No part of this publication may be reproduced, stored in a retrieval system or transmitted in any form or by any means, electronic, mechanical, photocopying, recording or otherwise, without the written permission of the publisher.

All views and comments printed in this book are those of the author and should not be attributed to the publisher.

Contents

A-Roads

All A Roads passing through Sheffield are listed below along with their start and end points.

Road	Start	End
A57	Liverpool	Lincoln
A61	Derby	Thirsk
A616	Newark-on-Trent	Huddersfield
A621	Sheffield	Baslow
A625	Sheffield	A623
A629	Rotherham	Skipton
A630	Sheffield	M18 Junction 4
A6101	Rivelin	Hillsborough
A6102	Greenhill	Deepcar
A6109	Sheffield	Rotherham
A6135	M1 Junction 30	M1 Junction 36
A6178	Sheffield	Rotherham
A6187	Castleton	Hathersage Rd

ABC

Sheffield new wave band ABC was formed by Mark White and Stephen Singleton (two thirds of earlier Sheffield group *Vice Versa)* in 1980 along with music journalist Martin Fry.

Their first album, *Lexicon of Love*, released in 1982 reached number 1 in the UK charts and has received platinum certification in the UK.

Chart singles *Poison Arrow*, *The Look of Love* and *All of my Heart* reached 6, 4 and 5 respectively in the UK charts in the same year.

ABC broke up in 1991. Martin Fry resurrected the group in 1997 and is still recording and performing.

Airport

Sheffield City Airport (SZD)

Opened 1997, last flight 2002, licence withdrawn and final closure in 2008.

The short runway, along with the opening of the much larger Robin Hood Doncaster Sheffield Airport were two contributory factors for the non-viability of Sheffield City Airport. The airport has since been redeveloped as the Sheffield Business Park, although the original control tower remains intact.

Destinations

Amsterdam, Belfast, Brussels,
Dublin, Edinburgh, Jersey, London.

Passenger Numbers

Year	Passengers
1998	46,000
1999	75,000
2000	60,000
2001	33,000
2002	13,000

Runway Length:

Heathrow: 3902m

Doncaster: 2893m

Sheffield: 1211m

Landing Requirements:

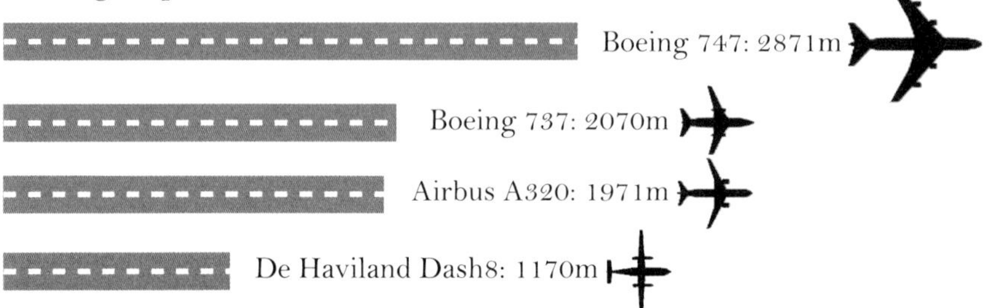

Allsorts

	Sheffield	Elsewhere
1842	Bassets founded in Sheffield by George Bassett	
1864		'Unclaimed Baby' jellied sweets first produced in Lancashire
1876	George Basset elected Mayor of Sheffield	
1880		Maynards founded in London
1899	Tray of sweets dropped creating 'Allsorts' mixture	
1918	Bassetts produced 'Peace Babies' to celebrate the end of the war	
1926	Bertie Bassett created as mascot for the company	
1933	Bassets moved to site in Owlerton	
1953	'Peace Babies' rebranded by Bassetts as 'Jelly Babies'	
1985		Trebor purchased Maynards for £7.5m
1989	Cadbury – Schweppes bought Bassetts for £91m	Cadbury – Schweppes purchased Trebor for £147m

2010 Kraft Foods purchased Cadbury - Schweppes for £11.5bn

2012 Kraft Foods renamed Mondelez

2016 Maynards and Bassetts brands combined within Mondelez empire - now 'Maynards Bassetts Liquorice Allsorts' and 'Maynards Bassetts Jelly Babies'

Coconut rolls | Cream Rock | Liquorice Cuttings | Aniseed jelly spogs | Liquorice sandwiches

B-Roads

All B Roads in Sheffield are listed below, along with their more commonly known street names

Road	Street Names
B6053	Mosborough Parkway, Station Rd
B6054	Bradway Rd, Greenhill Main Rd, Greenhill Parkway
B6057	Jordanthorpe Parkway
B6058	Station Rd (Mosborough)
B6063	Hollybank Rd, Hollinsend Rd, Gleadless Bank
B6064	Woodhouse Rd, Normanton Spring Rd, Coisley Hill, Sheffield Rd, Tannery St, Market St, Station Rd (Woodhouse)
B6065	Richmond Rd, Orgreave Rd, Laverack St
B6066	Beaver Hill Rd, Rotherham Rd, Highfield Lane
B6068	Abbey Lane
B6069	Brocco Bank, Clarkhouse Rd, Clarkson St
B6070	Duke St, City Rd
B6071	Granville St, Shrewsbury Rd, Talbot St, Bernard St, Bernard Rd, Foley St, Leveson St
B6073	Exchange Place, Exchange St, Furnival Rd, Lovetot Road
B6074	Hillfoot Bridge, Neepsend Lane, Mowbray St
B6075	Rutland Rd, Pitsmoor Rd, Minna Rd
B6076	Stannington Rd, Stopes Rd, Brookside Bank, Rye Lane, Cliffe Hill, Yews Lane, Main Rd, Briers House Lane, New Rd
B6077	Loxley Rd
B6080	Gower St, Sunderland St
B6081	Abbeydale Rd
B6082	Carlisle St (East), Holywell Rd, Tyler St, Green Lane
B6083	Newhall Rd
B6085	Worksop Rd, Darnall Rd, Main Rd, Catley Rd
B6086	Bellhouse Rd, Firth Park Rd, Stubbin Lane
B6087	Chaucer Rd, Yew Lane, Stocks Hill, Church St, Nether Lane
B6088	Manchester Rd (Stocksbridge)
B6158	Dyche Lane
B6200	Staniforth Rd, Main Rd, Handsworth Rd, Retford Rd
B6375	Whirlowdale Rd
B6388	London Rd, Myrtle Rd, Prospect Rd, Spencer Rd, Gleadless Rd, White Lane, High Lane
B6539	Corporation St, West Bar, West Bar Green, Tenter St, Broad Lane, Brook Hill
B6546	Market Place (Chapeltown), Lound Side, Hall Wood Rd
B6547	Glossop Rd

Banks, Gordon

30th Dec 1937 – 12th Feb 2019

Brought up in Tinsley, Banks left school at 15 and took up a job with a coal merchant. He had been a goalkeeper for Sheffield Schoolboys, but it was a chance opportunity to stand in for the regular goalkeeper of amateur side Millspaugh that led to him being scouted by professional outfit Chesterfield.

Banks played in every match of the England 1966 World Cup winning campaign, and in the 1970 World Cup made what was considered to be one of the greatest saves of all time against Pelé.

In 1972 Banks crashed his car, with the resulting injuries leading to the loss of sight in his right eye. Although this could easily have been the end of his career, it didn't stop Banks playing in goal, and in 1977 he joined Fort Lauderdale Strikers in America. Despite only having vision in one eye he won the North American Soccer League Goalkeeper of the Year award in 1977.

A brief spell as manager of Telford United followed in the late 1970s.

Banks was given the FIFA Goalkeeper of the Year award six times during his career, was awarded an OBE in 1970, and was the first person to be inducted into the Sheffield Walk of Fame.

At his funeral, goal keepers from each of his former clubs acted as pallbearers.

Years	Team	Appearances
1958-59	Chesterfield	23
1959-67	Leicester City	293
1967-73	Stoke City	194
1967	Cleveland Stokers (loan)	7
1971	Hellenic (loan)	3
1977-78	Fort Lauderdale Strikers	37
1961	England U23	2
1963-72	England	73

Bean, Shaun
aka Stark, Eddard..

...of House Stark, Lord of Winterfell, Lord Paramount of the North, Warden of the North, Hand of the King, Lord Regent of the Seven Kingdoms, Protector of the Realm.

Born: 17th April 1959

Education: Brook Comprehensive School (now Handsworth Grange), Rotherham College of Arts and Technology (Welding), RADA.

Film roles

1984 *Winter Flight*
1986 *Caravaggio*
1988 *Stormy Monday*
1989 *How to Get Ahead in Advertising, The Fifteen Streets, War Requiem*
1990 *Windprints, The Field*
1992 *Patriot Games*
1994 *Shopping, Black Beauty*
1995 *GoldenEye*
1996 *When Saturday Comes*
1997 *Anna Karenina*
1998 *Ronin, Airborn*
1999 *Bravo Two Zero*
2000 *Essex Boys* 2
2001 *Don't Say a Word, LOTR: The Fellowship of the Ring*
2002 *LOTR: The Two Towers, Equilibrium, Tom & Thomas*
2003 *LOTR: The Return of the King, The Big Empty*
2004 *National Treasure, Troy*
2005 *North Country, Flightplan, The Island, The Dark*
2006 *Silent Hill*
2007 *The Hitcher, Outlaw, Far North*
2010 *Black Death, Percy Jackson & the Olympians: The Lightning Thief, Cash, Death Race 2*
2011 *Age of Heroes*
2012 *Cleanskin, Soldiers of Fortune, Mirror Mirror, Silent Hill: Revelation*
2014 *Wicked Blood*
2015 *The Snow Queen 2: The Snow King, Any Day, Jupiter Ascending, Pixels, The Martian*
2016 *The Young Messiah*
2017 *Drone, Dark River*
2020 *Possessor*

Notable TV roles include Mellors in *Lady Chatterley*, Sharpe in *Sharpe*, Eddard Stark in *Game of Thrones*, Simon in *Accused* & Father Michael Kerrigan in *Broken.*

Bean has a "100% Blade" tattoo on his shoulder, and also another saying "9" to signify his role as Boromir as one of the Fellowship of 9 in *Lord of the Rings.*
Bean has won numerous television and film awards, has an honorary doctorate from both Sheffield's universities and was inducted into the Sheffield Walk of Fame in 2007.

Beer

Sheffield was declared the real ale capital of England in a 2016 study by er…the University of Sheffield. Even taking into account a bit of local bias Sheffield is right up there as a contender for the title. The report calculated that there are almost 5 times as many breweries per head of population in Sheffield as in London, brewing over 1,000 different beers each year. On any given day you can find over 400 different beers on tap in Sheffield.

Sheffield breweries and their core ranges are listed below – this feels like a list it would be well worth working your way down!

Abbeydale Brewery	ABV	Date	Score (5)	Comment
Heresy	4.5			
Moonshine	4.3			
Deception	4.1			
Absolution	5.3			
Black Mass	6.66			
Daily Bread	3.8			
Heathen	4.1			
Blue Bee Brewery	ABV	Date	Score (5)	Comment
Reet Pale	4.0			
Hillfoot Best Bitter	4.0			
Triple Hop	4.3			
Tempest Stout	4.8			
Bradfield Brewery	ABV	Date	Score (5)	Comment
Farmers Ale	3.9			
Farmers Blonde	4.0			
Farmers Stout	4.5			
Farmers Pale Ale	5.0			
Farmers Brown Cow	4.2			
Yorkshire Farmer	4.0			
Brew Foundation	ABV	Date	Score (5)	Comment
Apollo Thirsteen	3.9			
Wort' the Wait	4.5			
Pekkochu	3.9			
Lager than Life	4.5			
Pop	3.6			
Wheat Your Heart Out	6.0			
C-Bomb	4.2			

	ABV	Date	Score (5)	Comment
Janet's Treat Porter	4.8			
Laughing Water	4.3			
Crosspool Ale Makers	ABV	Date	Score (5)	Comment
On the Loose	5.1			
Sandygate	3.6			
CrossPale	4.0			
Straight Outta Crosspool	5.6			
Dead Parrot Beer Co.	ABV	Date	Score (5)	Comment
Aurornis Xui	4.6			
Bohemia	4.7			
Norwegian Blue	3.7			
Kato Nwar	4.8			
Emmanuales	ABV	Date	Score (5)	Comment
Ryejoice	5.4			
As the Deer Pants for Porter	5.0			
Oh Hoppy Day	6.1			
Jonah and the Pale	5.0			
Exit 33 Brewing	ABV	Date	Score (5)	Comment
Thirst Aid	4.0			
Mosaic	4.1			
Hop Monster	4.5			
Northern Best	4.2			
Oat Stout	5.0			
Blonde	4.0			
Fuggle Bunny	ABV	Date	Score (5)	Comment
New Beginnings	4.9			
Cotton Tail	4.0			
Orchard Gold	5.0			
24 Carrot	6.0			
Oh Crumbs	3.8			
Hazy Summer Daze	4.2			
Russian Rare-Bit	5.0			
Jammy Dodger	4.5			
La La Land	3.9			
Kelham Island Brewery	ABV	Date	Score (5)	Comment
Easy Rider	4.3			
Pale Rider	5.2			
Kelham Best	3.8			
Pride of Sheffield	4.0			
Riders on the Storm	4.5			

Little Critters Brewing Co.	ABV	Date	Score (5)	Comment
Little Hopper	3.6			
Blonde Bear	4.2			
Loxley Brewery	ABV	Date	Score (5)	Comment
Gunson	4.8			
Lomas	4.4			
Fearn	3.8			
Halliday	4.0			
Revill	4.0			
Mitchell's Hop House Brewing	ABV	Date	Score (5)	Comment
Madness	5.0			
Independent	4.0			
Marilyn	4.3			
Dennis	4.5			
Lets Have a Butchers	4.0			
Neepsend Brew Company	ABV	Date	Score (5)	Comment
Blonde	4.0			
Annona	4.2			
Breakfast IPA MK3	6.0			
Peppercorn Stout	4.4			
Triton	4.5			
Sheffield Brewery Company	ABV	Date	Score (5)	Comment
Blanco Blonde	4.2			
Crucible Best	3.8			
Five Rivers	3.8			
Get Thi'sen Outdooerz	4.0			
Razor Paste	5.8			
Ruskin	4.8			
Sheffield Porter	4.4			
Stancill Brewery	ABV	Date	Score (5)	Comment
Barnsley Bitter	3.8			
Porter	4.4			
No. 7	4.3			
India	4.0			
Ginger Pale	4.0			
Stainless	4.3			
Black	3.7			
Black Gold	5.0			
Blonde	3.9			

St Mars of the Desert	ABV	Date	Score (5)	Comment
Jack D'Or	6.4			
Tapped Brew Company	ABV	Date	Score (5)	Comment
Sheaf Street Pale	4.5			
Mojo	3.6			
Toha	3.6			
Jericho	4.0			
Ale	3.5			
Sorsby Stout	4.0			
Station Yard	4.9			
Station Porter	5.0			
Toolmakers Brewery	ABV	Date	Score (5)	Comment
Lynch Pin	4.0			
Razmataz	4.2			
Black Edge	5.2			
Triple Point Brewing	ABV	Date	Score (5)	Comment
Debut	5.5			
Gold	4.0			
Helles	4.1			
Pilsner	4.6			
S.IPA	4.5			
True North Brew Company	ABV	Date	Score (5)	Comment
Polaris	4.3			
Sheffield Pilsner	5.0			
Blonde	4.0			
Best Bitter	3.8			
No regular beers				
Lost Industry Brewing	ABV	Date	Score (5)	Comment
On the Edge Brewery	ABV	Date	Score (5)	Comment
Steel City Brewing	ABV	Date	Score (5)	Comment

Bell Ringing

The Sheffield and District branch of the Yorkshire Association of Change Ringers are a 200 strong network of bell ringers.

Towers lying within Sheffield (with number of 🔔):

Sheffield Cathedral	St Peter and St Paul	🔔🔔🔔🔔🔔🔔🔔🔔🔔🔔🔔🔔🔔
Ranmoor	St John the Baptist	🔔🔔🔔🔔🔔🔔🔔🔔🔔🔔
Bolsterstone (GF)	St Mary's	🔔🔔🔔🔔🔔🔔🔔🔔
Bradfield	St Nicholas	🔔🔔🔔🔔🔔🔔🔔🔔
Dore	Christ Church	🔔🔔🔔🔔🔔🔔🔔🔔
Handsworth	St Mary's	🔔🔔🔔🔔🔔🔔🔔🔔
Norton (GF)	St James'	🔔🔔🔔🔔🔔🔔🔔🔔
Sheffield Cathedral (RC)	St Marie's	🔔🔔🔔🔔🔔🔔🔔🔔
Beighton	St Mary the Virgin	🔔🔔🔔🔔🔔🔔
Walkley	St Mary's	🔔🔔🔔🔔🔔🔔

GF indicates a ground floor ringing chamber.

Chiming Only Towers:

Firvale	St Cuthbert's	🔔🔔🔔🔔🔔🔔🔔🔔
Fulwood	Christ Church	🔔🔔🔔🔔🔔🔔🔔🔔
Hillsborough	Sacred Heart	🔔🔔🔔🔔🔔🔔🔔🔔
Brocco Bank	St Augustine's	🔔🔔🔔🔔🔔

Other Swing Chiming Bells and Bells Hung Dead With Chiming Clappers or Chiming Hammers:

City Centre – Bochum Bell (static exhibit) 🔔, Bramall Lane – St Mary's 🔔, Chapeltown – St John's 🔔, Chapeltown – Former St John's Church Hall 🔔, Ecclesall – All Saints 🔔, Gleadless – St Peter's 🔔, Grenoside – St Mark's 🔔, Hyde Park – St John's 🔔, High Green – St Saviour's Mortomley 🔔, Norton Lees – St Paul's 🔔, Orchard Square clock 🔔🔔🔔🔔🔔, Oughtibridge 🔔, Parson Cross – St Bernard's 🔔, Stocksbridge – St Matthias 🔔, Tinsley – St Lawrence 🔔🔔🔔, Totley – All Saints 🔔, Wadsley 🔔.

The blue ribband of bell ringing is the peal. Peals must consist of at least 5000 changes, with no change repeated. To count as a legitimate peal, the sequence must start and finish on a round, ringers must ring the same bell continuously, and there must be no outside help or use of memory aids.

Betula Pendula

Sheffield is blessed with 4,500,000 trees and has a greater urban tree coverage than any other UK city.

Approximate numbers of the most common species are indicated below.

Birth Rate

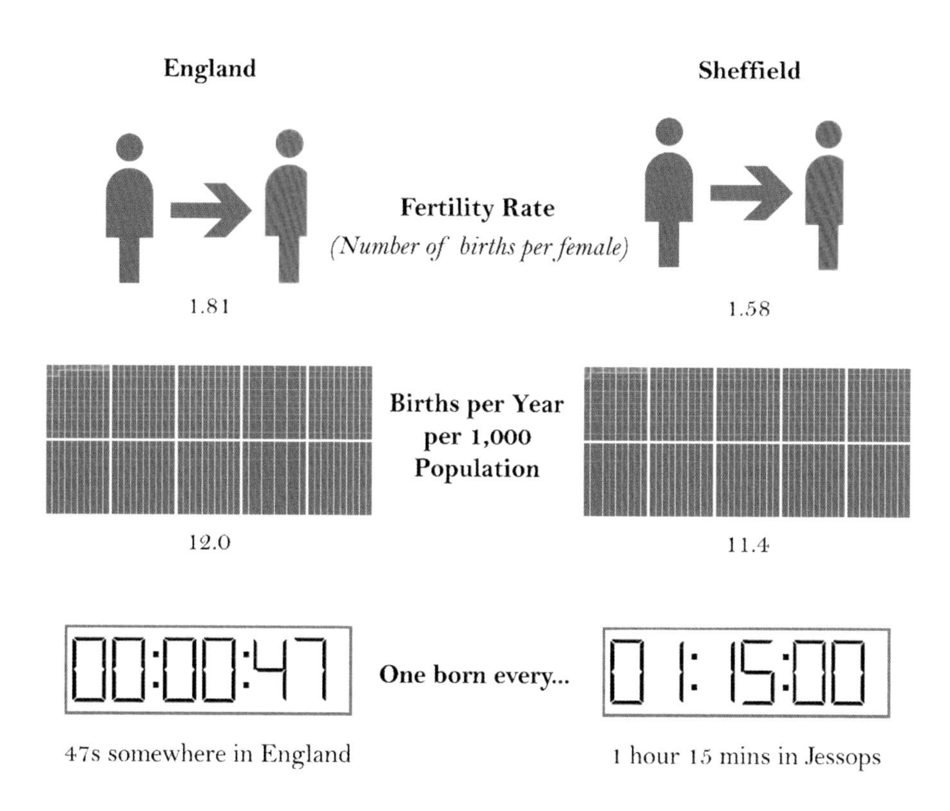

Despite the low fertility rate, the population of Sheffield is still growing. This is due to the death rate falling below the birth rate, and immigration to the city.

Blair Athol

The land around Banner Cross was originally owned by Lord John Murray, the son of the Duke of Atholl (hence Murray Road). Blair Athol Road is named after a village of the same name in Perthshire, close by the family seat of the Duke of Atholl's family at Blair Castle. Nearby Tullibardine Road references the title (Marquis of Tullibardine) of the Duke of Atholl's eldest son, Glenalmond Road is named after the Glenalmond valley in Perthshire, Glentilt Road after the River Tilt in Perthshire and Strathtay Road is named for one of the family titles of the Murray family.

Blitz, The Sheffield

With its steel and munitions industry vital to the war effort, Sheffield was the target of a number of German bombing raids during the Second World War.

Nights of bombing

1940		1941	
18/08	Wharncliffe Side	09/01	Dore
19/08	Sheffield	15/01	Sheffield
22/08	Stocksbridge	04/02	Sheffield
28/08	Sheffield & Ecclesfield	15/02	Sheffield
29/08	Stannington & Graves Park	14/03	Sheffield
30/08	Chapeltown	08/05	Sheffield
31/08	Sheffield	27/07	Sheffield
10/09	Sheffield	12/10	Sheffield
26/09	Tinsley	20/10	Sheffield
27/09	Sheffield		
28/09	Sheffield		
14/10	Sheffield & Ecclesfield		
12/12*	Sheffield, Chapeltown & Stocksbridge		
15/12*	Sheffield & Ecclesfield		

*The bombing raids of 12th and 15th December 1940 are commonly referred to as the 'Sheffield Blitz.'

The Germans dubbed these raids *Operation Crucible.*

Visible signs of bombing today

- The Moor was completely destroyed by the bombing – as evidenced by the lack of pre-war architecture anywhere along The Moor.
- Devonshire Green was a pre-war area of dense back-to-back housing that was completely destroyed and is now an open space as a direct result of the bombing.
- A crack running the full length of the floor of the entrance foyer of the Sheffield Library.
- Sheffield City Hall has shrapnel marks on its outside pillars.
- Visible repairs to the park walls on both sides of Mushroom Lane.

Night of 12th December 1940

122 Junker 88s, 151 Heinkel 111s, 7 Dornier 17s

>355 tonnes of explosives
>16,000 incendiary cannisters

7.41pm – 4.00am

Night of 15th December 1940

66 Heinkel 111s, 11 Dornier 17s

>140 tonnes of explosives
>11,000 incendiary cannisters

6.50pm – 10.05pm

Damage

660 killed, 1,500 injured, 40,000 homeless

3,000 destroyed, 3,000 badly damaged, 80,000 (50% of the housing stock) damaged

Marples Hotel destroyed, killing 70
8 schools destroyed, 106 damaged
Nether Edge & Jessops hospitals damaged
Weston Park Museum and Bramall Lane damaged
The Moor and Atkinsons dept store destroyed

Brown Bayley's steelworks, Hadfield's Hecla and East Hecla steelworks damaged

Bole Hill

A bole or bolehill was a wind-blown smelting fire, usually situated in an exposed location, associated with smelting Lead, with the wind used to stoke the fire up to the high temperatures needed. The bole at Totley is a scheduled historical monument on account of it being one of the best preserved examples in England. The remains of the large bole (7m x 3m) are visible, along with channels for the lead to flow to the casting pit. The site includes the remains of a smaller smelting oven and a pond for washing the slag. The Totley bole is thought to have been in use from the 12th to the 16th Century.

Bramall Lane

Bramall Lane sports ground was first opened in 1855 as home to six Sheffield cricket clubs, including the *Wednesday* Cricket Club, but quickly became a venue for local football too, and even had a banked cycle track built around the outside of the field for bicycle racing.

Yorkshire County Cricket Club was headquartered at Bramall Lane from 1863-93 before moving to Headingley. Yorkshire continued to play county cricket regularly at Bramall Lane until as late as 1973. England also played a test match on the ground in 1902 against Australia, with the tourists winning.

The first football match at Bramall Lane was played between Sheffield FC and Hallam FC in 1862. A local club *The Wednesday* also played at the ground and made Bramall Lane their official home from 1880-1887 before moving to their new ground at Olive Grove and then eventually Hillsborough.

Sheffield United Football Club was formed as the home team for the ground in 1889, and has been based at Bramall Lane ever since. While the club has a record home match attendance of 68,000 for an FA Cup fixture against Leeds United in 1936, they managed to squeeze 88,000 into the ground to hear Bruce Springstein perform in 1988. The ground is now fully seated and holds just over 32,000.

Bramall Lane hosted the first ever floodlit match in 1878, used to be a regular venue for FA cup semi-finals and hosted the FA Cup Final in 1912. Several international football games have taken place on the ground too (in fact, Bramall Lane claims to be oldest venue in the world still able to host international football matches). As well as being one of only two venues to have hosted international football, a test match and an FA cup final (the other is the Oval), Bramall Lane is also scheduled to be a venue for the 2021 Rugby World Cup.

Brierley, Harry

1871-1948

The son of a steel-worker, Harry Brierley left school at the age of twelve. Despite his relative anonymity today, he revolutionised the Sheffield steel industry, the fortunes of Sheffield, and eating utensils the world over.

In 1903 two of the great Sheffield steelmakers – John Brown & Company and Firth & Sons – joined forces to form Firth Brown. In 1908 they established Brown Firth Laboratories and recruited Brierley, who had established his reputation as a methodical researcher, to lead this project. At the time, research was driven by military considerations, in particular the search was on for more durable varieties of steel to use in the production of gun barrels. Brierley's experimentation with the addition of chromium as an alloying metal led to the discovery of 'rustless' steel. Brierley also noticed that acids used for etching steel had little effect on the new rustless steel, and quickly realised the new steel's potential to be used for cutlery – up until this point, it was only expensive silver cutlery that avoided the need for regular polishing to remove rust and stains.

The recipe for this new wonder material: 12.8% chromium, 0.44% manganese, 0.2% silicon, 0.24% carbon and 85.32% iron.

After the war William Herbert Hatfield developed the 18/8 variant of stainless steel that is widely used in cutlery today – 18% chromium and 8% nickel.

Brierley received the Bessemer Gold Medal from the Iron and Steel Institute in 1820, had a Thornbridge beer named after him in 2013, and has a mural painted of him on the side of the Howard Hotel.

Burkhill, John

John Burkhill will be recognised by anyone who has taken part in any organised running event in Sheffield. He has taken part in over 1000 organised events, at each one sporting a green wig and pushing a pram in which he collects money for MacMillan Cancer. He has raised over £750,000 in total.

In 2019, he rightly joined a select group of people, including Jessica Ennis and Nelson Mandela, when he was given the Freedom of the City of Sheffield in recognition of his fundraising efforts. He is also one of an extremely small number of people who have been awarded two British Empire Medals in the honours lists.

Carbon Capture

Sheffield's 4.5 million trees add to our quality of life in more ways than one.

As well as greening the city, they capture chemicals and particulates from the air, improve the air quality, and help protect the city from flooding by capturing water.

The amount of pollution captured annually by Sheffield's trees. This includes nasties such as ozone, carbon monoxide, nitrogen dioxide, sulphur dioxide and small particulates.

The amount of carbon captured annually by Sheffield's trees. Sheffield's trees store over half a million tonnes of carbon in total.

The amount of water captured by Sheffield's trees each year. Were it not for our trees, Sheffield's rivers and flood defences would have to deal with an extra 500 Olympic-sized swimming pools of water each year.

The value of Sheffield's trees, taking into account the cost of replanting them all as well as the environmental costs they save, has been estimated at £1.5 billion.

Carols

Carolling of epic proportions takes place in pubs across Sheffield from immediately after Armistice Day (yes, that is mid-November!) through to New Year's Day. Most of the carols originate from non-conformist chapels in villages to the north of the city and are often local to the village where they are sung. Church singing grew more sedate from the 1820s onwards, and the traditional carol singing moved into the pubs where it continues to this day. The 'Sheffield Carols' as they are known are therefore older (and more traditional) than the carols that most of us grew up learning.

The lyrics and tunes of the Sheffield carols are mostly unfamiliar at first, although you will recognise the words (or at least those of verses 1,2,3 and 6) of *While Shepherds Watched their Flocks by Night* being sung to a variety of different tunes.

Variants of 'While Shepherds'

- ♫ Cranbrook*
- ♫ Crimond
- ♫ Fern Bank
- ♫ Liverpool
- ♫ Lloyd
- ♫ Lyngham
- ♫ October
- ♫ Old Foster
- ♫ Pentonville
- ♫ Shaw Lane
- ♫ Sweet Chiming Bells
- ♫ Sweet Christmas Bells
- ♫ Winchester Old

*tune of *On Ilkla Moor Baht 'at.*

Other Sheffield Carols

- ♫ Diadem
- ♫ Egypt
- ♫ Hail Smiling Morn
- ♫ Home on the Swale
- ♫ Ho Reapers
- ♫ Jacobs Well
- ♫ Malin Bridge
- ♫ Mistletoe Bough
- ♫ Mount Moriah
- ♫ Portugal
- ♫ Shepherds Arise
- ♫ Spout Cottage
- ♫ Stannington
- ♫ Tinwood

Pubs

- Blue Ball, Worrall
- Blue Bull, Ecclesfield
- Crown & Glove, Stannington
- Old Red Lion, Grenoside
- Pheasant Inn, Oughtibridge
- Plough, Low Bradfield
- Rose & Crown, Stannington
- Royal Hotel, Dungworth
- Sportsman, Lodge Moor
- The Ale House, Woodseats
- Three Merry Lads, Lodge Moor
- Travellers Rest, Oughtibridge
- Wharncliffe Arms, Wharncliffe Side

Catchment Areas

For many, school catchment area is the biggest driver to where they live (and probably of their house price too!). Catchment areas are not an exact science, but this graphic is a good approximation.

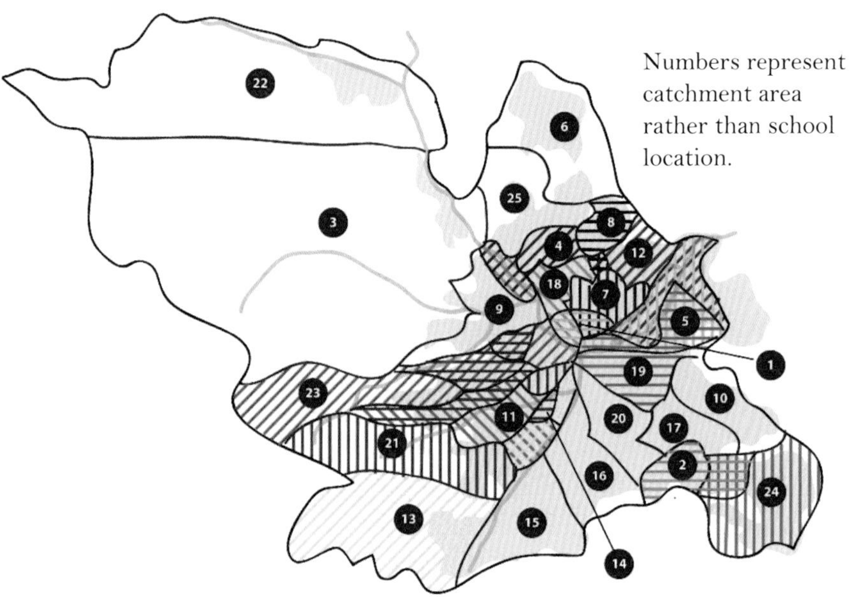

1. Astrea Academy
2. The Birley Academy
3. Bradfield
4. Chaucer
5. Don Valley Oasis
6. Ecclesfield
7. Fir Vale
8. Firth Park Academy
9. Forge Valley
10. Handsworth Grange
11. High Storrs
12. Hinde House
13. King Ecgbert
14. King Edward VII
15. Meadowhead
16. Newfield
17. Outwood Academy City
18. Parkwood Academy
19. Sheffield Park Academy
20. Sheffield Springs Academy
21. Silverdale
22. Stocksbridge High
23. Tapton
24. Westfield
25. Yewlands Academy

Alongside these, Mercia School recruits from the majority of the south and west. The two Catholic secondary schools – All Saints and Notre Dame serve the east and west halves of the city respectively.

Chaucer, Geoffrey

Sheffield's reputation for the production of cutlery ('that which cuts') is recorded as far back as tax records from 1297. Not long after, there is reference to a 'Sheffield knife' in Chaucer's Canterbury Tales.

> *Ther was no man, for peril, dorste hym touche. A Sheffeld thwitel baar* [knife] *he in his hose. Round was his face, and camus* [pug] *was his nose.*
>
> The Reeves Tale, Canterbury Tales (late 14th Century)

Cholera

The 19th Century saw Cholera spread across the globe in several waves. The second epidemic, reaching England in 1832 claimed the lives of 402 people from Sheffield, and millions globally.

The timeline below has particular resonance in light of the Covid-19 pandemic. It is interesting to note the differences and similarities that 200 years has brought to both the spread and response to a serious pandemic.

1817	First record of *Cholera Morbus* in India
1830	Cholera recorded as having arrived in Russia
Jan 1831	Ships arriving from Russia ordered to be quarantined to prevent spread of disease
1831	Cases recorded in northern Europe
1 Jul 1831	*Sheffield Courant* wrote "The alarm is entirely groundless"
Oct 1831	Port authorities of Sunderland ignored government instructions to quarantine all ships from the Baltic states resulting in Sunderland recording the first case of Cholera in England
29 Oct 1831	Formation of a Sheffield District Committee by medical professionals, which met daily, in order to advise on anti-cholera measures
7 Nov 1831	Town Trustees met "to determine the means to be adopted for preventing cholera … should that disease unfortunately appear in Sheffield"
Nov 1831	Town Trustees made a donation of £200 to the Cholera Fund

16 Dec 1831	*Sheffield Courant* wrote that "The Overseers of the Poor of Sheffield respectfully call upon the inhabitants to cleanse their houses, yards, premises, etc."
Feb 1832	First case recorded in London
16 Jun 1832	A 'house of recovery' (upper floors of the workhouse on Kelham Street) advertised in the local press to prepare to receive cholera victims
14 Jul 1832	The Privy Council in London formally constituted the Sheffield Board of Health
14 Jul 1832	The first official bulletin detailing the number of cases and deaths was issued by the Sheffield Board of Health
24 Jul 1832	*Sheffield Iris* - arrangements for burial published. A remote site by Clay Wood was chosen
13 Oct 1832	Report published on how the epidemic was handled
Nov 1833	Outbreak officially declared over
7 Oct 1834	Town Trustees contributed £20 towards the cost of a cholera monument, to be erected at the Clay Wood site
11 Dec 1834	Cholera monument cornerstone laid

In total 50,000 people in England died as a result of the 1832 cholera outbreak, representing 3 out of every 1000 people. In Sheffield the death rate was closer to 4 out of every 1000.

There were further smaller outbreaks of Cholera in 1849, 1854 and 1866.

Sheffield's grade II listed Cholera Monument still stands, despite being struck by lightning in 1990. The monument was designed by architect M.E. Hadfield who also designed Sacred Heart Church in Hillsborough and the Wicker Arches. Hadfield Road in Walkley is named after the anti-Corn Law MP George Hadfield.

Chocolate

The global giant Thorntons Chocolate grew from a single modest 'Chocolate Kabin' that was opened by Joseph Thornton in 1911 on Norfolk Street in Sheffield.

The business grew steadily, by 1927 running 8 shops across the north of England served by a small factory on the Penistone Road. Further growth led to moves to larger premises on Stalker Lees Road and then Archer Road, before it outgrew even this and moved production to Belper in 1947 and then eventually to Alfreton.

At their peak, Thorntons ran over 500 outlets across the world. Financial difficulties led to the brand being taken over by Italian company Ferrero in 2015 for a price of £112m.

Before the second world war, fudge and 'special' toffee formed the bulk of Thorntons sales. Post-war they branched into Continental, Belgian and Swiss chocolates which comprise the majority of Thorntons sales today.

"Chocolate Heaven since 1911"
"It's the Thorntons that Counts"

Clough, Grace

Born: 21st June 1991

Education: High Storrs, Leeds University (Sociology), Kellogg College, Oxford.

Grace Clough was born with Erbs Palsy (where nerves in the shoulder are damaged during birth). After playing competitive football Clough discovered rowing in her early 20s. She was talent-spotted and fast-tracked into the British Paralympic adaptive rowing mixed coxed four, going on to win several gold medals in the following years.

Gold Medals

2014	World Championships	Amsterdam
	World Rowing Cup	Aiguebelette
2015	World Championships	Aiguebelette
	World Rowing Cup	Varese
2016	Paralympic Games	Rio de Janeiro
2017	World Championships	Sarasota
2018	World Championships	Plovdiv

Clough was inducted into the Sheffield Walk of Fame in 2016 and awarded an MBE in 2017.

Coal

There is evidence of coal mining in the Sheffield area dating back to Roman times. However, it was the extension of the canal network in the late 18th Century that led to coal mining becoming commercially viable on a larger scale in South Yorkshire, as the coal could now be more easily transported by canal than road. The arrival of the railways in the 19th Century provided both a further means of transporting coal, and an additional demand for the black stuff. By 1900, at its peak, there were over 100,000 miners working 100 mines across South Yorkshire.

The coal industry was nationalised in 1947, and the National Union of Mineworkers (NUM) formed at the same time. By then, many of the collieries had already closed, but the Bramley Hall, Handsworth, High Hazel, Nunnery, Orgreave, Thorncliffe and Smithy Wood collieries in Sheffield were all still in operation.

By the time that the national pit closure programme was announced in 1984 all of the Sheffield collieries had ceased activity. The Orgreave coking plant was still in operation at this time and saw heavy clashes between police and miners.

Today, there is little left to see of this huge industry - the Advanced Manufacturing Park and Waverley housing estate cover the sites of the Orgreave and High Hazels collieries, the Parkway industrial area is on the site of the Nunnery colliery and little apart from the Miners Arms in Chapeltown serves as a reminder of the Thorncliffe and Smithy Wood coal mining activity.

The 'Paddy Mail' disaster occurred at the Nunnery Colliery on 3rd December 1923 and tragically resulted in the loss of seven lives. The Paddy Mail was an underground train consisting of small tubs that was either dragged up or braked down an incline by a steel rope connected to an engine. The cause of the accident was a snapped rope that sent 44 tubs containing a total of 90 men and 30 boys hurtling down a steep incline. It is miraculous that more lives were not lost.

Cobbett, William

> *If the people of Sheffield could only receive a tenth part of what their knives sell for by retail in America, Sheffield might pave its streets with silver.*
>
> Rural Rides (1830).

Cocker, John (Joe)

20th May 1944 – 22nd Dec 2014

Education: Sheffield Central Technical School

Cocker left school at 15 to a job as a gasfitter. His musical career kicked off properly in 1961 when he adopted the stage name 'Vance Arnold' as the lead singer of *Vance Arnold and the Avengers*. The *Avengers'* big moment was supporting *The Rolling Stones* when they performed at Sheffield City Hall in 1963. Cocker's first solo hit was recorded in 1964 and following this he reverted to 'Joe Cocker' and formed *Joe Cocker's Blues Band*. By 1966 this group had dissolved and Cocker had set up *The Grease Band*. The *Grease Band* stuck together for three years, during which time they rose from performing in UK clubs to playing Woodstock. Cocker's next outfit was *Mad Dogs and Englishmen* which managed a hectic two-year stint in the early 70s. His later career was a string of successful blues and soul studio albums and a number of well-received tours. In 1983 Cocker won a Grammy for *Up Where We Belong*, and was awarded an OBE in 2007. Following his death, Cocker's weekly record sales jumped from 1,000 to over 20,000.

Cocker's career was not without controversy, including being arrested in Australia in 1972 for possession of marijuana, throwing up on stage and a further arrest in Austria for refusing to perform with sub-standard sound equipment.

Joe Cocker was unrelated to Jarvis Cocker, despite rumours to the contrary. The two families did know each other though, Joe having babysat the younger Jarvis.

Studio Albums

- *With a Little Help from My Friends* (1969)
- *Joe Cocker!* (1969)
- *Joe Cocker* (1972)
- *I Can Stand a Little Rain* (1974)
- *Jamaica Say You Will* (1975)
- *Stingray* (1976)
- *Luxury You Can Afford* (1978)
- *Sheffield Steel* (1982)
- *Civilized Man* (1984)
- *Cocker* (1986)
- *Unchain My Heart* (1987)
- *One Night of Sin* (1989)
- *Night Calls* (1991/US: 1992)
- *Have a Little Faith* (1994)
- *Organic* (1996)
- *Across from Midnight* (1997)
- *No Ordinary World* (1999)
- *Respect Yourself* (2002)
- *Heart & Soul* (2004)
- *Hymn for My Soul* (2007)
- *Hard Knocks* (2010)
- *Fire It Up* (2012)

Coe, Sebastian

Born: 29th Sept 1956

Education: Tapton, Loughborough University

Coe joined Hallamshire Harriers running club at age 12 and quickly established himself as a talented middle-distance runner who would go on to b. Coe's international career spanned the 1970s and 80s, and was characterised by both a fierce rivalry with fellow Brit Steve Ovett, and a string of world records. There was a period of one hour during 1980 when Seb Coe held all of the 800m, 1000m, 1500m and mile world records (until Ovett stole the mile record back again).

Since retiring from athletics Coe has held a number of high profile and influential roles in both politics and sport.

He has racked up 4 Olympic medals, three Sports Personality of the Year awards, and any number of honours from the queen, but apart from his plaque on the Sheffield Walk of Fame, there appears to be little in Sheffield to celebrate his achievements.

World Records			
1979	800m	1:42.33	
1979	Mile	3:48.95	
1979	1500m	3:32.03	
1980	1000m	2:13.40	
1981	800m(i)	1:46.0	
1981	800m	1:41.73	still 3rd fastest ever
1981	1000m	2:12.18	still 2nd fastest ever
1981	Mile	3:48.53	
1981	Mile	3:47.33	
1982	4x800m	7:03.89	
1983	800m(i)	1:44.91	
1983	1000m(i)	2:18.58	

(i) indoor

Olympic Medals
Moscow 1980
1500m
800m
Los Angeles 1984
1500m
800m

Roles

1992 – 97	Conservative MP for Falmouth & Cambourne
1997 - 01	Chief of Staff to the Leader of the Opposition
2000 -	Member of the House of Lords – Life Peer
2004 – 13	Chair of Organising Committee for London Olympics and Paralympics
2008 – 12	President of the Organising Committee for the Summer Olympics
2012 – 14	Chairman of the British Olympic Association
2012 -	Chancellor of Loughborough University
2015 -	President of the International Association of Athletics Federations

Honours

1982	Appointed Member of the Order of the British Empire (MBE)
1990	Appointed Officer of the Order of the British Empire (OBE)
2000	Created Life Peer as Baron Coe of Ranmore*
2006	Appointed Knight Commander of the Order of the British Empire (KBE)
2013	Appointed Member of the Order of the Companions of Honours (CH)

*Ranmore (Surrey), not Ranmoor (Sheffield).

Crescents (in S11)

Alms Hill Crescent
Bents Crescent
Bingham Park Crescent
Brincliffe Crescent
Collegiate Crescent
Grange Crescent
Grange Crescent Road
Greystones Crescent
Greystones Grange Crescent
Hardwick Crescent
High Storrs Crescent
Huntingdon Crescent
Parkhead Crescent
Silverdale Crescent

Crucible Curse

The curse: first time winners of the World Snooker Championships at the Crucible have never successfully defended their title the following year.

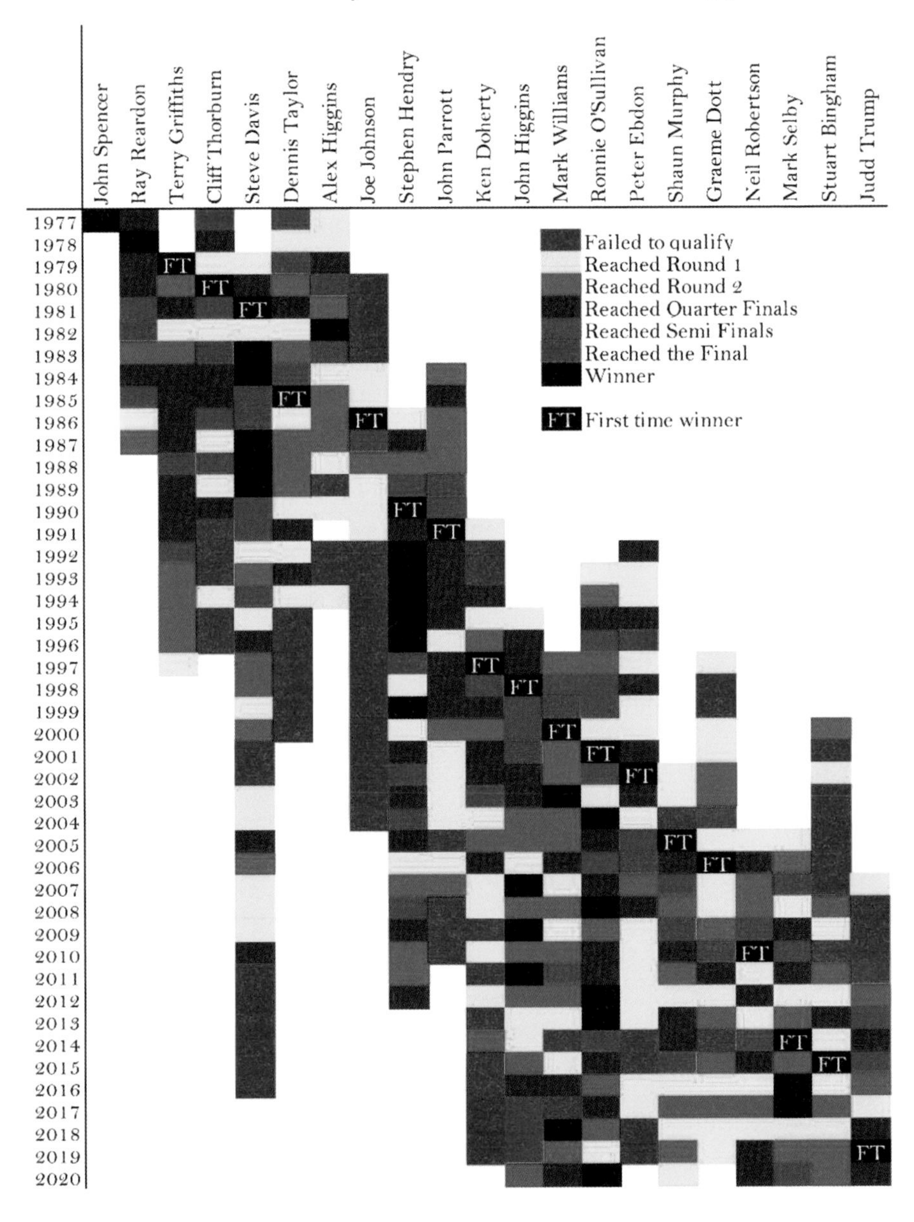

Cutlery, Anatomy of

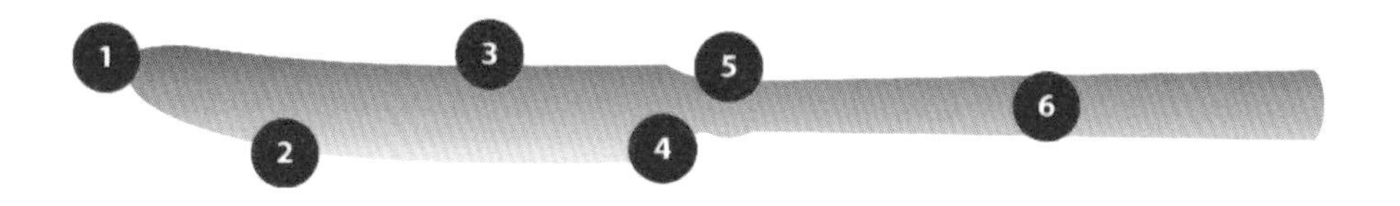

1. Point
2. Edge
3. Spine
4. Head
5. Guard
6. Handle

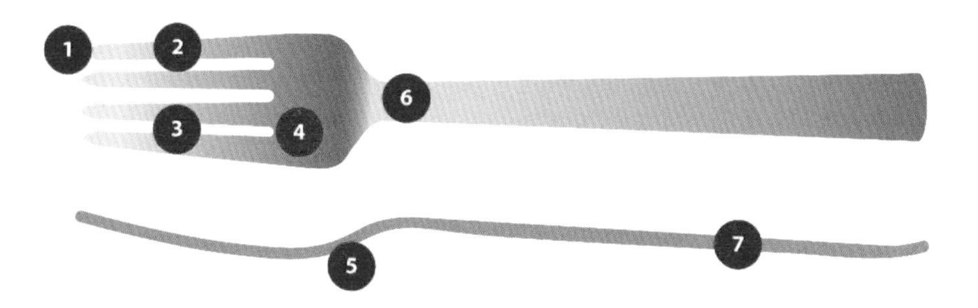

1. Point
2. Tine
3. Slot
4. Root
5. Back
6. Neck
7. Handle

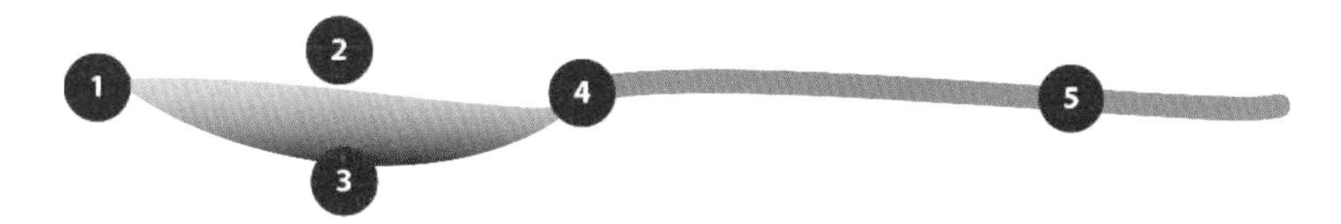

1. Tip
2. Bowl
3. Back
4. Neck
5. Handle

Dam Busters

Daah, dah dah dah da da da da daah, dah dah dah da da da da daah, ...

During World War II, an audacious attack on the Ruhr Valley dams was planned. By rupturing the dams and causing a destructive flood downstream, the British war planners hoped to wipe out a large portion of Germany's steel production and hydro-electric facilities in the heavily industrialised Ruhr. The problem was that a bomb dropped in the conventional way was likely to miss a narrow dam wall. It would also not detonate far enough underwater to cause sufficient damage to breach the dam wall. Barnes Wallace came up with a bouncing bomb that, while solving some problems, created others. To work, this four ton bomb had to be dropped at a precise distance from the dam, at a speed of exactly 240 mph and a height of just 60 feet. If that wasn't enough, all of this would have to be done at night in order to avoid detection.

Although it is widely known that Squadron 617, led by Wing Commander Guy Gibson, practiced and perfected their low flying bombing technique over Derwent Dam, they also used Ewden, Langsett and Dam Flask reservoirs to practice. The planes were flying so low that telephone wires crossing Dam Flask had to be taken down while the practice runs took place.

Operation Chastise took to the air on the night of the 16th and 17th May 1943, with the modified Lancaster bombers of Squadron 617 undertaking a low level flight over the Netherlands and Germany to avoid detection. They successfully breached both the Mohne and Eder dams, causing large scale flooding and damage.

Worried about possible retaliation, masts were erected either side of the four reservoirs in the Loxley valley with wires and suspended weights in between to foil any German copy-cat attacks. Smoke machines were also installed in order to quickly blanket the reservoirs with an impenetrable fog if needed.

Lancaster bombers were back over the Derwent Dam in 1954 for the creation of the *Dam Busters* film. The night-time low-level flying to recreate the bombing raids was deemed too dangerous and the scenes were instead filmed during the day-time with the film being over developed to create the night-time effect.

The *Dam Buster's March*, written by Eric Coates (but not originally composed for the film) has been adopted by the city as an unofficial anthem. It regularly features alongside favourites from the Last Night of the Proms at the annual *Classic in the Gardens* that takes place each July in Sheffield's Botanical Gardens.

'Dee Dah'

A national survey carried out in 2019 placed the Sheffield accent in a disappointing 41st place in a ranking of the sexiest UK accents. Who did we beat? Cornwall, Bristol, Hull and Birmingham!

Even if not everyone is a fan, the Sheffield accent *is* distinctive, with some of its quirks listed below.

"Dee Dah" is where a *d-* sound is used instead of *th-*. More common among the older population with *"Thee"* and *"Tha"* becoming *"Dee"* and *"Dah"*.

"The" is often shortened, but not consistently. For example, *"Going to the pub"* is *"Gun'ut' pub"*, whereas *"I am going to go the pub"* would be *"I'm gunna gu tert pub"*.

"h" is usually dropped, for example *"'ello"* or *"'ey up"*. Where the *h* is dropped in the middle of the word, an *"r"* sound is created, eg *"Oolaroop" (Hula Hoop)* or *"Medderall" (Meadowhall)*.

"t" often beomes an *r-* sound when two words are merged together *"Shurrup" (Shut up)* or *"Whorrabout" (What about)*.

"r" sounds before consonants are often not pronounced – for example *"father"* loses the *r* sound after the *a*..

The *"u"* and *"a"* sounds are almost always shortened. For example *"butter"* is pronounced with an *"uh"* sound.

"-ake" words are sometimes (but not always) shortened to "-ek." For example *"make, sake, take"* become *"mek, sek, tek"*, whereas *"bake"* and *"cake"* remain unchanged.

Other vowel sounds can be extended and contorted. For example *"board, floor, cheese, there, where"* become *"boo-erd, floo-er, chay-erz, they-er, we-er"*.

"-n't" is kept but the bit that comes before is often shortened. *"Wunt, shunt, dint"* for *"wouldn't, shoudn't, didn't"*.

"s" is often lost as a signifier of a plural. Eg *"ten pound"*.

"was" is pronounced without its *s*. This often sounds like a grammatically incorrect *"were."*

Deerlands

Exactly what it says on the tin – a place where there were deer. Doe Royd is named for the same reason.

Def Leppard

Def Leppard was formed by three Tapton school students (Rick Savage, Tony Kenning and Pete Willis) in 1977. Savage, along with Joe Elliott and Rick Allen (who joined shortly after its founding), are still members of the band.

Def Leppard were at the forefront of the British heavy-metal movement. They were also associated with glam-rock and are often credited with the birth of pop-metal.

Def Leppard are one of only five bands to have produced two albums (*Pyromania* and *Hysteria*) that have sold over 10 million copies each. They are in good company - the other four outfits are The Beatles, Led Zeppelin, Pink Floyd and Van Halen! As well as phenomenal record sales, Def Leppard also appear in the *Guinness Book of Records* for performing three concerts on three continents in one day (Sheffield, Tangiers and Vancouver).

In 1984 drummer Rick Allen lost his left arm in a car crash on the A57 just outside Sheffield. The arm was reattached at the time, but ultimately couldn't be saved. Allen defied the odds with an incredible comeback, learning to play the drums with his legs and persuading the rest of the band that he could drum just as well with three limbs as four.

Brian May of Queen inducted Def Leppard into the extremely exclusive Rock and Roll Hall of Fame in Cleveland, Ohio in 2019.

Def Leppard were inducted into the Sheffield Walk of Fame in 2006.

Studio Albums

- *On Through the Night* (1980)
- *High 'n' Dry* (1981)
- *Pyromania* (1983)
- *Hysteria* (1987)
- *Adrenalize* (1992)
- *Slang* (1996)
- *Euphoria* (1999)
- *X* (2002)
- *Yeah!* (2006)
- *Songs from the Sparkle Lounge* (2008)
- *Def Leppard* (2015)

Defoe, Daniel

As well as writing *Robinson Crusoe* and *Moll Flanders*, Daniel Defoe travelled the length and breadth of Britain, recording his observations in three volumes describing his travels.

> *This town of Sheffield is very populous and large, the streets narrow, and the houses dark and black, occasioned by the continued smoke of the forges, which are always at work: Here they make all sorts of cutlery-ware, but especially that of edged-tools, knives, razors, axes, and nails.*
>
> *Here is a very spacious church, with a very handsome and high spire; and the town is said to have at least as many, if not more people in it than the city of York. Whether they have been exactly numbered one against the other, I cannot tell. The manufacture of hard ware, which has been so antient in this town, is not only continued, but much encreased; insomuch that they told us there, the hands employed in it were a prodigious many more than ever dwelt, as well in the town, as in the bounds of that they call Hallamshire; and they talked of 30,000 men employed in the whole; but I leave it upon the credit of report.*
>
> A Tour Through the Whole of Great Britain (1724)

Defoe was impressed by *a fine engine or mill for raising water to the town, a fine hospital* and *a very large and strong bridge over the Don*, the latter probably Lady's Bridge. His high regard for the bridge was probably reinforced by the fact that not long before his visit the Don had flooded doing *a prodigious deal of damage* and *taking away with it two or three stone bridges.*

Delf

Delf can mean

1. Crockery
2. A mine or excavation
3. A square heraldic emblem

Within the Sheffield context, Delf Street, Delph House Road and Delves Avenue, Close, Drive, Place, Road and Terrace are all named after nearby quarries or mines.

Derby (Steel City)

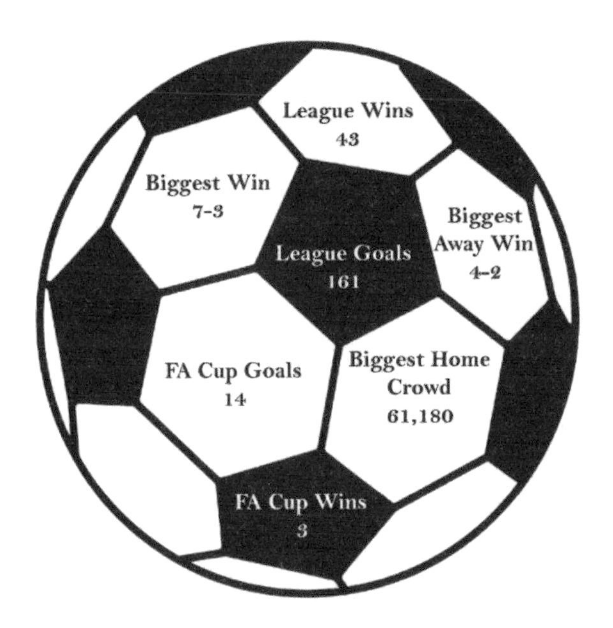

League Derby Results

Season – United at home – Wednesday at home

Season	United at home	Wednesday at home	Season	United at home	Wednesday at home	Season	United at home	Wednesday at home
1893-94	1-1	1-1	1914-15	0-1	1-1	1965-66	1-0	2-2
1894-95	1-0	2-3	1919-20	3-0	2-1	1966-67	1-0	2-2
1895-96	1-1	1-0	1926-27	2-0	2-3	1667-68	0-1	1-1
1896-97	2-0	1-1	1927-28	1-1	3-3	1970-71	3-2	0-0
1897-98	1-1	0-1	1928-29	1-1	5-2	1979-80	1-1	4-0
1898-99	2-1	1-1	1929-30	2-2	1-1	1991-92	2-0	1-3
1900-01	1-0	1-0	1931-32	1-1	2-1	1992-93	1-1	1-1
1901-02	3-0	1-0	1932-33	2-3	3-3	1993-94	1-1	3-1
1902-03	2-3	0-1	1933-34	5-1	0-1	2000-01	1-1	1-2
1903-04	1-1	2-0	1937-38	2-1	0-1	2001-02	0-0	0-0
1904-05	4-2	1-3	1938-39	0-0	1-0	2002-03	3-1	2-0
1905-06	0-2	1-0	1949-50	2-0	2-1	2005-06	1-0	1-2
1906-07	2-1	2-2	1951-52	7-3	1-3	2007-08	2-2	2-0
1907-08	1-3	2-0	1953-54	2-0	3-2	2008-09	1-2	1-0
1908-09	2-1	1-0	1954-55	1-0	1-2	2009-10	3-2	1-1
1909-10	3-3	1-3	1958-59	1-0	2-0	2011-12	2-2	1-0
1910-11	0-1	2-0	1961-62	1-0	1-2	2017-18	0-0	2-4
1911-12	1-1	1-1	1962-63	2-2	3-1	2018-19	0-0	0-0
1912-13	0-2	1-0	1963-64	1-1	3-0			
1913-14	0-1	2-1	1964-65	2-3	0-2			

FA Cup Derby Results

Season – Stage of competition met – Score(s) – Eventual outcome

Season	Stage	Score	Score	Outcome
1899-00	Last 16	1-1	0-2	Reached Q-Finals
1924-25	Last 32	3-2		Won FA Cup
1927-28	Last 16	1-1	4-1	Reached S-Finals
1953-54	Last 64	1-1	1-3	Reached S-Finals
1959-60	Q-Final	0-2		Reached S-Finals
1992-93	S-Final	2-1		Reached Final

League Cup and Full Members Cup Derby Results

Season – Stage of competition met – Score – Eventual outcome

Season	Stage	Score	Score	Outcome
1980-81	1st Round	1-1	2-0	Reached 3rd Round
2000-01	3rd Round	2-1		Reached Q-Finals

Dying

Sadly, we all have to go eventually.

The good news is that the death rate in Sheffield has been falling from around 13 per 1,000 population per year in 2000, to around 10 per 1,000 population now. That is quite an improvement and suggests better health and improved health care.

In Sheffield approximately 30% of all deaths are amongst those aged under 75. The breakdown of these is illustrated below.

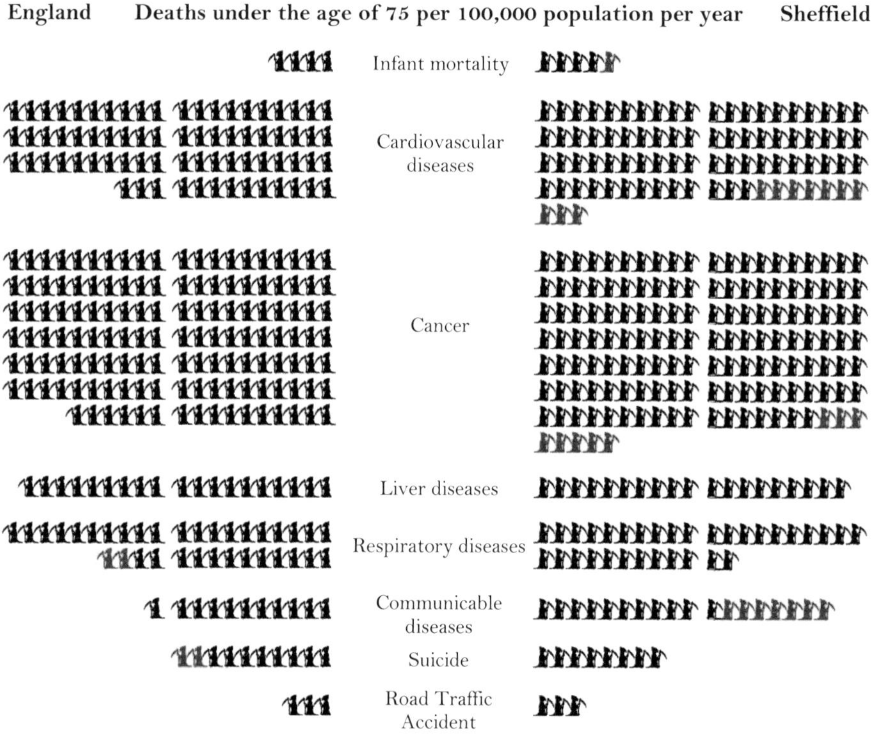

England **Deaths under the age of 75 per 100,000 population per year** **Sheffield**

Infant mortality

Cardiovascular diseases

Cancer

Liver diseases

Respiratory diseases

Communicable diseases

Suicide

Road Traffic Accident

Note that this data is pre-COVID.

Disasters

Sheffield has not been immune from tragedy, having survived all manner of disasters over the past centuries.

In the 19th Century several waves of **Cholera** spread across the globe. The Cholera Monument overlooking the city remembers the 400+ who died in Sheffield during the biggest outbreak that took place in 1832.

Only three decades later the **Great Sheffield Flood** of 1864 (still the largest man-made flooding disaster ever in England in terms of damage to property and loss of life), caused widespread destruction and devastation as the waters from Dale Dyke reservoir burst the dam wall and swept down the Loxley and Don valleys, destroying pretty much everything in their path.

Then of course, Sheffield played its part in both World Wars, losing an enormous number of lives in the process. Casualties from Sheffield on the front-line during **World War I** were high, and there was a large loss of life and damage to property in Sheffield during World War II, particularly during the **Blitz** of December 1940.

World War II also bore witness to the **Mi Amigo** plane crash in Endcliffe Park, recently commemorated with a fly past and BBC Breakfast TV coverage.

More recently, the **Hillsborough Disaster** of 1989 claimed the lives of almost 100 Liverpool fans, injuring many more. Some good eventually came from the Taylor Report into the disaster and the subsequent conversion of football grounds to all-seating.

Throughout the city's history, the Fire Service have been a constant, playing a major part in the response to all disasters and emergencies that have befallen it, not to mention their role as first responders to major **Fires.**

At the time of writing, the COVID-19 epidemic looks as though it too will appear in future accounts of the history of Sheffield as a major disaster for the city, whether the biggest long term impact for Sheffield will be human or economic is too early to say.

Divisions

So, in how many ways can you carve up a city like Sheffield?

In Anglo-Saxon times, Sheffield as we know it was divided into the ancient kingdoms of Mercia and Northumbria – the Limb Brook, River Sheaf and Meersbrook formed part of the boundary. 'Limb' derives from the Latin *Limbus* meaning border, Meersbrook translates in Old English as 'Boundary Brook', and one of the meanings of Sheaf is 'divide'.

In 1951 the Peak District was declared the first national park in England. A line, more or less north to south places one third of Sheffield within the Peak District.

In the early 1970s **Postcodes** arrived and, like the rest of the country, Sheffield was divided up into new postal regions.

The current organisation of the City into 28 Wards, each voting for three Councillors took place in 2004. While still on politics, the boundaries of the **Parliamentary Constituencies** are regularly modified, with the most recent Boundary Commission having taken place in 2010.

For many, Sheffield can be viewed as a set of distinct school **Catchment Areas** that dictate the desirability (and house prices) of different areas of Sheffield.

The other type of catchment area, dictated by geography and river valleys, create well-defined regions that have their own individual identities, delineated by higher ground on either side.

And of course, just as **Football** is a game of two halves, Sheffield is very much a city of two halves (with perhaps a small number of ambivalents!).

Anglo Saxon Kingdoms

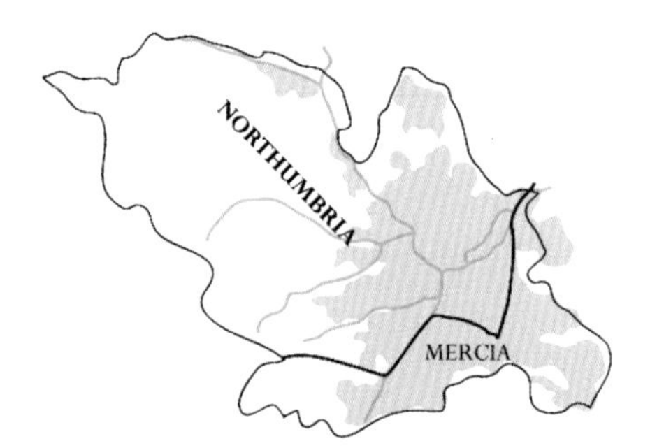

National Parks

Postcodes

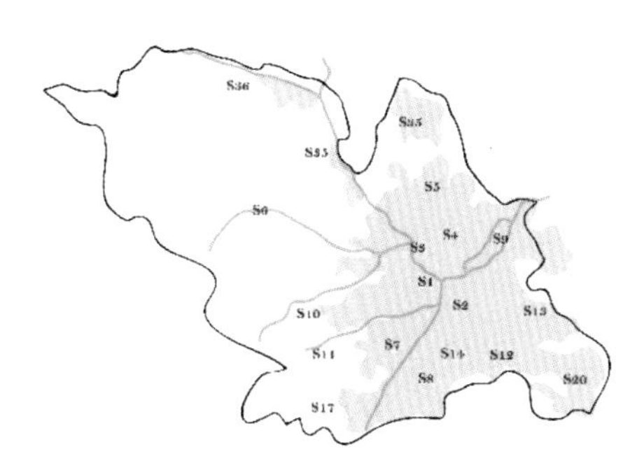

City Council Wards

Parliamentary Constituencies

School Catchment Areas

River Catchment Areas

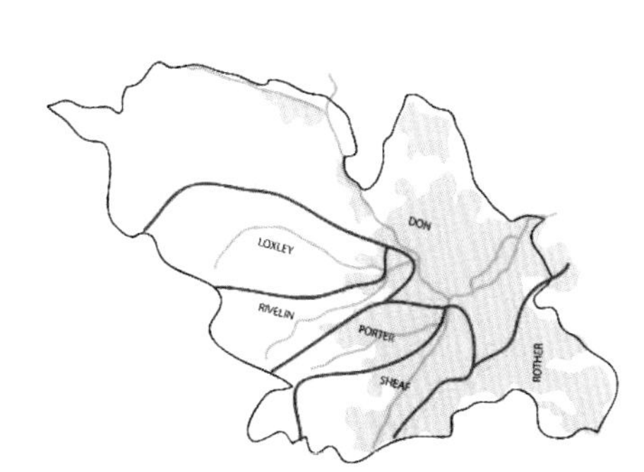

Football Affiliation

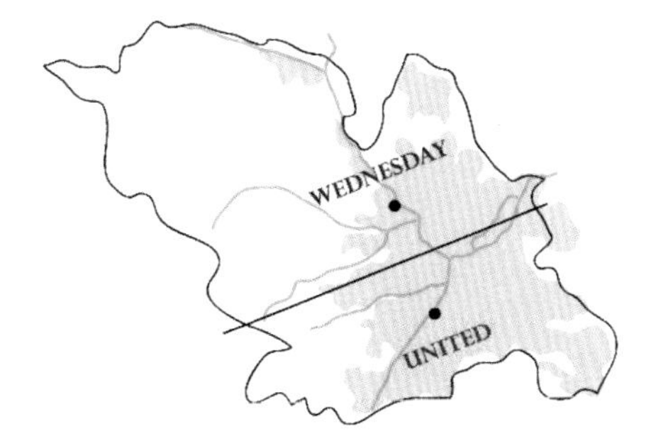

Doctor, The

The first full episode featuring Jodie Whittaker as the Thirteenth Doctor Who was largely filmed in Sheffield, with the steel city also making appearances in subsequent episodes in the series.

Shoot locations included Ecclesall Road and Hunter Road, the HTC plant near Meadowhall and Park Hill flats.

Most of the references to Sheffield within the dramatisation are at least fairly accurate:

- It produces Sheffield Steel and has a history of mining coal. So far, so good.
- It is in the Hallamshire area of South Yorkshire and is home to the University of South Yorkshire. Stretching things a bit now, but we can see where they are coming from.
- The Battle of Hope Valley in the 9th Century saw a human army beat off a Dalek scout who had been sent ahead to earth. What?
- While the Dalek was destroyed in the battle, the Kaled mutant inside was not. To safeguard the human race, three warriors who would become known as the *Three Custodians* cut the Kaled mutant into three parts and carried them off to far corners of the planet. One of the Custodians was killed as he crossed what is now Sheffield. Over a thousand years later the body of the Custodian was discovered in sewers underneath Sheffield Town Hall. On New Years Day 2019 the piece of Kaled mutant that had been buried with the Custodian was exposed to ultraviolet light. This awakened the Dalek which, using a spatial shift, was able to reconstruct itself and continue its conquest of earth. Maybe a bit far-fetched, but it's a good story!
- Best of all though, The Time Lord fixed her sonic screwdriver with our very own Steel.

"Swiss army sonic – now with added Sheffield Steel"

Domesday Book

The Domesday Book was a survey of England and Wales completed in 1086 by William the Conqueror in order to establish the taxes that were due to him. There are 19 settlements listed in the Domesday Book within the area of modern-day Sheffield. All can still be located on a contemporary map - the majority have become established areas of Sheffield, while a few are still little more than small clusters of buildings.

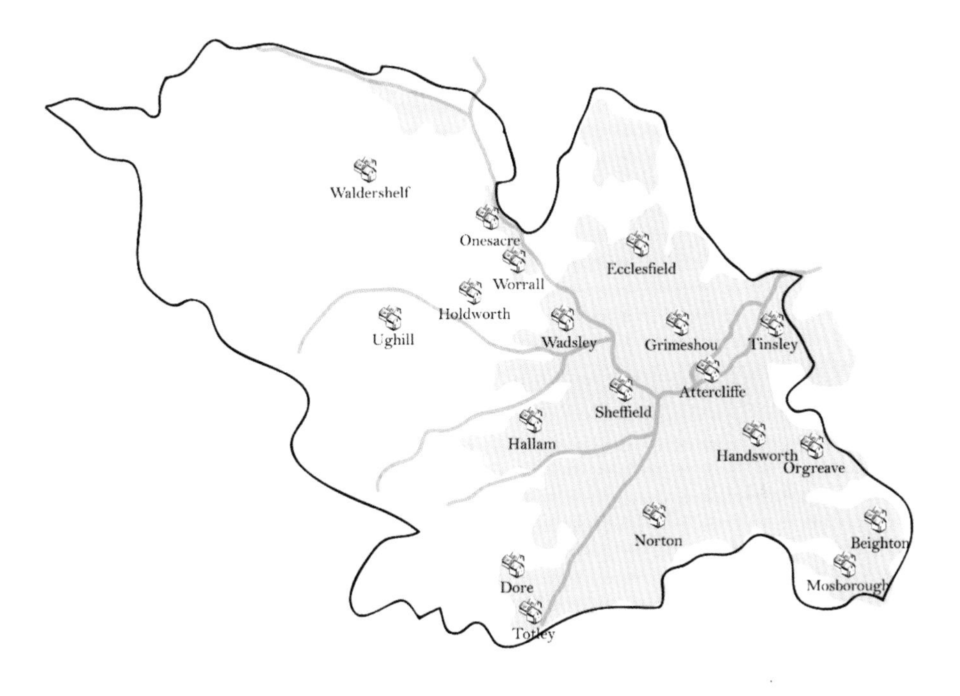

Each entry records the following information about each settlement.

- Population (often not recorded)
- Resources
- Value of the settlement to the Lord
- Tenant in Chief
- Lord (landowner)

Attercliffe

-
3 ploughlands
-
Countess Judith
Roger of Bully

Beighton

2 villagers
0.8 ploughlands, 1 men's plough team, 1 acre meadow, 1 x 0.5 leagues woodland
£0.6s.2d
Roger of Poitou
Roger of Poitou

Dore

-
0.5 ploughlands
-
Roger of Bully
Roger of Bully

Ecclesfield

2 villagers, 2 smallholders
3 ploughlands, 1 lord's plough team, 1 men's plough team, 1 x 1.5 leagues woodland
£0.10s
Roger of Bully
Roger of Bully

Grimeshou

3 villagers, 3 smallholders
2 ploughlands, 1 lord's plough team, 1 men's plough team, 3 x 2 furlongs woodland
£1
Roger of Bully
Roger of Bully

Hallam

33 villagers
20 ploughlands, 2 lords plough teams, 12.5 men's plough team, 8 acres meadow, 1 x 4 leagues woodlands
£2
Countess Judith
Roger of Bully

Handsworth

11 villagers, 6 freemen, 4 smallholders
7 ploughlands, 1 lord's plough team, 7.5 men's plough team, 1 x 3 leagues woodland
£2
Count Robert of Mortain
Richard of Sourdeval

Holdworth

-
1 ploughland
£1
Roger of Bully
Roger of Bully

Mosborough

13 freemen
3 ploughlands, 5 men's plough team, 3 acres meadow, 1 x 1.5 leagues woodland
-
Ralph son of Hubert
Ralph son of Hubert

Norton & Little Norton

3 households
7 acres meadow, 1 x 3 leagues woodland
-
King William
King William

Onesacre
- -
- 0.5 ploughlands
- £0.16s
- King William
- King William

Orgreave
- -
- 2 ploughlands
- -
- Roger of Bully
- Roger of Bully

Sheffield
- -
- 2 ploughlands
- -
- Countess Judith
- Roger of Bully

Tinsley
- 1 villager, 3 freemen
- 4 ploughlands, 1 men's plough team, 10 acres meadow, 1 league x 8 furlongs woodland
- £2
- Count Robert of Mortain
- Richard of Sourdeval

Totley
- -
- 1 ploughlands, 1 x 0.5 leagues woodland
- £0.1s
- King William
- King William

Ughill
- -
- 2 ploughlands, 1 x 1 leagues woodland
- £1
- Roger of Bully
- Roger of Bully

Wadsley
- -
- 2 ploughlands, 1 x 1 leagues woodland
- £1
- Roger of Bully
- Roger of Bully

Waldershelf
- -
- 0.5 ploughlands
- £0.16s
- King William
- King William

Worrall
- -
- 2 ploughlands, 1 x 1 leagues woodland
- £1
- Roger of Bully
- Roger of Bully

Don Bridges

The Don may not be on the scale of other big city rivers, and its transit of the city is often hidden away rather than celebrated, but its journey through Sheffield takes in a vast amount of history. Developments such as the Five Weirs Walk and the re-modelling of the area around Kelham Island are improving access to this artery of the city and its historical past. The river and its many bridges provide a fascinating insight into the transformation of Sheffield over time.

Working downstream from Stocksbridge, the bridges are as follows:

- Soughley Lane Bridge
- Soughley A616 Bridge, 1988
  Carries the Stocksbridge Bypass.
- Woodhead Line R'way Bridge, 1845
- Station Road Bridge
  Leads to site of former Deepcar Station.
- Bridge by More Hall Farm
  Private bridge
- Oughtibridge Station Lane Bridge
  Bottom of Jawbone Hill close to the site of the former Oughty Bridge Station.
- Rocher Bridge (F)
  Footbridge. Only crossing of the Don on the 4km stretch from Oughtibridge to Leppings Lane.
- Leppings Lane Bridge
  Originally 'Leapings Lane' after stepping stones in the river.
- Hillsborough Stadium Footbridge, 1996
- Cadbury's Works Bridges, 1934
  Two private bridges built by Basset's to connect the factory with the other side of the Don.
- Wardsend Bridge, 2007
  Original Bridge built in the 18th Century to access Wardsend Cemetery, rebuilt after the 2007 Sheffield flood.
- Hillfoot Bridge, 1885
  Original bridge rebuilt after the Great Sheffield Flood. Grade II listed.
- Rutland Road Bridge, 18th C
  Originally known as 'Neepsend Bridge'
- Ball Street Bridge, 1865
  Rebuilt after the Great Sheffield Flood
- Borough Bridge, 1853
  Grade II Listed
- Iron Footbridge, c1865
  Original wooden bridge built in 1726. Replaced in 1795 by one of first 10 iron bridges in the world. Rebuilt after the Great Sheffield Flood.
- A61 Roundabout East Side Bridge, 2007
- Nursery Street Bridge, 2005
  Footbridge.
- Lady's Bridge, 1485
  Oldest recorded bridge in Sheffield. Grade II listed.
- Blonk Street Bridge, 1827
- Willey Street Footbridge, 2010
  Design based on butterfly wings.
- Derek Dooley Way Bridge, 2000
  Originally 'Cutlers Gate'. Renamed in 2008.
- Wicker Railway Viaduct, 1848

- Cobweb Footbridge, 2002
  Suspended underneath the Wicker Railway Viaduct.
- Bailey Bridge, 2006
  Footbridge – part of the Five Weirs Walk. This is an original WWII Bailey Bridge.
- Midland Railway Viaduct, 1870
- Norfolk Bridge, 1856
- Washford Bridge
  Recorded in a will in 1535. Rebuilt several times, including after WWII bombing damage.
- East Coast Road Bridge
- Scrapyard Railway Bridge
- Stevenson Road Bridge
- Newhall Road Bridge
  Originally a 17th C packhorse bridge.
- Amberley Street Footbridge
- Abyssinia Bridge, 1908
  Carries the outer ring road. Rebuilt in 1968 and named after the battle of the same year.
- Forgemaster Works Bridges
  Two roads and one pipe – all private.
- Weedon Street Bridge
  Also known as 'Brightside Bridge'.
- Sheffield District Railway Bridge, 1900
- Meadowhall Way SW Bridge
  This busy collection of bridges were all opened in 1990 at the same time as the Meadowhall Shopping Centre.
- Meadowhall Works Bridge
- Meadhowall Interchange Footbridge
- Meadowhall Way North Bridge
- Meadowhall Coach Park Bridge
- Meadowhall Coach Footbridge
- Supertram Bridge, 1994
- South Yorkshire R'way Bridge, 1854
- M1 Tinsley Viaduct, 1961
- Halfpenny Footbridge, 2001
  On the site of a ferry crossing where passage was half a penny.
- Blackburn Meadows Bridge

Dominoe Grove

Road in S9 named after 'Dominoe Joe' who led a protest march in 1893. The cause of the demonstration was a reduction in the wages paid to miners by the Birley Vale and Woodhouse Colliery owners.

Dooley, Derek

13th Dec 1929 – 5th Mar 2008

Brought up in Abbeydale, Banks left school at 15 and took up a job with a coal merchant. He had been a goalkeeper for Sheffield Schoolboys, but it was a chance opportunity to stand in for the regular goalkeeper of amateur side Millspaugh that led to him being scouted by professional outfit Chesterfield.

The 1951-52 season saw Dooley score 46 goals for Wednesday – this is still the club record for a single season. In February 1953 Dooley was injured in a collision with another player. Following treatment, it was discovered that his leg had become infected and had to be amputated.

Dooley returned to Wednesday to manage the club from 1971-73. Shortly after being sacked as manager, he was offered the role of Commercial Manager for Sheffield United, eventually becoming Chair of United's Club Board.

At the Sheffield derby in 1992, while still employed by United, Dooley received a standing ovation from both sets of fans. Similarly, when he died in 2008 both halves of the city came together to commemorate one of the city's greatest players. He was awarded an MBE in 2003, inducted into the Sheffield Legends Walk of Fame in 2007, and had a section of the ring road named after him in 2008.

Years	Team	Appearances	Goals
1946-47	Lincoln City	2	2
1947-53	Sheffield Wednesday	61	62
1971-73	Sheffield Wednesday	Manager	
1974-08	Sheffield United	Various roles	

Dore Stone

Dore means 'gateway', in this case between the Anglo-Saxon kingdoms of Northumbria and Mercia. The boundary was marked by the Limb Brook, the River Sheaf and the Meersbrook.

During the 820s King Egbert of Wessex had brought all of the regions of England, including Mercia, under his dominion. There was just one exception – Northumbria. The Anglo-Saxon Chronicles record that in 827 Egbert marched his army northwards and at Dore received the submission of King Eanred of Northumbria. The Dore Stone, bearing a plaque commemorating the moment at which Egbert became King of the whole of England, was erected on the village green in 1968.

Egbert has managed to gain a 'c' at some point during the past 1200 years. King Ecgbert School is today fittingly part of the Mercia Learning Trust.

Drabble, Margaret

Born: 5th June 1939

Education: Quaker boarding school, York, and Newnham College, Cambridge University.

Margaret Drabble was a prolific novelist. Her writing often drew on her own experiences - her early novels depict young women growing up in the 1960s and 70s. As well as fiction, Drabble authored biographies and screen plays, and was also a vocal anti-American (or at least anti-Bush) critic following the 2003 invasion of Iraq.

Drabble was appointed Commander of the British Empire (CBE) in 1980 and upgraded to a Dame Commander of the British Empire (DBE) in 2008. She was awarded the Golden PEN Award in 2011 and inducted into the Sheffield Walk of Fame in 2012.

Novels

- *A Summer Bird-Cage* (1963)
- *The Garrick Year* (1964)
- *The Millstone* (1965)
- *Jerusalem the Golden* (1967)
- *The Waterfall* (1969)
- *The Needle's Eye* (1972)
- *The Realms of Gold* (1975)
- *The Ice Age* (1977)
- *The Middle Ground* (1980)
- *Hassan's Tower* (1980)
- *The Radiant Way* (1987)
- *A Natural Curiosity* (1989)
- *The Gates of Ivory* (1991)
- *The Witch of Exmoor* (1996)
- *The Peppered Moth* (2001)
- *The Seven Sisters* (2002)
- *The Red Queen* (2004)
- *The Sea Lady* (2006)
- *The Pure Gold Baby* (2013)
- *The Dark Flood Rises* (2016)

Dungworth

This unattractively named hamlet is perched above Dam Flask reservoir. It is home of Our Cow Molly ice-cream and the Royal Hotel pub where Sheffield carols are sung from mid-November through to New Years Day. Dungworth dates back to the 13th Century and has been used as a local surname for at least as long. The name probably derives from a dwelling that was either partly underground or had a dung-covered roof.

DVLA Registrations

Standard car registration plates in England all carry an area code. Since 2001 the area code has been the first two letters of the registration plate, indicating the broad area where the vehicle was first registered. The two digit number is an age identifier and the last 3 letters are random letters.

The two letter area identifiers for the Sheffield region are listed below. The area identifiers of our nearest 'neighbours' are also given – a good number of these can also be seen on Sheffield's roads.

The Sheffield area identifiers allow a theoretical maximum of 243,340 unique registrations each year.

Leeds

YA, YB, YC, YD, YE, YF, YG, YH, YJ, YK, YL*

Beverley

YV*, YW, WX, YY

Manchester

MA, MB, MC, MD, ME, MF, MG, MH, MJ, MK, ML, MM,

Sheffield

YL*,YM, YN, YO, YP, YR, YS, YT, YU, YV*

Nottingham

FA, FB, FC, FD, FE, FF, FG, FH, FJ, FK, FL, FM, FN, FP

*These identifiers are shared, depending on demand.

Earl Marshal

The office of Earl Marshal is a hereditary position, held by the incumbent Duke of Norfolk. Apart from the Royal Family it is the highest hereditary office in the United Kingdom, and is ranked eighth of the nine Great Officers of State in terms of seniority. The Duke of Norfolk is therefore often referred to as "the first peer of the realm".

Duties today are largely ceremonial. In particular, the Earl Marshal has the important job of signing off on any new coats of arms.

Great Officers of State

1. Lord High Steward
2. Lord High Chancellor
3. Lord High Treasurer
4. Lord President of the Council
5. Lord Keeper of the Privy Seal
6. Lord Great Chamberlain
7. Lord High Constable
8. Earl Marshall
9. Lord High Admiral

In 1606 Thomas Howard (who's family held the hereditary titles of Earl of Arundel and Duke of Norfolk) married Alathea Talbot (who's family held the title of Earl of Shrewsbury, and owned much of Sheffield), thereby inheriting large parts of modern day Sheffield.

The Norfolk connection to Sheffield was therefore established, as was that of the title of Earl Marshal. Earl Marshal school is no more, having been 'rebranded' as Fir Vale, but Earl Marshall Road still reminds us of that link.

Edward Fitzalan-Howard is the 24th Duke of Norfolk and is the current Earl Marshal.

Eclipses

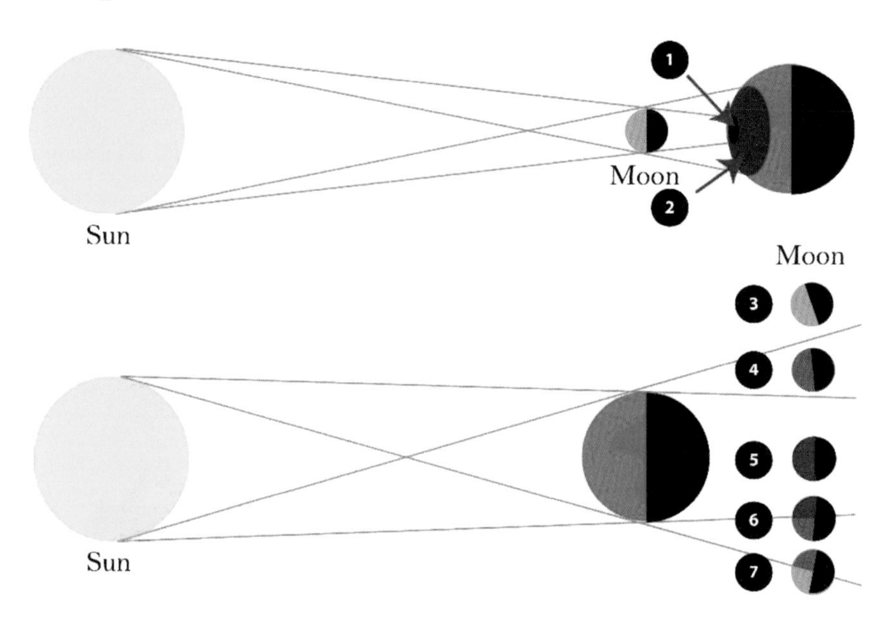

1 Total solar eclipse. If you are standing in this area the sun is completely obscured by the moon.

2 Partial solar eclipse. If you are standing in this area the sun is partly obscured by the moon.

3 No eclipse! Nothing is blocking anything else. Your relative position to the moon and sun will determine whether you see a full moon, a new moon, or something in between.

4 Lunar eclipse. The earth's shadow falls across the whole of the moon.

5 Partial lunar eclipse. The earth's shadow falls across part of the moon.

6 Penumbral eclipse. The earth partially blocks light falling across the entire surface of the moon.

7 Partial penumbral eclipse. The earth partially blocks light falling across part of the surface of the moon.

All the eclipses observable from Sheffield during the next 10 years are listed below. The 12th August 2026 looks to be the most dramatic date during the next decade from a heavenly body point of view.

If you are after a total solar eclipse viewable from Sheffield, you will sadly need to wait until 2051. Total solar eclipses are few and far between - the last time the moon came completely between the sun and Sheffield was all the way back in 1715.

Date	Time
10th June 2021	11:15am
19th Nov 2021	6:02am
16th May 2022	5:03am
25th Oct 2022	10:57am
28th Oct 2023	9:14pm
25th Mar 2024	6:02am
18th Sept 2024	3.44am
14th Mar 2025	6:20am
29th Mar 2025	11:04am
7th Sept 2025	7:46pm
12th Aug 2026	7.10pm
28th Aug 2026	5:12am
20th Feb 2027	11.12pm
2nd Aug 2027	10.00am
12th Jan 2028	4.13am
26th Jan 2028	4.31pm
6th July 2028	9.41pm
31st Dec 2028	4.51pm
12th June 2029	4.41am
26th June 2029	4.22am
20th Dec 2029	10:41pm
1st June 2030	6:25am
15th June 2030	9.32pm
9th Dec 2030	10:27pm

Education

Sheffield has around 200 schools and special schools, the vast majority state-funded. One in five Sheffield schools are rated "Outstanding" by OFSTED and almost nine out of ten are either "Good" or "Outstanding".

Decisions about where to live (**Catchment Areas**) and which primary school to apply to (**Feeders**) are important considerations for many. While **Educational Outcomes** for children in the city are still varied, this is perhaps more a function of deprivation than the performance of individual schools.

Sheffield was underserved in terms of its ability to educate its young people until the mid 20th Century, particularly in terms of having sufficient capacity in its **Secondary Schools.** In fact, many of today's secondary schools were only built in the decades following World War II. It is also interesting to notice the surprising amount of re-organisation/merging of secondary schools that has taken place, not to mention the renaming/rebranding of some schools - the secondary school landscape in some parts of the city today would be completely unrecognisable to the generation of our grandparents.

Sheffield is also proud to boast two prestigious universities that are both among the biggest employers in the region. The universities each have a student population of around 30,000 and have strong links with employers and industry – locally, nationally and internationally. The University of Sheffield and Sheffield Hallam University are both huge drivers for the economy of the city.

There is an urban myth that Sheffield has the highest 'retention rate' of graduates. This isn't quite true – after **University Graduation**, 42% of students remain in the city which *is* above the national average, but there is then a higher tendency than average for graduates to move out of the city over the longer term.

Educational Outcomes

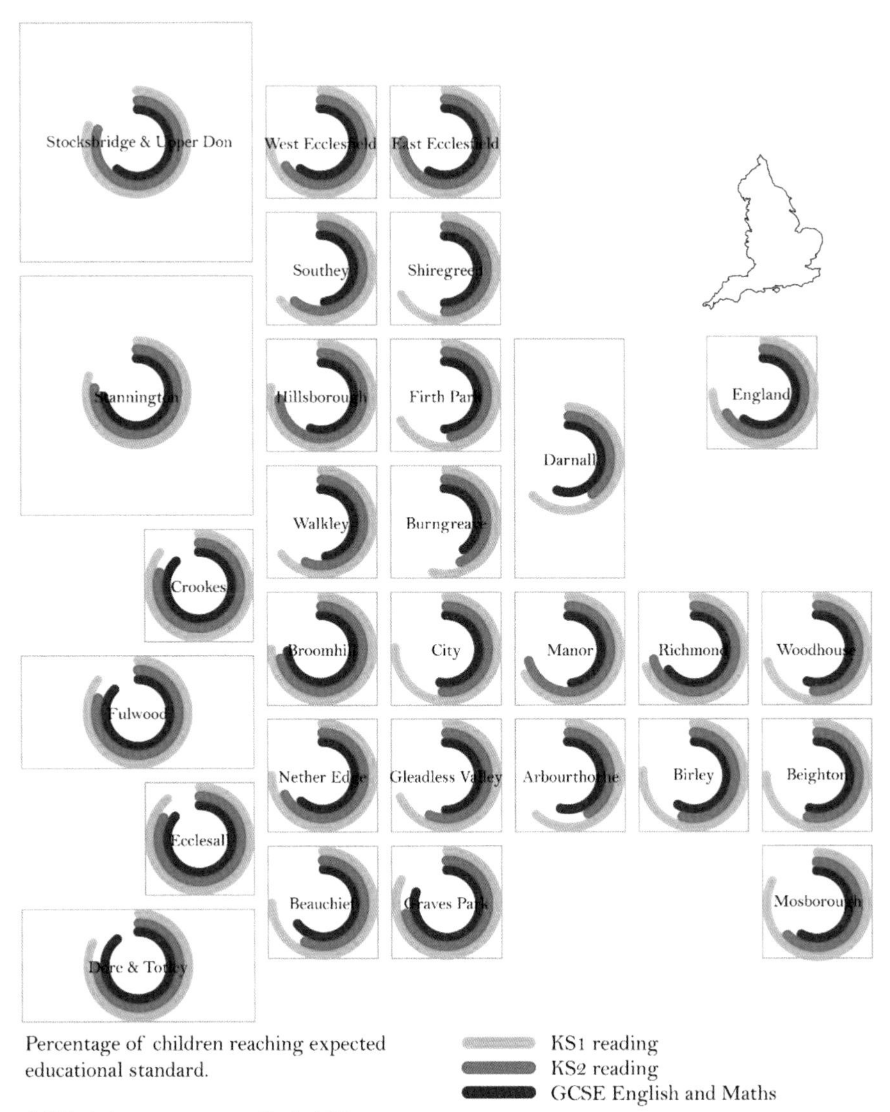

Percentage of children reaching expected educational standard.

A full circle represents 100% of children

Edward VII (King)

The list below catalogues royal visits made to Sheffield during the reign of Edward VII (1901-1910).

 Reigning monarch  Prince/Princess/Consort  Other royal

May 1905		Princess Henry of Battenburg to unveil the Queen Victoria Memorial, in Town Hall Square.
July 1905		Prince & Princess Arisugawa of Japan to inspect the guns being made for the Battleship *Katori* at the River Don Works.
July 1905		Edward VII and Queen Alexandra to open the University of Sheffield.
1906		Princess Christian to attend an NSPCC event at the Cutlers' Hall.
1909		George & Mary, Prince & Princess of Wales to open new University of Sheffield buildings.

Edward VIII (King)

There was just one royal visit to Sheffield during the Edward VIII's reign (1936).

 Reigning monarch  Prince/Princess/Consort  Other royal

1936		George, Duke of Kent to visit the Painted Fabrics Colony, Mappin and Webb, James Neill and Co., and the Royal Hospital

Elephants (the Herd of Sheffield)

A herd of 58 colourful elephants appeared in various locations around Sheffield during the summer of 2016. The seemingly bizarre choice of elephants was made as 2016 marked 100 years since the employment of 'Lizzie' the elephant in Sheffield during the First World War to haul munitions and machinery. The ever-resourceful citizens of Sheffield conscripted Lizzie, as well as a group of camels to help move the loads.

The 2016 herd of elephants were decorated by local artists, organisations and businesses. They were auctioned off in October 2016, raising over £400,000 for the Sheffield Children's Hospital.

The 10 most expensive elephants at auction are below.

Name	Creator	Exhibition location	Auction price
Marjorie	Pete McKee	Kelham Island	£22,000
AM	Matthew Cooper	Sheffield Town Hall	£16,500
Jungle Jim	Jenny Leonard	Peace Gardens	£15,000
Hendophant	Matt Cockayne	Leavygreave Rd	£11,300
Sheffield Elephant	Josh and Aimee Williams	Orchard Square	£11,000
The Elephant in the Hive	Caroline Greyling	Ponds Forge	£11,000
Bugsy	Liz Hall	Weston Park	£11,000
Izzy	Steve Millington	Sheffield Cathedral	£8,700
Elmer the Patchwork Elephant	Sheffield Children's Hospital patients	Weston Park	£8,500
Inconelly	Pressure Technologies	Fargate	£8,200

Elizabeth II (Queen)

The list below is a selection of the royal visits to Sheffield during the reign of Elizabeth II (1952-). All visits by Queen Elizabeth herself are recorded.

 Reigning monarch  Prince/Princess/Consort  Other royal

Apr 1953	Princess Margaret to open Rowlinson Secondary School, Norton.
Oct 1953	Alice, Duchess of Gloucester to open the Charles Clifford Dental Hospital.
Nov 1953	Philip, Duke of Edinburgh to open the British Iron Steel Research Labs.
Mar 1957	Princess Alexandra of Kent to open Silverdale Secondary School and St Mary's Church, Bramall Lane.
Oct 1957	Philip, Duke of Edinburgh to celebrate the centenary of Sheffield Football Club.
1958	Queen Mother to lay the foundation stone of the Royal Hallamshire Hospital.
1966	Queen Elizabeth the Queen Mother to open Hyde Park Redevelopment Scheme and the University of Sheffield Arts Tower.
1967	Philip, Duke of Edinburgh to open Granville College.
Feb 1969	Philip, Duke of Edinburgh to open the Engineering Industry Training Board.
May 1969	Katherine, Duchess of Kent to open new wards at Nether Edge Hospital.
1970	Princess Anne to open Weston Park Hospital.
1975	Queen Elizabeth II royal visit to South Yorkshire.
1977	Queen Elizabeth II Silver Jubilee visit.
1979	Charles, Prince of Wales to open Royal Hallamshire Hospital.
Jul 1980	Princess Anne to visit Manor Top Territorial Army Centre.

Oct 1980	♛	Prince and Princess Michael of Kent to open new arts block at Brook School, Richmond Road.
1984	♛	Prince and Princess of Wales royal visit.
Apr 1986	♛	Diana, Princess of Wales visit to Lodge Moor and Jessop Hospitals.
Dec 1986	♛	Queen Elizabeth II to open the roofed Spion Kop at Hillsborough, and the extension to the Assay Office.
Mar 1988	♛	Katherine, Duchess of Kent to open new South Yorkshire Fire Service HQ.
Nov 1988	♛	Prince Charles to visit the Leadmill.
1989	♛	Charles and Diana to visit victims of the Hillsborough Disaster.
Sep 1989	♛	Birgitte, Duchess of Gloucester to visit the Ryegate Centre.
Nov 1989	♛	Diana, Princess of Wales to visit the Children's Hospital and Family Service Unit.
Mar 1990	♛	Anne, Princess Royal for Ponds Forge topping out ceremony.
May 1990	♛	Anne, Princess Royal to attend Cutler's Feast.
Sep 1990	♛	Prince Edward for Duke of Edinburgh Award Scheme and to visit the Lyceum Theatre and new Meadowhall Shopping Centre.
Apr 1991	♛	Anne, Princess Royal to open the Ponds Forge International Sports Centre.
May 1991	♛	Queen Elizabeth II to open the Sheffield Arena; Philip, Duke of Edinburgh to attend the Cutler's Feast.
Jul 1991	♛	Anne, Princess Royal to attend the World Student Games.
Jun 1993	♛	Edward, Duke of Kent to attend opening Ceremony of the Hillsborough Memorial Garden.
Dec 1993	♛	Princess Margaret to open the Northern General Hospital's Firth Wing.
Mar 1994	♛	Queen Elizabeth II to open Sheffield Hallam University campus.

May 1994	♛	Anne, Princess Royal to open Supertram and visit Weston Park.
1995	♛	Anne, Princess Royal to open Manor Development Centre.
1998	♛	Philip, Duke of Edinburgh to open Sheffield Airport.
2000	♛	Andrew, Duke of York to unveil HMS Sheffield tribute at Sheffield Cathedral.
2002	♛	Birgitte, Duchess of Gloucester to visit Owler Brook School.
May 2003	♛	Queen Elizabeth II and Philip, Duke of Edinburgh to open the Winter Gardens.
Sep 2003	♛	Charles, Prince of Wales to open the Botanical Gardens Pavilions.
2006	♛	Edward and Sophie, Duke and Duchess of Wessex to visit Hinde House School and Red Cross HQ.
Jun 2007	♛	Charles, Prince of Wales to visit flood damage at Forgemasters.
Sep 2007	♛	Richard, Duke of Gloucester to visit flood damage.
2008	♛	Andrew, Duke of York to visit Sheffield Park Academy and the Advanced Manufacturing Park.
Feb 2010	♛	Edward, Duke of Wessex to re-open the Crucible theatre
Nov 2010	♛	Queen Elizabeth II and Philip, Duke of Edinburgh to open the Motor Neurone Disease Study Centre.
2011	♛	Camilla, Duchess of Cornwall to visit Emmaus Primary School.
2012	♛	Andrew, Duke of York to visit Madina Masjid Mosque.
2015	♛	Queen Elizabeth II to distribute Maundy Money
2019	♛	Harry, Duke of Sussex to visit Hallamshire Hospital, Hallam University and Invictus trials.
2020	♛	Duchess Catherine to visit Baby Basics charity.

Ennis-Hill, Jessica

Born: 28th Jan 1986

Education: Sharrow Primary School, King Ecgbert Secondary School, University of Sheffield (Psychology).

Jessica Ennis-Hill is Britain's greatest ever Heptathlete. Her international career was bookended by a bronze medal in the 2006 Melbourne Commonwealth Games and a silver medal in the Rio Olympics in 2016.

The highlight of her career was undoubtedly rising to the huge pressure of being the golden-girl for the London 2012 Olympics and producing a lifetime best performance to secure Olympic gold.

In recognition of her Olympic success Ennis-Hill was given the freedom of the City of Sheffield, had a postbox on the corner of Division Street and Holly Street painted gold, and Henderson's produced a commemorative gold-labelled bottle of relish in her honour.

Ennis-Hill was appointed Member of the Order of the British Empire (MBE) in 2011 and was inducted into the Sheffield Walk of Fame in the same year. She was runner up to Bradley Wiggins in the 2012 *Sports Personality of the Year*, and was appointed Commander of the Order of the British Empire (CBE) in 2013.

Heptathlon Events Personal Bests

Event	Record	Points	Event	Year
100m hurdles	12.54s	1,195	London Olympics	2012
High jump	1.95m	1,171	Desenzano del Garda, Competition	2007
Shot put	14.67m	839	Daegu, World Championships	2011
200m	22.83s	1,096	London, Olympics	2012
Long jump	6.63m	1,049	Ratingen, Competition	2016
Javelin	48.33m	828	Loughborough, Competition	2013
800 m	2:07.81	997	Daegu, World Championships	2011
Heptathlon	6,955 pts	7,175*	London, Olympics	2012

*Potential best

Faith

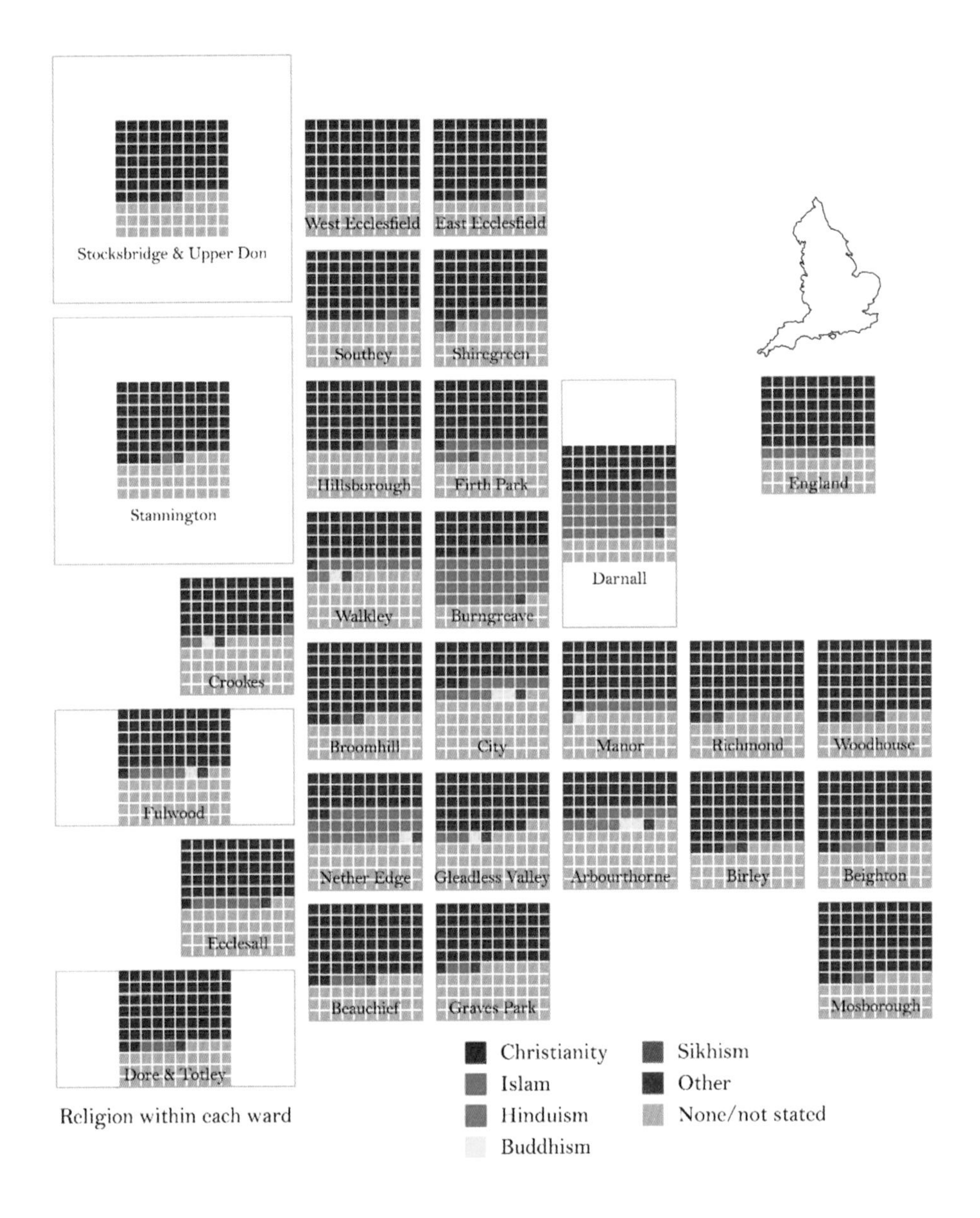

Religion within each ward

Feeder Schools

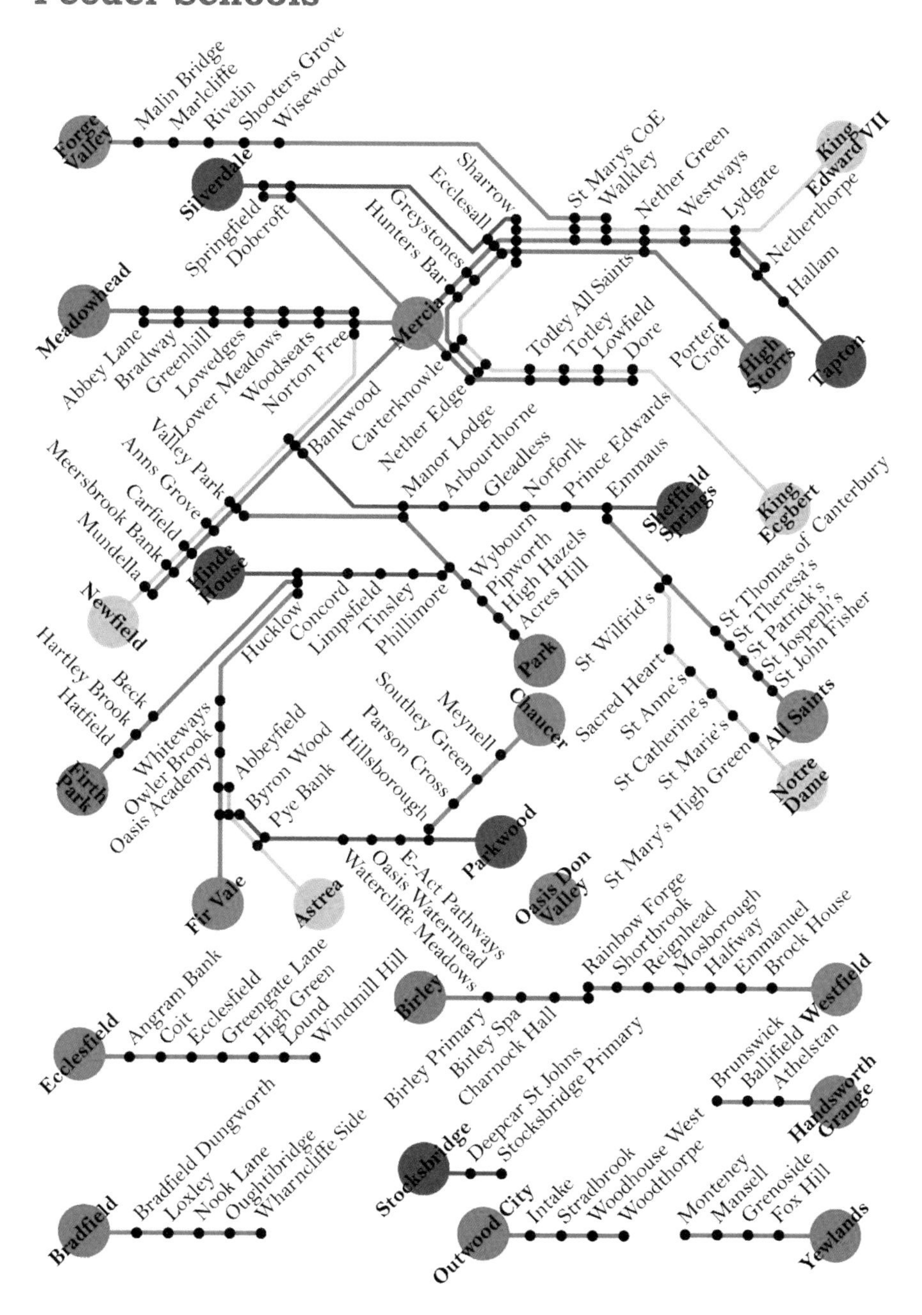

Filmed in Sheffield

- **Among Giants**
  Director: Sam Miller 1998
  Starring: Pete Postlethwaite, Rachel Griffiths, James Thornton

- **Four Lions**
  Director: Chris Morris 2010
  Starring: Riz Ahmed, Kayvan Novak, Nigel Lindsay, Arsher Ali, Adeel Akhtar

- **The Full Monty**
  Director: Peter Cattaneo 1997
  Starring: Robert Carlyle, Mark Addy, William Snape, Steve Huison

- **Funny Cow**
  Director: Adrian Shergold 2017
  Starring: Maxine Peake, Paddy Considine, Tony Pitts. Music by Richard Hawley

- **Hard Steel**
  Director: Norman Walker 1942
  Starring: Wilfrid Lawson, Betty Stockfeld, John Stuart

- **The History Boys**
  Director: Nicholas Hytner 2006
  Starring: Richard Griffiths, James Cordon, Russell Tovey, Frances de la Tour

- **Looks and Smiles**
  Director: Ken Loach 1981
  Starring: Graham Green

- **The Navigators**
  Director: Ken Loach 2001
  Starring: Dean Andrews, Thomas Craig, Joe Duttine, Steve Huison

- **Threads**
  Director: Mick Jackson 1984
  Starring: Karen Meagher, Reece Dinsdale

- **When Saturday Comes**
  Director: Maria Giese 1996
  Starring: Sean Bean, Emily Lloyd, Pete Postlethwaite

Fire

Major fires in Sheffield

Mar 1864	Surrey Theatre on West Bar burned down.
Jan 1887	All but tower and spire of St John's Ranmoor burned down.
Dec 1893	Fire at Hovey & Sons on Angel Street. Several businesses and stock destroyed. Value of damages estimated at £30m in today's money.
July 1898	Rawsons Brewery, Pond Street, destroyed by fire.
Jan 1904	Major fire at Birley Colliery. Amazingly, there were no fatalities.
April 1921	Sheaf Bank Works entirely destroyed by fire.
Dec 1940	Sheffield Blitz – large number of fires following the dropping of incendiary devices on the nights of 12th and 15th Dec.
Aug 1968	Fire and explosions at the Little Mermaid Café, Norfolk Street. Two firemen lost their lives.
June 1968	Large fire at the Queens Road Arnold Laver timber depot. In July 2002 a similar disaster was averted at the Arnold Laver Halfway depot – two forklift trucks caught fire, but fortunately were extinguished before the fire could spread.
Oct 1973	Gasworks explosion on Effingham Road. Three killed, many injured.
Feb 1974	Explosion at British Steel Works in Tinsley.
Dec 1984	Enormous fire at the Brightside storage warehouse on Carlisle Street. Probably Sheffield's largest ever single blaze.
June 2007	Gatecrasher night club burned down.
April 2012	Sheffield Ski Village destroyed by fire.
July 2013	Large fire at the Attercliffe recycling plant, close by the Parkway. Smoke visible for miles.
Sept 2014	Large fire at Ecclesfield industrial site.
July 2020	Large warehouse fire on the Parkwood Industrial Estate.

The National Emergency Services Museum on West Bar originally opened as the Sheffield Fire and Police Museum.

Football

UNITED		vs		WEDNESDAY
1889		Founded		1867
The Blades		Known as		The Owls
Bramall Lane		Home ground		Hillsborough Stadium
1899, 1902, 1915, 1925	🏆🏆🏆🏆	FA Cup winners	🏆🏆🏆	1896, 1907, 1935
1901, 1936	🏆🏆	FA Cup runners-up	🏆🏆🏆	1890, 1966, 1993
1897-98	🏆	Division One champions	🏆🏆🏆🏆	1903, 1904, 1929, 1930
away vs Port Vale, 1892 at home vs Burnley, Jan 1929	10-0	Biggest league win	9-1	at home vs Birmingham City, Dec 1930
away vs Middlesbrough, Nov 1933	3-10	Heaviest league defeat	0-10	away vs Aston Villa, Oct 1912
at home vs Leyton Orient, 2016	6-0	Biggest cup win	12-0	at home against Halliwell, Jan 1891
at home vs Bolton Wanderers, FA Cup 2nd Round, 1890	0-13	Heaviest cup defeat	1-6	away vs Blackburn Rovers, FA Cup Final 1890
vs Leeds United, FA Cup 5th Round, Feb 1936	68,287	Highest all-time home attendance	72,841	vs Manchester City, FA Cup 5th Round, Feb 1934
during 1925-26	102	Most goals in a league season	106	during 1958-29
during 2016-17	100	Most points in a season	93	during 2011-12

most recently in 2017-18	8	Longest winning run of matches	9	during 1904-05
during 1899-00	22	Longest unbeaten run of matches	19	during 1960-61 & also 2011-12
during 1975-76	7	Longest losing run of matches	8	during 2000-01
during 1975-76	19	Longest run without a win	20	during 1974-75
Joe Shaw, 1948-66	631	Most league appearances by a single player	501	Andrew Wilson, 1900-20
Jack Smith, 1935-48	203	Most consecutive appearances	214	Martin Hodge, 1983-87
Harry Hammond vs Bootle, 1892 & Harry Johnson vs West Ham, 1927	5	Most goals in a single league match	6	Douglas Hodge vs Norwich, 1938
Jimmy Dunne, 1930-31	41	Most league goals in a season	46	Derek Dooley, 1951-52
Louis Reed, 2014	16 yr 257 days	Youngest player ever	15 yr 269 days	Peter Fox, 1973
Jimmy Hagan, 1958	39 yr	Oldest player ever	46 yr	Jerry Jackson, 1923
Oli McBurnie from Swansea City, Aug 2019	£17m	Highest transfer fee paid	£8m	Jordan Rhodes from Middlesbrough in July 2017
David Brooks to AFC Bournemouth, July 2018	£11.5m	Highest transfer fee received	£3m	Chris Brunt, transferred to West Bromwich Albion, Aug 2007

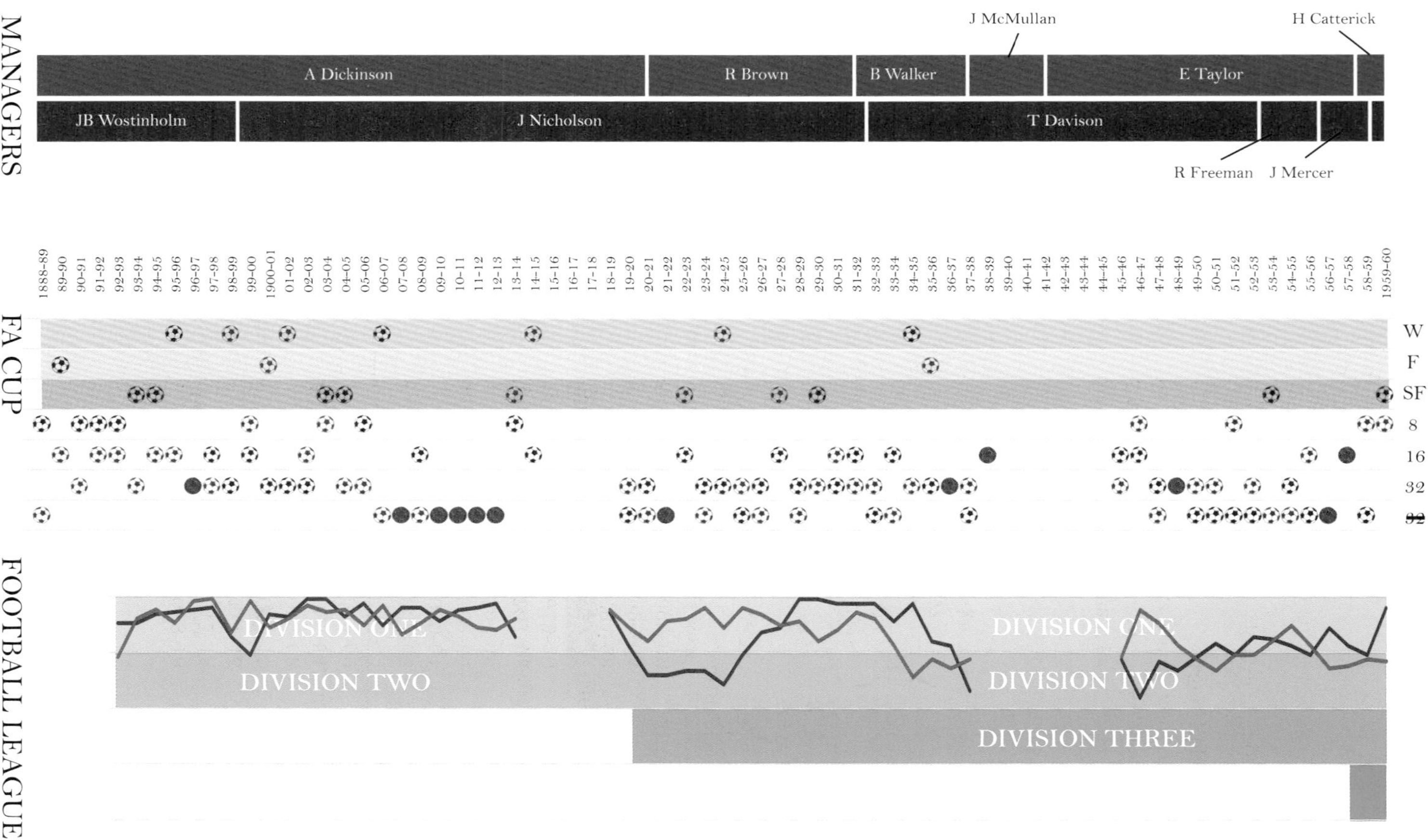

MANAGERS
A Dickinson
R Brown
B Walker
J McMullan
E Taylor
H Catterick
JB Wostinholm
J Nicholson
T Davison
R Freeman
J Mercer
1888-89
89-90
90-91
91-92
92-93
93-94
94-95
95-96
96-97
97-98
98-99
99-00
1900-01
01-02
02-03
03-04
04-05
05-06
06-07
07-08
08-09
09-10
10-11
11-12
12-13
13-14
14-15
15-16
16-17
17-18
18-19
19-20
20-21
21-22
22-23
23-24
24-25
25-26
26-27
27-28
28-29
29-30
30-31
31-32
32-33
33-34
34-35
35-36
36-37
37-38
38-39
39-40
40-41
41-42
42-43
43-44
44-45
45-46
46-47
47-48
48-49
49-50
50-51
51-52
52-53
53-54
54-55
55-56
56-57
57-58
58-59
1959-60
FA CUP
W
F
SF
8
16
32
FOOTBALL LEAGUE
DIVISION ONE
DIVISION TWO
DIVISION ONE
DIVISION TWO
DIVISION THREE

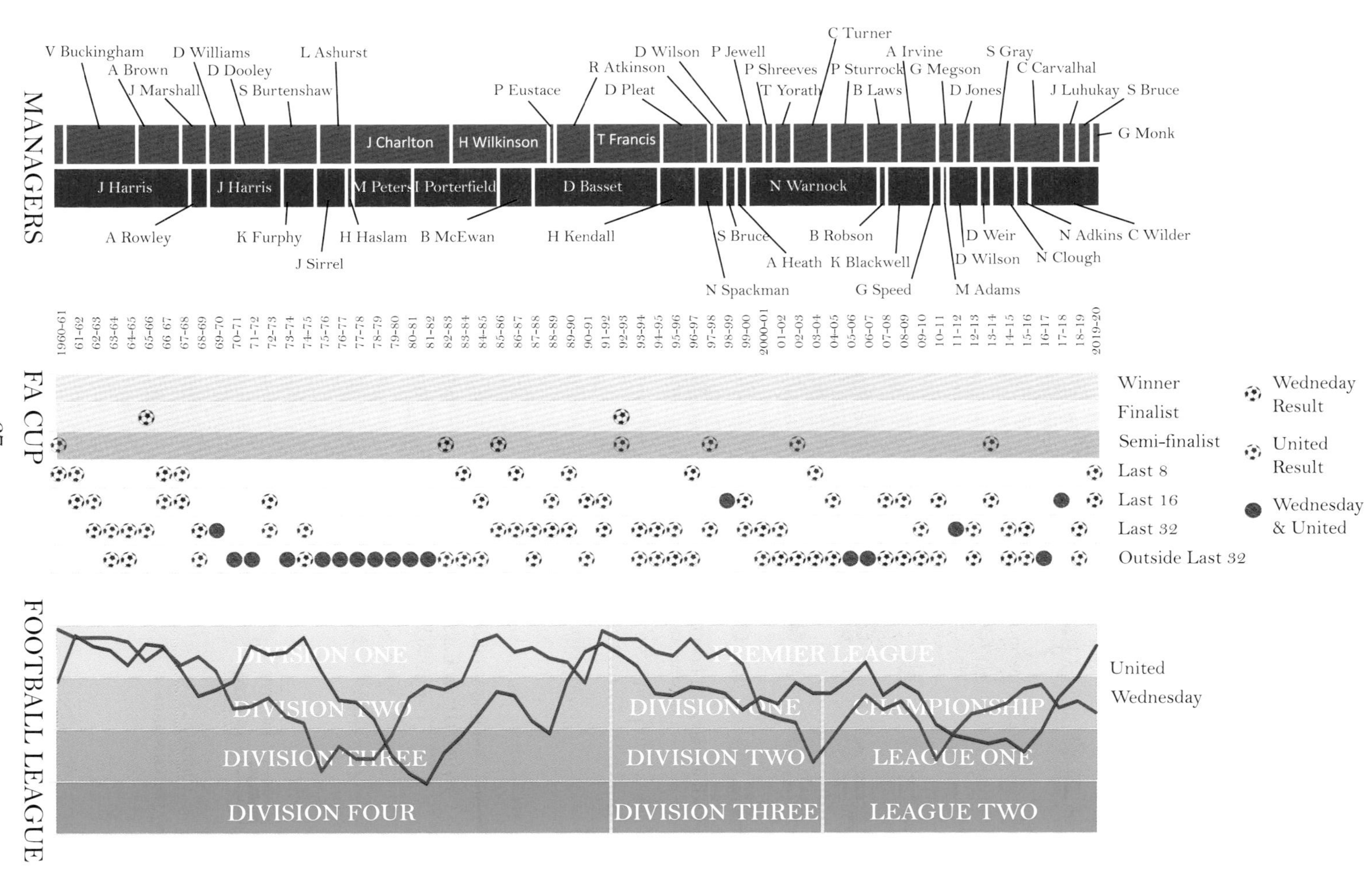
MANAGERS
V Buckingham
A Brown
J Marshall
D Williams
D Dooley
S Burtenshaw
L Ashurst
J Charlton
H Wilkinson
P Eustace
R Atkinson
D Pleat
T Francis
D Wilson
P Jewell
P Shreeves
T Yorath
C Turner
P Sturrock
B Laws
A Irvine
G Megson
D Jones
S Gray
C Carvalhal
J Luhukay
S Bruce
G Monk
J Harris
J Harris
M Peters
I Porterfield
D Basset
N Warnock
A Rowley
K Furphy
J Sirrel
H Haslam
B McEwan
H Kendall
S Bruce
N Spackman
A Heath
B Robson
K Blackwell
G Speed
D Weir
D Wilson
M Adams
N Clough
N Adkins
C Wilder
FA CUP
Winner
Finalist
Semi-finalist
Last 8
Last 16
Last 32
Outside Last 32
Wedneday Result
United Result
Wednesday & United
FOOTBALL LEAGUE
DIVISION ONE
DIVISION TWO
DIVISION THREE
DIVISION FOUR
PREMIER LEAGUE
DIVISION ONE
DIVISION TWO
DIVISION THREE
CHAMPIONSHIP
LEAGUE ONE
LEAGUE TWO
United
Wednesday

General Cemetery

This is the largest cemetery in Sheffield, having taken 87,000 burials right up until the 1970s. Difficult to imagine today, when it was opened in 1836 it was '*at some distance in the countryside…in a remote and undisturbed location*'.

The General Cemetery is the final resting place of a large number of Sheffield notables, some of whom are listed below. It also contains the largest single plot burial in England – one grave containing the bodies of 96 paupers.

The General Cemetery is open to the public – it scores an impressive (and perhaps surprising) 4.5 out of 5 on Tripadvisor.

- George Bassett (1818–1886)
  Founder of Bassetts and creator of Allsorts. Mayor of Sheffield (1876).
- George Bennett (died 1841)
  Founder of the Sheffield Sunday School movement. The memorial to him (c.1850) is Grade II listed.
- John, Thomas, and Skelton Cole
  Founders of the Cole Brothers department store in 1847.
- Francis Dickinson (1830-1898)
  Soldier who fought in the Charge of the Light Brigade during the Crimean war.
- William Dronfield (1824–1891)
  Founded the Alliance of Organised Trades, which was a forerunner of the Trades Union Congress.
- Mark Firth (1819 –1880)
  Steel manufacturer, Master Cutler (1867), Mayor of Sheffield (1874), and founder of Firth College that later became the University of Sheffield.
- William Flockton (1804 – 1864)
  Architect who built Wesley College (now King Edward VII school, Tapton Hall and a number of listed Sheffield churches.
- John Gunson (1809–1886)
  Chief engineer of the Sheffield Water Company when the Dale Dyke reserevoir wall collapsed causing the Great Sheffield Flood. Around a third of the flood's 240 victims are also buried in the General Cemetery.
- Samuel Holberry (1816–1842)
  A leading figure in the Chartist movement, Holberry was jailed after his plans to organise a 'Sheffield Rising' were discovered. His funeral was attended by one third of the population of Sheffield.
- Isaac Ironside (1808–1870)
  Chartist and local politician. We have Ironside to thank for the paving of our streets and the laying of underground sewers in the city.

- James Montgomery (1771–1854)
  Although originally buried in the general cemetery, the grave and Grade II listed monument to the poet James Montgomery were moved to the grounds of Sheffield Cathedral in 1971. Montgomery Road in Nether Edge is named after him.
- James Nicholson (died 1909)
  Prominent Sheffield industrialist. The Florentine pub in Ranmoor was built as a residence for his family.
- William Parker (died 1837)
  One of the first people to be buried in the cemetery. The monument that was erected at his grave is also one of the finest.
- William Prest (died 1885)
  Co-founded Sheffield Football club.

Other Cemeteries

- Abbey Lane Cemetery
- Bowcroft Cemetery
- Bradfield View Natural Burial Ground
- Burncross Cemetery
- Burngreave Cemetery
- City Road Cemetery
- Darnall Road Cemetery
- Ecclesfield Cemetery
- Intake Cemetery
- Loxley Cemetery
- Norton Cemetery
- Sheffield Jewish Cemetery
- Shiregreen Cemetery
- South Yorkshire Woodland Burial Ground
- St Mary's Cemetery, Walkley
- St Michael's Cemetery, Rivelin
- Tinsley Park Cemetery
- Wardsend Cemetery
- Wisewood Cemetery
- Woodhouse Cemetery

Crematoria

- City Road
- Grenoside
- Hutcliffe Wood

Geography and Climate

Sheffield is generally acknowledged to be more geographically diverse than any other English city. There is a greater diversity of habitats in Sheffield than in any other European city and a large number of **Nature Reserves** within the city boundary.

The geology of the region, with plentiful **Coal** and other minerals **Under Your Feet**, has provided the raw materials for Sheffield's industry, and the three-dimensional landscape meant that residents were able to harness the local **Waterpower** to their advantage. More recently, the local gritstone rock, best seen at **Stanage** has been a significant factor behind Sheffield's status as the climbing capital of England.

Sheffield's **Hills** and **Triangulation Points** serve as great vantage points from which to survey the landscape. **Rivers** provide green corridors that transport you quickly from the city into the countryside, taking you from an urban landscape, through woodland and agricultural land up onto high moorland. In times of heavy rainfall the steep hillsides and fast flowing rivers channel water quickly down the valleys, often leading to localised flooding. **Reservoirs** on the higher ground to the west of the city are an integral part of the landscape.

The landscape affects the weather in the city too. While the climate of Sheffield is best described as temperate, the variation in altitude of different parts of the city (ranging from 30m above sea level in the east to over 500m on the western moorland with most of the housing at a height between 100m and 200m) means that different parts of the city experience greater weather extremes than others. Heavier and earlier snowfall, heavier rain and higher winds all tend to be experienced on the higher ground. **Weather Records** show the range of weather experienced in Sheffield and **Snow** catalogues those winters of heaviest snowfall.

Sheffield has more trees per head of population than any other city – 9 trees per person. In fact there are almost twice as many silver birches (**Betula Pendula**) alone as there are people in Sheffield. The numerous areas of **Woodland** provide a high level of **Tree Canopy Cover** throughout the city.

George V (King)

The list below catalogues royal visits to Sheffield during the reign of George V (1910-1936).

Reigning monarch   Prince/Princess/Consort   Other royal

1915	King George to visit Wharncliffe War Hospital & Hadfields Ltd.
1918	King George and Queen Mary to visit the Grimesthorpe Steel and Ordnance Works
1919	King George & Queen Mary to present WWI honours.
1920	Prince Purachatia of Siam to visit Brown Bayley Steel Works.
July 1921	Edward, Prince of Wales to open Prince of Wales Road and visit Vickers and Hadfields.
Nov 1921	George, Duke of York to visit Hadfields and Blackburn Meadows Power Station.
1923	Edward, Prince of Wales to open the extension to the Town Hall and to visit Vickers and Hadfields.
1924	Albert, Duke of York to visit the King Edward VII Hospital.
1925	Princess Mary to visit the Royal Infirmary and the Painted Fabrics Colony.
Mar 1928	King & Queen of Afghanistan to visit Hadfields.
Aug 1928	Mary, Princess Royal to visit the Painted Fabrics Colony.
1929	Princess Mary, to open the Earl Haig Memorial Homes, to inaugurate the new block-printing department at the Painted Fabrics Colony and to receive the YMCA purses.
1930	Prince George to visit the Royal Infirmary and the Painted Fabrics Colony.
Apr 1933	Prince George to open Blackburn Meadows generating station.
Oct 1933	Mary, Princess Royal to present purses.

1934	♛	Elizabeth, Duchess of York to open the Central Library and Graves Art Gallery, and to visit the Painted Fabrics Colony and Royal Infirmary.
1935	♛	Edward, Prince of Wales and Mary, Princess Royal, to visit the Painted Fabrics Colony.

George VI (King

The list below catalogues royal visits to Sheffield during the reign of George VI (1936-1952).

 Reigning monarch  Prince/Princess/Consort  Other royal

April 1937	♛	Mary, Princess Royal to lay the foundation of an extension to Sheffield Cathedral
Oct 1937	♛	King George VI and Queen Elizabeth coronation visit
Mar 1938	♛	Albert, Duke of York to open part of the Royal Hospital
June 1938	♛	George, Duke of Kent industrial visit.
Jul 1938	♛	Alice, Duchess of Gloucester to lay the foundation stone of the Jessop Hospital.
1939	♛	Mary, Princess Royal to visit extension to Cathedral.
June 1940	♛	Mary, Princess Royal to open the new Princess Mary Nurses Home, Southey Hill.
Dec 1940	♛	Mary, Princess Royal to visit blitz casualties.
Jan 1941	♛	King George VI and Queen Elizabeth to inspect blitz damage.
Oct 1941	♛	King George VI and Queen Elizabeth visit to Sheffield.
Jan 1942	♛	Mary, Princess Royal to visit Auxiliary Territorial Service Girls on anti-aircraft gun sites.

Apr 1942		King Haakon of Norway.
May 1942	♛	Mary, Princess Royal visit to Sheffield.
Jun 1942	♛	George, Duke of Kent visit to Auxiliary Territorial service.
Aug 1942	♛	Mary, Princess Royal visit to Women's Voluntary Service.
Jan 1944	♛	Alice, Duchess of Gloucester to visit the Jessop Hospital.
Feb 1944	♛	Marina, Duchess of Kent to visit Arthur Balfour and Co. Ltd., and Walker and Hall Ltd.
1945		King George VI & Queen Elizabeth to open Ladybower Reservoir
Mar 1946	♛	Mary, Princess Royal to open a nursing exhibition at Fargate House.
Jul 1946	♛	Mary, Princess Royal to open the Regional Blood Transfusion Service and to visit the King Edward VII Hospital and Painted Fabrics Colony.
1948	♛	Princess Margaret to attend the Pageant of Production and to open the *Sheffield on its Mettle* Exhibition.
1949	♛	Mary, Princess Royal to open Sheffield National Centre for Radiotherapy.

Ghosts

Sheffield's most haunted locations (allegedly!):

- Bunting Nook, Norton
- Carbrook Hall
- Endcliffe Hall
- Former Star Building
- Highcliffe Road
- Mosborough Hall Hotel
- Northern General (Vickers Corridor)
- Old Queens Head
- Sheffield Fire and Police Museum
- Stocksbridge Bypass

Golf

Golf courses cover over 0.5% of all land in England. Sheffield's contribution is below.

Data on each hole is given as Yardage $^{\text{Par}}_{\text{Stroke Index}}$

Hole	Abbeydale	Beauchief	Birley Wood	Concord	Dore & Totley	Hallamshire	Hillsborough	Lees Hall	Stocksbridge	Tinsley
1	370 $^{4}_{13}$	326 $^{4}_{9}$	361 $^{4}_{13}$	283 $^{4}_{13}$	495 $^{5}_{13}$	455 $^{4}_{6}$	423 $^{4}_{3}$	324 $^{4}_{10}$	251 $^{4}_{15}$	424 $^{4}_{8}$
2	139 $^{3}_{17}$	199 $^{3}_{11}$	358 $^{4}_{3}$	482 $^{5}_{5}$	417 $^{4}_{5}$	175 $^{3}_{17}$	128 $^{3}_{13}$	346 $^{4}_{6}$	135 $^{3}_{9}$	162 $^{3}_{16}$
3	446 $^{5}_{9}$	394 $^{4}_{3}$	275 $^{4}_{9}$	290 $^{4}_{17}$	131 $^{3}_{17}$	409 $^{4}_{11}$	354 $^{4}_{1}$	309 $^{4}_{16}$	432 $^{4}_{17}$	483 $^{5}_{1}$
4	432 $^{4}_{1}$	162 $^{3}_{13}$	462 $^{5}_{7}$	470 $^{5}_{11}$	468 $^{5}_{9}$	390 $^{4}_{7}$	379 $^{4}_{5}$	499 $^{5}_{14}$	329 $^{4}_{3}$	314 $^{4}_{14}$
5	387 $^{4}_{7}$	371 $^{4}_{5}$	155 $^{3}_{15}$	420 $^{4}_{1}$	154 $^{3}_{16}$	474 $^{5}_{2}$	355 $^{4}_{11}$	150 $^{3}_{18}$	341 $^{4}_{5}$	282 $^{4}_{18}$
6	460 $^{5}_{11}$	275 $^{4}_{17}$	546 $^{5}_{5}$	145 $^{3}_{7}$	413 $^{4}_{3}$	177 $^{3}_{13}$	189 $^{3}_{9}$	535 $^{5}_{8}$	148 $^{3}_{11}$	346 $^{4}_{6}$
7	365 $^{4}_{3}$	424 $^{4}_{1}$	164 $^{3}_{11}$	190 $^{3}_{3}$	333 $^{4}_{7}$	306 $^{4}_{9}$	233 $^{4}_{17}$	355 $^{4}_{2}$	397 $^{4}_{1}$	282 $^{4}_{17}$
8	329 $^{4}_{15}$	292 $^{4}_{15}$	270 $^{4}_{17}$	310 $^{4}_{15}$	372 $^{4}_{1}$	359 $^{4}_{4}$	342 $^{4}_{7}$	207 $^{3}_{12}$	414 $^{5}_{13}$	408 $^{4}_{4}$
9	361 $^{4}_{5}$	223 $^{3}_{7}$	403 $^{4}_{1}$	303 $^{4}_{9}$	488 $^{5}_{11}$	143 $^{3}_{15}$	484 $^{5}_{15}$	528 $^{5}_{4}$	280 $^{4}_{7}$	155 $^{3}_{11}$
10	123 $^{3}_{18}$	455 $^{4}_{2}$	380 $^{4}_{4}$	326 $^{4}_{12}$	324 $^{4}_{15}$	407 $^{4}_{1}$	177 $^{3}_{12}$	271 $^{4}_{17}$	163 $^{3}_{10}$	377 $^{4}_{13}$
11	462 $^{5}_{14}$	162 $^{3}_{10}$	279 $^{4}_{10}$	114 $^{3}_{6}$	453 $^{4}_{2}$	311 $^{4}_{10}$	477 $^{5}_{6}$	165 $^{3}_{11}$	402 $^{4}_{8}$	364 $^{4}_{10}$
12	160 $^{3}_{10}$	244 $^{4}_{18}$	107 $^{3}_{18}$	244 $^{4}_{14}$	372 $^{4}_{8}$	123 $^{3}_{18}$	343 $^{4}_{10}$	460 $^{4}_{5}$	358 $^{4}_{6}$	391 $^{4}_{2}$
13	431 $^{4}_{2}$	268 $^{4}_{14}$	358 $^{4}_{8}$	149 $^{3}_{4}$	273 $^{4}_{6}$	334 $^{4}_{3}$	125 $^{3}_{18}$	449 $^{4}_{1}$	153 $^{3}_{16}$	353 $^{4}_{12}$
14	464 $^{5}_{4}$	152 $^{3}_{16}$	119 $^{3}_{16}$	126 $^{3}_{16}$	412 $^{4}_{4}$	420 $^{5}_{14}$	418 $^{4}_{2}$	178 $^{3}_{15}$	160 $^{3}_{12}$	362 $^{4}_{3}$
15	134 $^{3}_{12}$	191 $^{3}_{8}$	432 $^{4}_{2}$	246 $^{4}_{2}$	378 $^{4}_{14}$	518 $^{5}_{5}$	399 $^{4}_{4}$	418 $^{4}_{3}$	364 $^{4}_{4}$	152 $^{3}_{15}$
16	387 $^{4}_{8}$	503 $^{5}_{4}$	303 $^{4}_{12}$	92 $^{3}_{18}$	124 $^{3}_{18}$	415 $^{4}_{8}$	305 $^{4}_{14}$	148 $^{3}_{9}$	162 $^{3}_{2}$	496 $^{5}_{5}$
17	379 $^{4}_{6}$	358 $^{4}_{12}$	147 $^{3}_{14}$	140 $^{3}_{10}$	339 $^{4}_{12}$	123 $^{3}_{16}$	282 $^{4}_{16}$	352 $^{4}_{13}$	124 $^{3}_{18}$	180 $^{3}_{7}$
18	144 $^{3}_{16}$	354 $^{4}_{6}$	371 $^{4}_{6}$	268 $^{4}_{8}$	414 $^{4}_{10}$	454 $^{5}_{12}$	588 $^{5}_{8}$	477 $^{5}_{7}$	354 $^{4}_{14}$	368 $^{4}_{9}$
	71	67	69	67	72	71	71	71	66	70

A player with a handicap of 12 is given a stroke deduction on all those holes with a stroke index of 1 to 12. Stronger players have lower handicaps and therefore will have strokes deducted less frequently than weaker players who have higher handicaps.

Great Sheffield Flood

Twere in t'year eighteen sixty fooer
That people in Sheffield erd a gret rooer
Which cozzed citeh to drahn frum Bradfield to Dooer

An left hundreds a fooak wi no ouse anymooer

Felix Noonan, Sheffield poet.

Dale Dyke reservoir was constructed in the early 1860s to help provide adequate water for a Sheffield population that had grown four-fold in only 60 years. The Sheffield Waterworks Company, under the direction of John Gunson, were responsible for the building of the reservoir and at the time of the flood were filling it for the first time.

On the night of 11th March 1864, a crack was observed in the dam wall, but wasn't thought to be immediately dangerous. Shortly afterwards, the dam wall breached. An estimated 700 million gallons of water poured down the Loxley Valley, through Malin Bridge and Hillsborough before joining the Don and continuing its path of destruction through the Wicker, Attercliffe and further downstream, destroying almost everything in its path.

In total 240 lives were lost, over 100 homes destroyed and 500 damaged, 15 bridges swept away and 6 damaged. The damage claims amounted to £455,000 (£58 million in today's money) – one of the largest amounts paid out in compensation during the Victorian period. The cause of the crack was never identified, but a subsequent investigation led to profound changes in the construction of reservoirs.

Dale Dyke reservoir was reconstructed, slightly further upstream, in 1875.

There have only been 4 recorded dam breaches in the United Kingdom, all of which are recorded overleaf. Of these the Great Sheffield Flood caused the largest loss of life.

UK Dam Breaches	Year	Fatalities	Notes
Bilberry Dam, Holme Valley	1852	80	Breached after heavy rainfall.
Dale Dyke, Sheffield	1864	240	Defective construction.
Llyn Eigiau dam and Coedty reservoir, Dolgarrog	1925	17	Heavy rain and cost-cutting during construction.
Nant y Gro Dam, Elan Valley	1942	0	Testing of underwater explosives for Dambusters raid.

Notable Non-UK Breaches	Year	Fatalities	Notes
Edersee Dam, Germany	1943	70	Destroyed in *Operation Chastise* – aka Dambusters raid.
Mohne Dam, Germany	1943	1,600	Destroyed in *Operation Chastise* – aka Dambusters raid.
Vajont Dam, Italy	1963	2,000	Geological failure in valley wall.
South Fork Dam, Pennsylvania	1889	2,200	Poor maintenance.
Machchu 2 Dam, India	1979	5-10,000	Heavy rain.
Banqiao and Shimantan Dams, China	1975	171,000	Extreme rainfall. 11 million people lost their homes.

Green Fingers

An allotment is traditionally measured in poles, an old measurement dating back to Anglo-Saxon times. 10 poles is the accepted size of an allotment, a pole being an area 5 ½ yards by 5 ½ yards. A standard allotment is therefore approximately 250 square metres, or about the size of a doubles tennis court.

Sheffield Allotment Charges

Plot size	Up to 100m^2	Up to 200m^2	Up to 300m^2	301m^2 and up
Rent	£27	£54	£77	£117
Water	£14	£30	£40	£50
Total	**£41**	**£84**	**£117**	**£167**

Sheffield's 3681 allotments are spread across 81 different locations as below.

Location	Allotments
Archer Lane	114
Ash Street	1
Beauchief	54
Birley Moor Drive	3
Birley Moor Way	6
Bolehill Quarry	15
Bracken Moor	27
Brushes	27
Burncross	33
Corker Bottoms	60
Crimicar Lane	5
Crookes Marsh Lane	44
Crookes Quarry	39
Ecclesall	19
Edgefield	12
Elm Crescent	14
Ferncroft Avenue	7
Finchwell/Finchwell Rd	29
Francis Fields	27
Glen Cottages	2
Grimesthorpe	106
Grimesthorpe Rd/Pigeons	9
Hagg House	144
Hagg Lane	173
Hangingwater	112
Harris Road	40
Hawthorne Avenue	3
Heeley Common	24
High Storrs	73
High Wincobank	85
Highcliffe Road	55
Hinde House	20
Hinde House Lane	14
Holberry Gardens	21
Hollinsend	23
Hollinsend Rec	12
Junction Road	4
Lambcroft Municipal	37
Longley	12
Malin Bridge	13
Manor	72
Mauncer Drive Pigeon	8
Meersbrook	440
Meeting House Lane	1
Mickley Lane	52
Moor Crescent	3
Morley Street	178
Morley Street Gas	40
Moss Way	102
Mouse Hole	10
Norton Lees	61
Norton St Pauls	22
Norwood	64
Old Haywoods	9
Ouse Road	27
Oxley Park	9
Park Rifles	36
Park Road	7
Parson Cross Family Garden	109
Plumbley Lane	32
Reignhead Farm	36
Richmond	7
Rodney Hill	54
Roe Wood	47
Roscoe Bank	17
Roscoe Plantation	123
Rustlings Road	69
Sharrard Road	25
Sharrard Road Leisure G'ns	27
Shirecliffe	52
Soaphouse Lane	41
Sothall Green	13
South View	1
Stanley Road	22
Stubbin	36
Vicarage Lane	30
Victoria Road	70
Walkley Bank	36
Warminster Road	5
Woodseats	140
Wortley Road	7

Hallam Chase

The Hallam Chase is a fell race that always runs on the Tuesday after the 2nd bank holiday in May, starting at 8pm.

The course is a 3 ¼ mile route from Hallamshire Cricket Ground in Crosspool to Stannington Church and back, with over 800 feet of climbing in total. Slowest runners start first and the fastest runners going off last, the intention being that all runners finish more or less together.

The Hallam Chase is claimed to be the oldest continually run fell race in the country, having taken place (war years excepting) every year since 1863. There used to be many other similar local 'steeplechases', often attracting large crowds – the 1883 Chase was watched by 20,000 spectators – but today the Hallam Chase is the only remaining such local event.

Male record:	19:42	Trevor Wright	1962
Female record:	24:22	Jessica Turnbull	1998

Hancock, Barry

Born: 25th Jan 1946

Professor Barry Hancock was inducted into the Sheffield Walk of Fame in 2010 following a distinguished career at the University of Sheffield.

Hancock contributed an enormous amount to cancer research during his career and was recognised through a lifetime achievement award from the British Oncological Association and an OBE in 2009.

The internationally recognised clinical research centre at Weston Park was established by Hancock, and his legacy lives on through all of those who he trained.

Hancock has continued to support Weston Park in his retirement – in August 2016 he visited each of Northern Rail's 137 stations by rail within a single day to raise money for Weston Park Cancer Charity.

Health and Wellbeing

Sheffield is known as the 'outdoor city'. With the Peak District within the city boundaries and a wealth of footpaths to walk or run, cycle tracks and country roads to explore, grippy millstone grit to climb at **Stanage**, and all manner of variations on the above, it is easy to see why.

In terms of public amenities, there are allotments a-plenty (**Green Fingers**), a huge number of **Parks**, great leisure centres including the international swimming venue at **Ponds Forge**, several indoor climbing venues, and of course the English Institute of Sport.

There are a large number of mass participation sporting events – from the hugely well attended **parkruns** (almost 1500 Sheffielders turn out each week to participate in one of the six local events) to the ever popular Sheffield half marathon (**Twenty Six Point Two**), with Round Sheffield runs and oversubscribed Percy Pud races in between. Recent additions include the Sky Ride and Lets Ride events that have seen literally thousands take part in organised cycling events on closed roads.

All of the above is about proactively staying healthy in mind and body. The good news is that Sheffielders are also well-looked after when care is needed. The Sheffield Teaching Hospitals NHS Trust (Northern General, Royal Hallamshire, Charles Clifford Dental, Weston Park Cancer and Jessop Wing Maternity hospitals) employs 17,000 people locally, is nationally renowned for specialist cancer, neurology and cardiology treatment amongst others, and is one of three Major Trauma Centres for the Yorkshire and Humber region.

We don't live quite as long as the national average – sadly **Life Expectancy** is not consistently high across the city, with social deprivation being a contributory factor, and there is more **Dying** among the under 75s than across the country as a whole. Back in 1842, only two thirds of those born in Sheffield made it to age 5, and of these life expectancy was just 51 years.

Hendo's

Henry Henderson perfected the recipe for 'the black stuff' in 1885 and Sheffield has never looked back since. The recipe is a closely guarded secret, with only three family members of the firm party to it. Almost every shop in Sheffield will gladly sell you a bottle of Henderson's Relish, but it is almost impossible to get hold of outside of Sheffield. Henderson's produce 500,000 bottles a year, which means that on average the half million residents of Sheffield get through nearly a bottle each every year!

The orange and black labels are iconic in their own right, but Henderson's also produce both blue & white and red & white striped bottles for the more partisan consumer, and there was a gold label produced to celebrate Jessica Ennis' Heptathlon gold in London 2012.

The tiny premises by the University tram stop were in use by Henderson's until 2013 when they moved to a site off the Parkway.

Both the lack of awareness of Henderson's in the rest of the country, and the fierce defence any Sheffielder will make of both its authenticity and quality are perhaps best summed up by a brief exchange over 'Hendogate'. The first extract below is taken from the Hansard report of the debate into Intellectual Property that took place in the House of Commons on 20th Jan 2014. The speaker is Jim Dowd (MP for Lewisham West and Penge). The second is an extract from the open letter that was sent in reply by Nick Clegg (then MP for Sheffield Hallam, and Deputy Prime Minister).

> *This issue was brought home to me… last Saturday when I was in The Hare & Billet pub in Blackheath, which is well known to my hon. Friend the Member for Lewisham East (Heidi Alexander), whom I see on the Front Bench. I was having lunch and I asked whether there was any Worcestershire sauce—everybody knows the famous manufacturers of it and, being a simple soul from south-east London, I thought there was only one Worcester sauce. The nice chap serving us said there certainly was, and he came back with a bottle shaped like the one I always remember containing the marvellous concoction that is Lea & Perrins Worcestershire sauce. Not only was this bottle the same shape and size, but, amazingly, its label was orange with black lettering. However, it was something from Sheffield, from someone called Henderson's, whoever they are. I am sure that Mr Henderson and his company are perfectly estimable, and I am sure they pursue an entirely legitimate business, but I could not help feeling, "Of all the colours they could choose for their label and all of the shapes they could have for their bottle!" I did not even know there was such a thing as Sheffield sauce until then.*

Henderson's Relish has been made in Sheffield for over 100 years and is a much loved local institution. Its aroma and flavour are unique. It is used by thousands of Sheffielders and, as Henderson's appeal grows, many more people throughout the country and indeed around the globe. Given the history behind Henderson's Relish, I hope you can appreciate that Sheffielders are fiercely proud of it. We are confident it would win in any blind taste test, whether at a pub in Blackheath or anywhere else.

High Sheriff of South Yorkshire

Although the High Sheriff is officially the sovereign's judicial representative in each county, today it is largely a ceremonial title held by nominated individuals. The Lord Lieutenant holds a similarly redundant position as the sovereign's personal and military representative.

The word sheriff derives from *Shire Reeve* (senior official responsible for keeping the peace within a shire or county). Each ceremonial county, including South Yorkshire has a high sheriff.

The term of office is one year, starting each 25th March (until 1752 this was taken as the first day of the year, to coincide with the Catholic Feast of the Annunciation – 9 months before Christmas).

Duties

- Attendance at Royal visits to the county.
- Proclamation of the accession of a new sovereign.
- Acting as the returning officer for parliamentary elections in county constituencies ('any parliamentary constituency that contains more than a small rural element'); in practice this is normally delegated to an acting returning officer.
- Attendance at the opening ceremony when a High Court judge goes on circuit.
- Annual appointment of undersheriffs to act as deputies.

High Sheriffs of South Yorkshire (1974 – present)

- 74-75 John Basil Peile
- 75-76 Edward John Thornely Taylor
- 76-77 John Mark Mansell Jenkinson
- 77-78 Eric Wilkes
- 78-79 Nigel Haywood Wilton Lee
- 79-80 Peter Edward Reynard
- 80-81 Charles Gerard Buck
- 81-82 Joye Powlett Smith

- 82-83 Sir Basil Edward Rhodes
- 83-84 Hon. Edward Neil Turner
- 84-85 Richard Neale Horne
- 85-86 Jeremy Ronald Archdale
- 86-87 Hon. Mark Robin Balfour
- 87-88 James Edward Eardley
- 88-89 William Wentworth Ping
- 89-90 John Anthony Boddy
- 90-91 Stewart McKee Hamilton
- 91-92 Ian Stephen Porter
- 92-93 David Beatson Clark
- 93-94 Christopher Shelley Barker
- 94-95 Michael Frampton
- 95-96 Peter Wilton Lee
- 96-97 William Warde-Norbury
- 97-98 Michael John Mallett
- 98-99 Kathryn Elizabeth Riddle
- 99-00 David Baxter Shaw
- 00-01 Ian Geoffrey Norton
- 01-02 Adrian M. C. Staniforth
- 02-03 Marian Rae
- 03-04 David Barker Moody
- 04-05 Pamela Liversidge
- 05-06 Sarah Elizabeth Lee
- 06-07 John Biggin
- 07-08 Jonathan C. V. Hunt
- 08-09 Robert John Giles Bloomer
- 09-10 Helena Muller
- 10-11 Anthony P. Cooper
- 11-12 Andrew Jackson Coombe
- 12-13 Mrs J. A. Kenny
- 13–14 Lady Sykes
- 14–15 John C. Bramah
- 15–16 John Raymond Holt
- 16–17 Dr Julie MacDonald
- 17–18 Stephen Ingram
- 18–19 Barry Reginald Eldred
- 19–20 John Pickering

Hills

A city built like Rome, on seven hills

Anon

It turns out, pinning down these seven hills is a bit tricky. The thing is, travelling around Sheffield, you definitely spend a lot of time going uphill and downhill, but there aren't actually that many geographical features that you'd say are a hill in the true sense of the word. Most of the topography of Sheffield is actually a series of ridges that fan outwards separating the river valleys. Finding 'hills' in the true sense of the word, ie places from where every direction is down, is harder than you might think.

The following page shows the high ground of Sheffield along with those hills that meet the definition of a *Tump* (those hills that have a vertical height drop of 30m in all directions before encountering another *Tump*. Something that we may consider a hill (Greno Knoll for example) doesn't meet this definition as there is not a vertical drop of 30m in the direction of Wharncliffe Chase which is slightly higher and a little to the Northwest (but just outside the geographical boundary of Sheffield and therefore not included on our map).

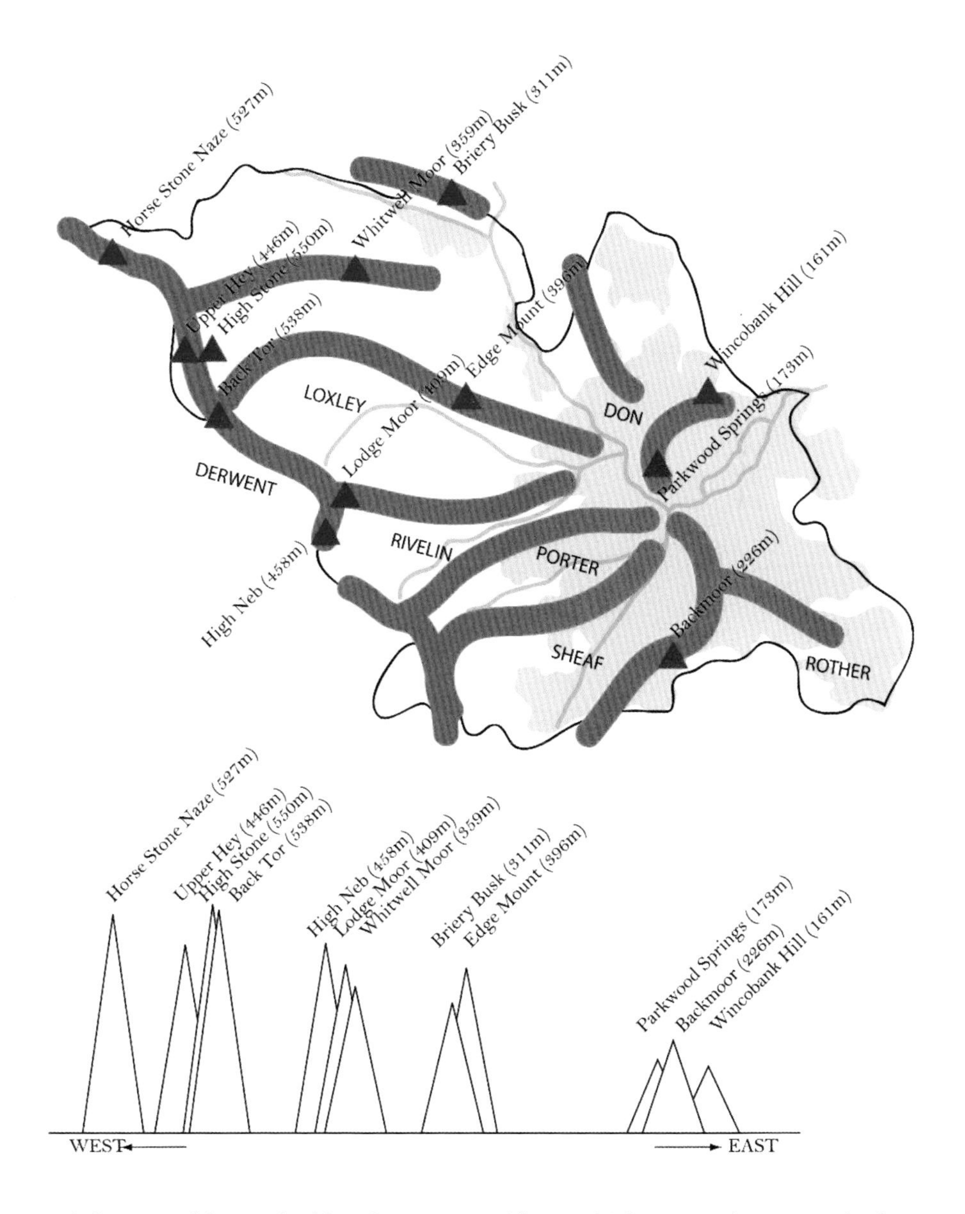

High ground is marked by the orange ridges which act as the watersheds between Sheffield's main rivers. These are the 'hills' of Sheffield.

Tumps are marked by red triangles.

Hillsborough Disaster

The Hillsborough disaster of 15th April 1989 was our country's worst ever sporting disaster. A total of 96 Liverpool fans died as a result of crushing in the pens at the Leppings Lane entrance to the ground. Over 750 others were injured. Of those who died, 38 were under the age of twenty. Although the effect of the disaster on Sheffield was huge, it paled in comparison to the impact on the people of Liverpool.

A tragedy for all those affected, blame was initially put on the 'unruly' behaviour of the Liverpool fans. It took the Taylor Report of 1990, the Hillsborough Independent Panel review in 2009 and a second coroner's inquest in 2014-16 to conclude that the deaths were as a result of negligence on the part of match officials and members of South Yorkshire Police.

As well as laying the ground for the long-awaited justice for the families of the victims, the Taylor Report had a lasting effect on football ground safety. Perimeter fencing was removed from grounds and top-flight stadia converted to all-seating. With very few exceptions, all new grounds are seating only.

Memorials in Sheffield to commemorate the disaster

- A memorial at Hillsborough stadium reads: *In memory of the 96 men, women, and children who tragically died and the countless people whose lives were changed forever. FA Cup semi-final Liverpool v Nottingham Forest. 15th April 1989. 'You'll never walk alone.'*
- A memorial garden is situated in Hillsborough Park.
- There is a memorial headstone at the junction of Middlewood Road, Leppings Lane and Wadsley Lane.

The flames on the crest of Liverpool Football Club were added to commemorate those who died at Hillsborough.

Hillsborough Stadium

Area	Built	Fans	Capacity
North Stand	1960-61	Home	9,255
North-West Corner	1965-66	Away	-
West Stand	1961-65	Away	6,658
South Stand	1913-15	Home	11,352
Spion Kop	1914	Home	11,210

History

Sheffield's history dates back to the Carboniferous Period 300-350 million years ago when the area that would become Sheffield was underwater and when the layers of rock and minerals that would go on to form the peak district and to provide Sheffield with its mineral wealth were first laid down.

By the time of the Caenozoic Period around 60 million years ago further rock formation and tectonic movement had set out the basic topography of the area. Although erosion and subsequent ice-ages have further altered it, today's landscape would have been broadly recognisable.

There are plenty of clues in the landscape that point to human activity in a **Prehistoric Sheffield** during the iron and bronze ages. There was a period of Roman occupation too.

'Sheffield', *a clearing in the forest by the River Sheaf*, is believed to have been first established by the Anglo Saxon's between the 6th and 9th Centuries.

The boundary between the ancient Kingdoms of Mercia and Northumbria ran through modern day Sheffield, and it was at Dore in 829 that Northumbria was surrendered to King Egbert.

Vikings invaded not long after this - the period of Danelaw that followed accounts for the etymology of many of Sheffield's place names (**What's in a Name**).

The Normans conquered in 1066, and at some point around this time Baron William de Lovetot acquired land in and around Sheffield. The **Domesday Book** of 1086 references both Sheffield itself, and also a number of small settlements in and around modern-day Sheffield.

The 12th Century saw the building of both Sheffield Castle and the first Lady's Bridge over the Don by William de Lovetot.

By the 13th Century cutlery production was already an established industry. Sheffield castle ownership passed to the Furnivals via marriage and a Royal Charter of 1296 allowed Sheffield to hold a weekly market.

The early 15th Century saw the **Talbot** family (Earls of Shewsbury) marrying into the Furnival family and inheriting land and property in Sheffield. This period also witnessed the building of the first of Sheffield's **Reservoirs** at Barker's Pool and the construction of the Old Queens Head at **Ponds Forge** (the oldest surviving domestic building in Sheffield).

During the 16th Century both Cardinal Wolsey and Mary Queen of Scots were imprisoned in the Manor Lodge, and Beauchief Abbey was dissolved.

The 17th Century witnessed land and property in Sheffield pass to the Howard family (Dukes of Norforlk) via marriage into the Talbot family. It also saw the formation of the Company of Cutlers to oversee cutlery production in the town. Sheffield Castle was demolished following uprisings in the English Civil War.

During the 18th Century the Crucible Process, Sheffield plate and Britannia metal were invented in quick succession to revolutionise the city's cutlery industry. At this point in time, Sheffield's exploitation of **Waterpower** to support its growing industry was greater than that of any other UK city.

The 19th Century saw a **Cholera** epidemic, the arrival of the railways, Bessemer's converter, the birth of football in this country as we know it, the **Great Sheffield Flood**, the formation of both Wednesday and United along with the discovery of a certain well-known recipe by **Henderson's**.

The first part of the 20th Century was in many ways the peak of Sheffield's industrial prowess. This period saw the heyday of both the steel and coal industries in Sheffield. It was also perhaps the golden age of **Football** in the city with FA Cup wins coming thick and fast. Stainless steel was invented in Sheffield during this time, as were Bassets **Allsorts**. The two World Wars were both Sheffield's finest hour and its darkest days. The contribution from the Steel industry to the war effort was immense, but the loss of life, on the front line of **World War I** and II, and at home during the **Blitz** was a high price to pay. The latter half of the century witnessed the opening of the Peak District national park, the M1 and Sheffield City **Airport**, not forgetting of course significant musical and **On Screen** contributions from Sheffield musicians and actors. The World Student Games were hosted by Sheffield and tragedy struck at the **Hillsborough Disaster** of 1989.

The 21st Century is only just upon us, but has already seen plenty of extreme weather, the closing of the airport, the demolition of the **Tinsley Towers**, Olympic Champions, regeneration of the city centre, a lot of resurfacing, a resurgence of Sheffield as the Real Ale Capital of England, the academisation of the majority of the city's schools, the **Tramways** Music Festial and, most recently, the COVID-19 pandemic.

A **Timeline** of Sheffield's history captures these and some of the other key moments in the city's history in a graphic representation.

Over the past two hundred years there have been a number of Royal visits during the reigns of **Victoria, Edward VII, George V, Edward VIII, George VI and Elizabeth II**. These chart a fascinating insight into some of the more recent key moments in Sheffield's history.

HMS Sheffield

There have been three Royal Navy vessels named HMS Sheffield, but none are any longer in commission. The building of a fourth, a Type 26 frigate, was signed off in 2018. This is expected to be in service by the mid-2020s.

HMS Sheffield (C24)

Class:	Town-class light cruiser
Commissioned:	1937
Decommissioned:	1967 (scrapped)
Displacement:	9,100 tonnes
Length:	170m
Beam:	19m
Max speed:	32 knots
Complement:	748

Battle honours:

- Norway 1940
- Spartivento 1940
- Atlantic 1941–43
- *Bismarck* 1941
- Mediterranean 1941
- Malta Convoys 1941
- Arctic 1941–43
- North Africa 1942
- Barents Sea 1942
- Biscay 1943
- Salerno 1943
- North Cape 1943

HMS Sheffield (D80)

Class:	Type 42 guided missile destroyer
Commissioned:	1975
Decommissioned:	1982 (foundered)
Displacement:	4.820 tonnes
Length:	125m
Beam:	14.3m
Max speed:	30 knots
Complement:	270

Battle honours:

- Falklands 1982

HMS Sheffield was struck by a missile in the Falklands War and sank whilst being towed to South Georgia Island. There were 20 fatalities.

HMS Sheffield (F96)

Class:	Type 22 frigate
Commissioned:	1988
Decommissioned:	2002 (sold to Chile – still in service)
Displacement:	5,300 tonnes
Length:	148m
Beam:	15m
Max speed:	30 knots
Complement:	250

Battle honours:

- None

HMS Sheffield

Class:	Type 26 frigate
Commissioned:	N/A
Decommissioned:	N/A
Displacement:	6,900 tonnes
Length:	150m
Beam:	21m
Max speed:	>26 knots
Complement:	157

Battle honours:

- N/A

Hollin

As in Hollins Lane, Hollindale Drive, etc, the word *hollin* means Holly. Holly used to be grown extensively as a nutritious winter feed for livestock and there are many references to this in and around Sheffield.

House Prices

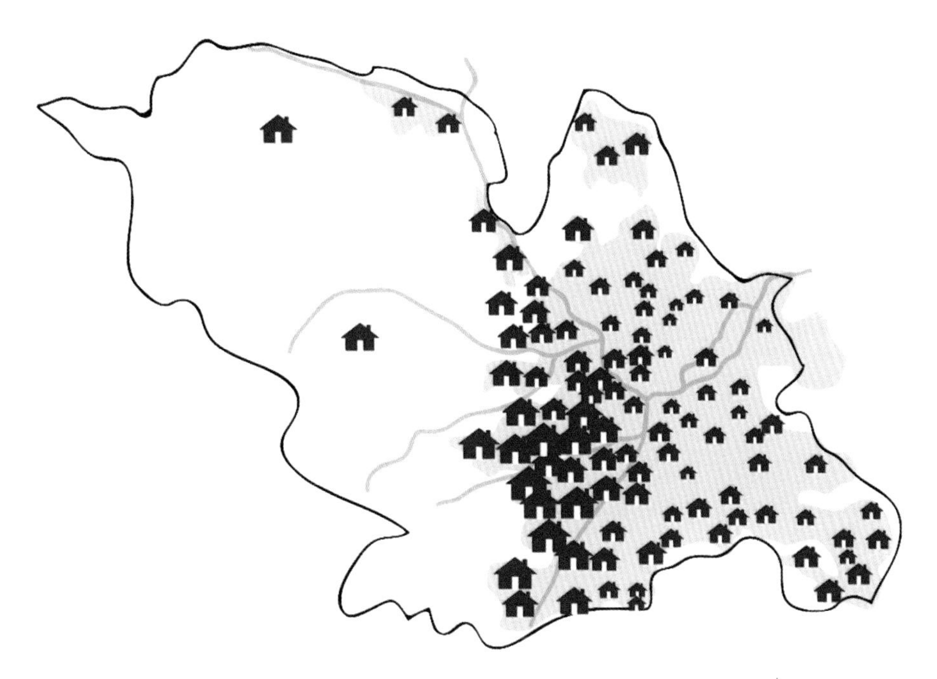

Average house price in different Sheffield neighbourhoods.

The average price is dependent on both the typical size and type of property in each neighbourhood, as well as any premium that individual areas might command.

£50,000 £150,000 £300,000

£100,000 £200,000 £400,000

Hunters Bar

Ecclesall Road was built in 1810 as a toll road, with tolls being collected until 1884. Present day Hunters House Hotel was the 'Hunters' and the 'bar' was a gate across the road. The gate itself was trashed by delighted locals when tolls ceased being collected, but the original gate posts still sit pride of place in the middle of the roundabout that has been named after them.

Toll gates were common in the 18th and 19th Centuries as a means of paying for the construction of turnpike roads. West Bar is another reference to a toll gate, as of course are Toll Bar Avenue, Close, Drive, etc in Gleadless.

Huntsman, Benjamin

1704 - 1776

Benjamin Huntsman began his working life as a clock and lock maker in Doncaster. At the time local cutlery makers made their cutlery from imported German steel – Huntsman moved to Handsworth in Sheffield to try his hand at producing good quality local steel.

Huntsman's experimentation was successful and he managed to produce cast steel using a crucible. Although higher quality than the German imported steel, this cast steel was harder to work with and therefore not as appealing to the local cutlers. As a result Huntsman wasn't able to find a local market for his steel, and instead exported his steel to France. It wasn't long before Huntsman's cast steel found its way back to Sheffield, but this time in the form of higher quality finished French cutlery. This presented the local cutlers with a new problem and Sheffield's cutlers were left with no option but to buy Huntsman's cast steel in order to preserve their own business interests. Unfortunately for Huntsman, he failed to take out a patent on his process, and it wasn't long before his crucible method was stolen by local iron workers and adopted more widely.

Benjamin Huntsman was buried at Attercliffe Chapel.

There is a city centre pub named after him as well as Huntsman Road in S9. Oh yes, and Sheffield earned itself the name of 'Steel City'.

Income

Median household income for each ward.

Each coin represents a £5,000 band. ie 6 coins would indicate a median household income of £25-30,000.

Ingle, Brendan

19th June 1940 – 25th May 2018

Ingle was an ex-professional boxer from Ireland, who moved to Wincobank in Sheffield. A local vicar asked him to do some community work for the youth of the area as they were 'out of control'. He originally offered to organise a weekly youth dance, but the youngsters ended up fighting afterwards and he would get the gloves out and referee to try to calm things down. So was born St Thomas' Boys and Girls Club and the beginnings of Ingle's legacy on both Sheffield and the boxing world.

This tiny club, under the coaching and direction of Ingles has produced more boxing champions than any other gym in the world. In total, Ingle trained four world champions, six European champions, fifteen British champions and six Commonwealth Champions, including the likes of Herol 'Bomber' Graham, Johnny Nelson, Junior Witter, Ryan Rhodes, Kell Brook, Kid Galahad, Richard Towers and Prince Naseem Hamed.

Ingle was made an MBE in 1998 for services to boxing and inducted into the Sheffield Walk of Fame in 2008.

In Print

A selection of novels set in Sheffield:

- 🕮 Enemy Within (1994) — Paul Adams
- 🕮 The Bantams of Sheffield (1891) — Guy Balguy
- 🕮 Put Out the Light (2010) (C) — Terry Deary
- 🕮 Granny Was a Buffer Girl (1986) — Berlie Doherty
- 🕮 Dear Nobody (1991) — Berlie Doherty
- 🕮 The China Bird (2000) — Bryony Doran
- 🕮 Now You See Me (2001) — Lesley Glasiter
- 🕮 Trick or Treat (1991) — Lesley Glaister
- 🕮 The Northern Clemency (2008) — Philip Hensher
- 🕮 Suzu's Petals (2016) — Sue Hepworth
- 🕮 The Evergreen in Red and White (2014) — Steven Kay
- 🕮 Two Caravans (2007) — Marina Lewycka
- 🕮 Black Car Burning (2019) — Helen Mort
- 🕮 Put Yourself in His Place (1870) — Charles Reade
- 🕮 Bleak Water (2002) — Danuta Reah
- 🕮 Lawless and Tilley Series (1997-99) — Malcolm Rose

🕮 Ours Are the Streets (2011)	Sanjeev Sahota
🕮 Meet Me by the Steelmen (1997) (C)	Teresa Tomlinson
🕮 Lestrade and the Sawdust Ring (1993)	MJ Trow
🕮 Our Human Constitution (1901)	Anthony Ward
🕮 Love in the Time of Britpop (2018)	Tim Woods

(C) Children's book

Ironside, Isaac

17th September 1808 – 20th August 1870

Ironside was the son of Wesleyan lay preacher. Aged 12, he became an apprentice stove-grate fitter, but managed to spend time studying in the evenings. As a result, in 1833 he was able to join the accountancy firm that his father had recently set up. He went on to make a success of the firm, providing him with substantial financial means.

Ironside became involved in local politics in 1830 when he started campaigning for universal suffrage. He became a leading Chartist and spoke alongside other local Chartists, including Ebenezer Elliot, at a large protest gathering at Paradise Square in 1838.

Ironside served on the council from 1846-68, and we have him to thank for, among other things, the paving of Sheffield's streets and the laying of the first deep sewers in the city. He also set up a number of educational establishments and a model workhouse farm at Hollow Meadows.

He died of an illness at his home (Alma Grange) on Carr Road. Ironside is buried in Sheffield's General Cemetery.

Ironside was not as militant as earlier Chartist Samuel Holberry. The latter organised what was known as the 'Sheffield Rising' that attempted to take over the Town Hall in 1840. Holberry organised a militia that were set on using live firearms to achieve their objective. The plot was exposed by a pub landlord from Rotherham who had infiltrated the group. Holberry was imprisoned and died in gaol. He also made it to Sheffield General Cemetery, with his funeral attended by 50,000 people (over a third of Sheffield's population at the time).

Ironside has a handful of roads named after him in Hemsworth. The eight large water features in the Peace Gardens are named the *Holberry Cascades*.

Jenkin Road

There is much debate as to which road in Sheffield holds the official title of steepest road. Jenkin Road is certainly a contender - when it featured in the 2014 Tour de France, the *Côte de Jenkin Road* was the steepest bit of tarmac in the whole of that year's race, seeing off numerous Alpine and Pyrenean passes!

Blake Street possesses a higher average gradient, but the profile of Jenkin Road masks a short brutal ramp of 25% about half-way up which is steeper than any stretch of Blake Street.

Blake Street may however ultimately have greater claim to the title as it has been officially crowned as Britain's third steepest residential street, coming in behind Vale Street, Bristol and Old Wyche Road in the Malverns.

Going out towards the Peak District (but still officially in Sheffield), New Road rising up from Broomhead Reservoir has a short stretch in excess of 30% which is likely to be the most vertical bit of tarmac possessing a Sheffield postcode.

Four 'favourites' are considered below.

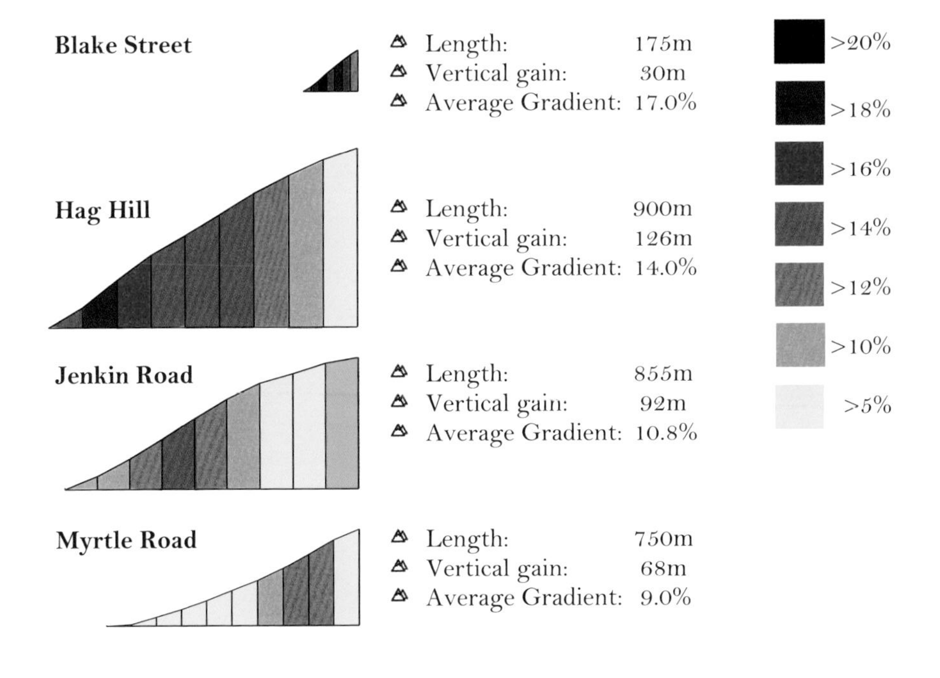

Karabiners & Friends

Belay device – a mechanical piece of equipment that allows a belaying partner to safely belay a climber in an efficient way. Depending on the angle the rope is held, the device either allows the rope to be pulled freely through the device (so the belay partner can easily pull in slack rope), or provides a friction brake that reduces effort for the belaying partner and that can arrest a fall.

Cams – also known as 'climbing friends,' are spring loaded devices that can be placed in cracks and connected to the climbing rope. Any pressure on the cam (eg caused by a climber fall) results in the moving parts of the cam being forced apart, wedging the cam tightly in position.

Chalk – rubbed on hands to absorb moisture from sweaty palms and to increase grip.

Helmet – not just to protect a climber's head from user error, but also from falling rocks and debris from above.

Hexes & nuts – metal prisms of various sizes, that are jammed into cracks in rocks as protection. The hexes are then attached to the climbing rope with a karabiner. Hexes are designed to be wedged into cracks, rather than hammered, and therefore don't damage the rock. Smaller hexes are referred to as nuts.

Karabiners – a loop of metal with a spring loaded (often screwed) gate that is used to quickly connect various items, eg hexes or cams to a climbing rope.

Nut Key – tool to help climbers remove cams, nuts and hexes at the end of a climb.

Quickdraws – for connecting protection (cams, nuts, hexes) 'quickly' to the climbing rope. Consists of two bespoke karabiners connected by a short bit of semi-rigid material. The specific design of the gates on the two karabiners and the stiffness of the connecting material makes quickdraws 'quick' to use.

Rope – climbing ropes are made from nylon and are 'dynamic' in that they will stretch 6-7% of their original length to reduce impact force in the event of a fall. Climbers need to think about durability, ease of use (how easily the rope will move through equipment), weight, thickness (essentially how strong) and price of their rope.

Slings – a sling or 'runner' is a loop of webbing material that can be used in a variety of ways, eg wrapped around a section of rock or attached between a cam and the climbing rope so that the climbing rope has a straighter route and therefore suffers lower drag.

Life Expectancy

The graphic shows the life expectancy in each ward of Sheffield. On average, residents of Sheffield live 8 months less than a typical person in England.

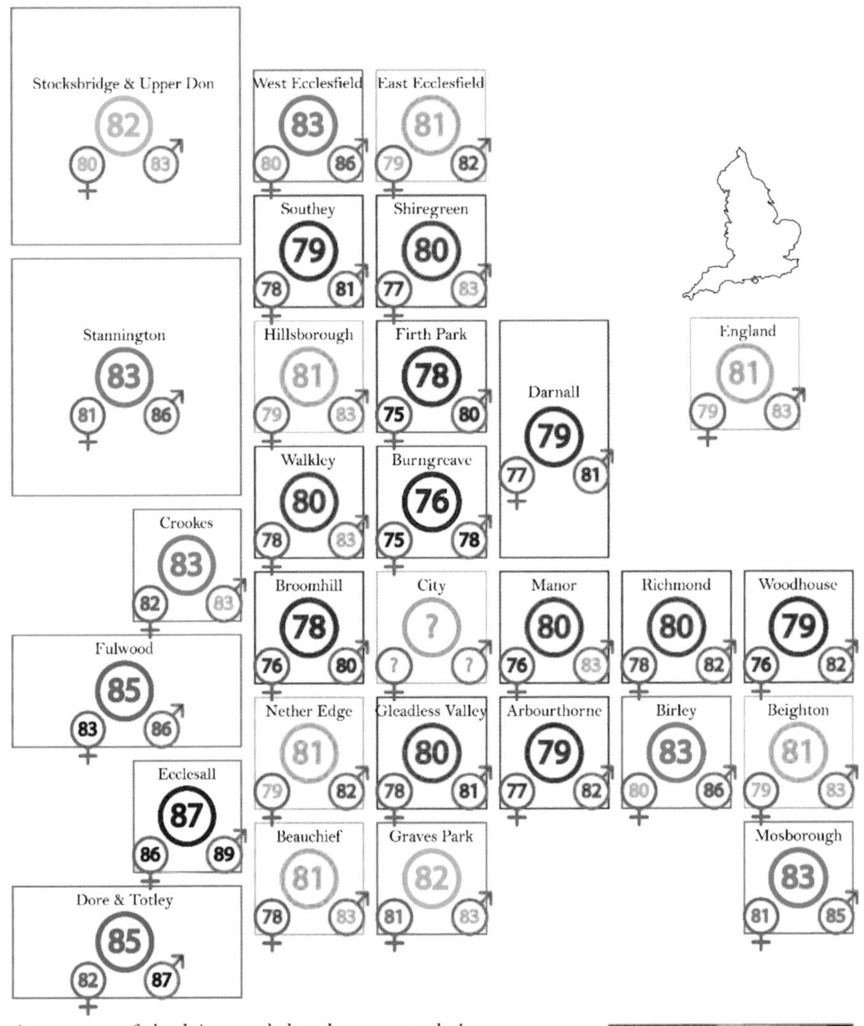

Average age of death in rounded to the nearest whole year.

Insufficient deaths in City ward to generate data.

Die Younger | Live Longer

Life expectancy the same as the national average

Lime Tree Avenue

In 1905 there were high rates of unemployment in Sheffield. A proposal to build a road from Malin Bridge out towards Hollow Meadows along the bottom of the Rivelin valley was proposed in order to provide employment, at the same time replacing the network of tracks and lanes that existed at the time. This was to become the Rivelin Valley Road. As part of the project, 700 lime trees were planted along the road. One hundred years later this is now the second longest avenue of lime trees in England. The longest is in nearby Clumber Park.

Sheffield has approximately 4,500,000 trees, of which around 36,000 are planted along Sheffield's roads. The Rivelin Valley Road avenue of lime trees therefore constitutes 2% of all Sheffield's road-side trees.

Slightly more controversial was the contract between Sheffield City Council and Amey that very nearly led to 17,500 long-standing street trees being felled and replaced with smaller saplings. The Rustlings Road stand-off over their lime trees and the consequent national media coverage eventually led to a rethink on this strategy, but not before 6,000 road-side trees across the city had been replaced.

There are two 'Lime Streets' in Sheffield, one in S6, the other in S19.

Tree Species with Sheffield Roads Named after them:

- Acorn
- Alder
- Ash
- Beech
- Birch*
- Broad Elms
- Cherry Tree
- Chestnut Avenue
- Cypress
- Fir
- Holly
- Larch
- Lime
- Maple
- Oak – Durmast, Golden, Holme, Apple, Red, Scarlet
- Palm**
- Pear
- Rowan
- Sycamore
- Tulip tree (yellow poplar)
- Willow
- Yew

*Named after a person rather than a tree.

**Derivation unknown – but unlikely to be the tree.

Coppice, Orchard, Forrest, Grove, Tree Root and Wood also feature in Sheffield street names.

Listed Buildings

Categories

There are three categories of listed status for buildings in England and Wales (numbers of buildings in Sheffield in brackets):

- **Grade I**: buildings of exceptional interest (5)
- **Grade II***: particularly important buildings of more than special interest (42)
- **Grade II**: buildings that are of special interest, warranting every effort to preserve them (>1000)

Selection criteria

- **Age and rarity:** The older a building is, the more likely it is to be listed. All buildings constructed before 1700 that "contain a significant proportion of their original fabric" will be listed whereas buildings less than 30 years old are rarely listed unless they are of outstanding quality and under threat.
- **Aesthetic merits:** i.e. the appearance of a building. Some buildings with limited visual appeal may be listed on the grounds of representing particular aspects of social or economic history.
- **Selectivity:** where a large number of buildings of a similar type survive, only the most representative or significant examples are listed.
- **National interest:** significant or distinctive regional buildings; e.g. those that represent a nationally important but localised industry.

Sheffield's listed structures include industrial buildings, churches, phone-boxes, pubs, bridges, mile posts, schools, farm houses, retaining walls, old railway stations, sewer gas lamps, ruined buildings and an obelisk.

Grade I

- Abbeydale Industrial Hamlet (Works) — 1785-1876
- Church of St. Nicholas, Bradfield — c.1200-c.1500
- Church of St. Mary, Ecclesfield — c.1200
- Sheffield Cathedral — 1430-1966
- Town Hall — 1897

Grade II*

- Abbeydale Works (counting house, workmen's cottages, managers house and stable)
- Beauchief Hall and adjoining steps, forecourt walls and gates
- Beehive Works
- Bishops House
- Botanical Gardens glasshouses
- Broom Hall
- Butchers Wheel
- Carbrook Hall public house
- Cathedral church of St Marie
- Church of St James, Midhopestones
- Church of St James the Great, Norton
- Church of St John, Ranmoor
- Church of St Mary, Bramall Lane
- Church of St Mary the Virgin, Beighton
- Church of St Paul, Parson Cross
- Church of St Thomas a Becket and Remains of Beauchief Abbey Church
- City Hall
- Cornish Place Works, East & West Ranges
- Cutlers' Hall
- Darnall Works, crucible steel shops
- Endcliffe Hall
- Fair House farmhouse, Bradfield
- General Cemetery, chapel, lodges and gateway with screen and flanking walls
- Globe Works
- Green Lane Works, entrance gateway
- Heritage House
- King Edward VII Upper School
- Leah's Yard
- Loxley United Reformed Church
- Lyceum Theatre
- Manor Lodge, Turret House
- Mappin Art Gallery
- Mount Pleasant Community Centre
- Norton Hall Hospital with colonnade and orangery
- Oakes Park, gateway, walls and steps and Adjoining Terrace Wall and Steps
- Old Hall Farmhouse, Brightholmlee
- Old Queens Head public house
- Onesacre Hall
- Paradise Square (1-15, 14 - 22, 17, 19, 24, railings outside 12 & 14)
- Park Hill Flats
- Portland Works
- Rolling mill, Bradfield
- Sharrow Mills
- Sheffield United Gas Light Company offices
- Sheffield War Memorial, city centre
- Shepherd Wheel and attached dam goit and weir
- Terminal Warehouse
- The Mount
- The Old Bank House and attached railings
- Priory, Ecclesfield
- University of Sheffield, Library and Arts Tower
- Well Meadow Street, ranges and crucible furnace attached to no 35
- Whitley Hall Hotel
- Wicker Arch and adjoining viaduct and buildings

Little Mesters

Cutlery means 'that which cuts', and it was the production of knives (both table knives and penknives) for which Sheffield's cutlers were most renowned.

The process of producing knives was originally carried out by a single tradesman from start to finish. By the 18th Century, with the increase in the variety of products being made, there was a growing need for craftsmen with particular specialisms. The Little Mesters were the army of workers who carried out these specific processes - either the forging, grinding or finishing. Little Mesters usually specialised on just one particular type of blade (table-knife, pocket-knife, razor blade, etc), and operated out of small workshops, very often in their own backyards. By the mid-19th Century wealthy businessmen known as *factors* were renting out space in larger buildings to these craftsmen, once again bringing all of the processes back under one roof.

The various stages involved in the production of steel blades are outlined below.

Forging Process

The process starts with a steel ingot.

Mooding: Heated sheet of steel was flattened, straightened and cut into rectangular piece of the correct length and width for the blade.

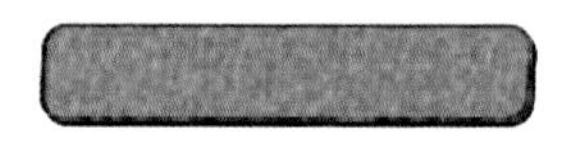

Tanging: The end of the blade attached to the handle was shaped.

Smithing: While still hot the cutting edge of the blade was thinned. The makers mark was added at this stage. For a pocket-knife, the nail nick would also have been created.

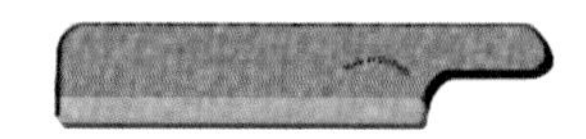

Hardening: The blade was heated to a very high temperature and then rapidly cooled. At this stage the blades were hard, but brittle.

Tempering: The blades were heated more gradually and then again rapidly cooled. At this point, the blades retained their hardness, but had become more flexible.

Grinding Process

Rough Grinding: Used to correctly shape the blade and to remove any marks from the forging process. The larger the knife, the larger the grindstone used.

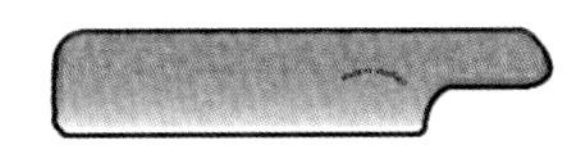

Whittening: Finer grinding using a harder grindstone than in the rough grinding stage.

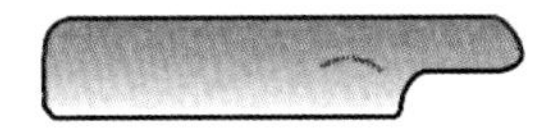

Glazing: Finer treatement using abrasive powders stuck to leather-rimmed wheels. This process was carried out twice – rough glazing, followed by fine glazing.

Buffing: This process gave the blades their final polished appearance. The buffing device was a wheel with a buffalo leather rim (hence the term 'buff'-ing).

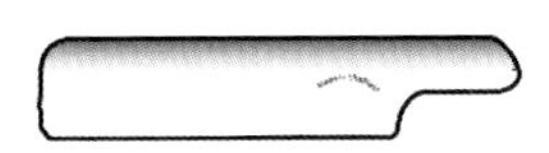

Finishing Process

The fitting of the blade to the handle was carried out either by a table-knife cutler or a spring-knife cutler.

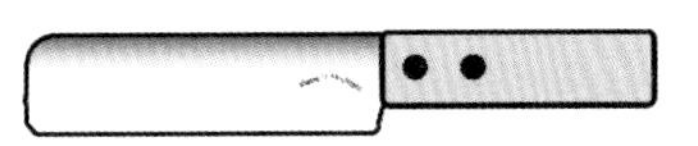

Local Phrases

9 while 5 - *9 until 5*

Agen - *against*

Beck - *Stream/Brook*

Be rayt - *It will be fine*

Breadcake - *Bread roll*

Chucky Egg - *Soft boiled egg*

Gennel/Jennel - *A passageway, usually between two houses*

Gi'o'er! - *Stop it!*

Going off - *Going on*

Got a rayt dab on - *Sweaty*

Goz – *Saliva*

Love - *Mate, Pal, Duck. Used with people of either the same or different genders.*

Mi'sen - *Myself*

Mardy - *Moany/Whingy*

Maungy - *Whingy*

Mithering - *Bothering*

Nah Then **–** *Hello*

Nanan **-** *Grandmother*

Nesh - *Soft. eg complains about the cold.*

Pack up - *Packed lunch*

Snided – *Full/rammed*

Sylin' it down - *Raining heavily*

Thi'sen - *Yourself*

Us - *My, Our*

Yourn – *Your, Yours*

Lord Lieutenant of South Yorkshire

Forms of Address

- Written: '(Title and name), Her Majesty's Lord Lieutenant'.
- Salutation: 'Dear Lord Lieutenant'.
- In a speech: 'My Lord Lieutenant'.
- In conversation: '(Title and name)' or 'Lord Lieutenant'.
- Plural: 'Lord lieutenants'.

Lord lieutenants were originally responsible for the militia within each region. Today the lord lieutenant of a county acts as the monarch's personal representative in a largely ceremonial role. Until South Yorkshire's formation in 1972, Sheffield was under the lord-lieutenancy of the West Riding.

Present day Responsibilities of Lord-Lieutenants

- Arranging visits of members of the royal family and escorting royal visitors;
- Presenting medals and awards on behalf of the sovereign, and advising on nominations for honours;
- Participating in civic, voluntary and social activities within the lieutenancy;
- Acting as liaison with local units of the Royal Navy, Royal Marines, Army, Royal Air Force and their associated cadet forces;
- Chairing the Advisory Committee on Justices of the Peace;
- Chairing the local Advisory Committee for the Appointment of the General Commissioners of Income Tax.

As the sovereign's representatives, lord-lieutenants must be non-political and may not hold office in any political party. Unless the sovereign removes them, they are appointed for life with a usual retirement age of 75. The position is unsalaried.

Lord-lieutenants of South Yorkshire

- 1974 – 1985: Gerard F Young CBE
- 1985 – 1996: J. Hugh Neill CBE TD
- 1996 – 2003: Richard A Lumley, 12th Earl of Scarbrough
- 2004 – 2015: David B Moody CVO
- Current: Andrew J Coombe

Banner of the lord-lieutenants

Made in Sheffield

Sheffield first built its reputation on its **Cutlery** and **Steel** production. Several important industrial processes were pioneered in Sheffield that played a significant role in supporting the growth of this industry. Around 1740 Benjamin Huntsman developed the Crucible Process along with his converter. This produced a better quality steel than was locally available before, in turn leading to better quality cutlery. Shortly afterwards Thomas Boulsover invented 'Sheffield Plate' which enabled the coating of cheaper metal with a layer of silver. In 1769 Britannia Metal was first produced in Sheffield by James **Vickers.** Harry **Brierley's** invention of stainless steel in Sheffield in 1913 meant that good quality cutlery became affordable for the masses, and Sheffield was ready to meet the demand.

Little Mesters were the skilled craftsmen who, until fairly recently, carried out the labour-intensive processes of forging, grinding and finishing cutlery. Cutlery is still made in Sheffield, but it is the high-end product rather than the mass-produced knife and fork that now trade off the Sheffield name. Cutlers such as David **Mellor** are still turning out exquisite pieces.

Sheffield steel has many other uses than cutlery and, in particular, made a massive contribution to the war efforts. More controversially, in the 1990s Sheffield steel was in the news with the **Supergun** affair.

Today the city is embracing technology with innovative collaborations such as the Advanced Manufacturing Research Centre (AMRC) so that it remains well-positioned to capitalise on its technical expertise and knowledge.

Aside from steel, some of Sheffield's most famous exports are aimed at those with a sweet tooth. Both Bassets **Allsorts** and **Thorntons** started with humble beginnings in Sheffield before eventually going global.

The city's greatest culinary contribution though must be Henderson's Relish. Difficult to source outside of Sheffield, **Hendo's** is generally accepted as improving whatever is on your dinner plate.

Today 'Made in Sheffield' is a globally recognised mark of quality that Sheffield manufacturers meeting the required standard can add to their products.

Mappin, Frederick

The progress of Sheffield in my lifetime has been something wonderful. Why, in my young days it was a little bit of a place of no consequence and no trade. When I think of the small notions and little minds of the public men of old Sheffield I can hardly realise that the City has become the fine important flourishing place it is today, one of the largest Cities of the Empire.

Quoted in Sidney Pollard, *A History of Labour in Sheffield*, (1959).

Matthews, Nick

Born: 25th July 1980

Education: High Storrs

Nick Matthews is Britain's most successful male squash player. He has won the British National Squash title 8 times and was the first Brit to win the World Championships in 2010. Since then he has gone on to win the World Championships on two further occasions, becoming one of only 5 players to have won the title three times. He was ranked number 1 in the world during 2010, has won a total of 33 international titles, and was a finalist on 71 occasions. There are 4 Commonwealth Games gold medals in his collection, but unfortunately no Olympic medals as squash has not yet been given Olympic sport status.

Since retiring in 2018, Matthews has set up the Nick Matthews Academy at the Hallamshire Tennis and Squash club. The show court is also named after him.

Matthews was made an OBE in 2015, and inducted into Sheffield's Walk of Fame in 2013.

World Championships

- Bermuda 2007 singles
- Khobar 2010 singles
- Rotterdam 2011 singles
- Doha 2012 singles
- Manchester 2013 singles
- Doha 2014 singles

Commonwealth Games

- Delhi 2010 singles
- Delhi 2010 doubles
- Glasgow 2014 singles
- Glasgow 2014 doubles

Megatron

This is possibly Sheffield's largest, but best kept secret.

The land around Ponds Forge used to be marshy and prone to flooding. It was here that the Porter joined the Sheaf, which in turn joined the Don shortly afterwards. In the 1860s the Midland Railway Company bought up the rights to the Porter and Sheaf and enclosed the Sheaf and part of the Porter in a stone and brick culvert. With the flow of water managed, the culvert could be built over and the area developed. In 1870 the current railway station, then known as Ponds Station, was opened above the culvert.

The Sheaf culvert starts at the bottom of Granville Road. It quickly becomes three connected parallel culverts and runs under the station until a short open stretch by Pond Street. The River Porter joins the Sheaf underground somewhere underneath the station taxi-rank..At Pond Street, the Sheaf returns underground and runs underneath the international sports centre. Here the three parallel culverts open out into a single expansive underground space, known affectionately as the *Megatron Cathedral*, on account of its cathedral-like dimensions.

After the Megatron, the culvert continues a short distance further, with the Sheaf emerging from underground and joining the River Don by Blonk Street.

The Sheaf culvert is 1300m long and in places up to 10m wide and 6m high – a remarkable feat of Victorian engineering.

In 1991 the River Sheaf flooded Sheffield station. On platform 5 you can find a substantial log with a plaque that references this event. The log was part of the flood debris.

The Porter culvert runs under Waitrose and then Decathlon before finally going underground a final time to join the Sheaf. The Porter culvert is more varied with a mixture of stone, brick and concrete construction. In 2017 a hole appeared in Decathlon car park when the culvert roof gave way, giving a brief glimpse into Sheffield's underground world.

Mellor, David

5 October 1930 – 7 May 2009

Education: Sheffield College of Art, Royal College of Art

Designer David Mellor initially specialised in producing silverware items. He was also an early adopter of the 'new' stainless steel and his *Symbol* design of cutlery (manufactured by Walker and Hall) was the first stainless steel cutlery to be produced in any serious quantity.

Although best known for his cutlery, most people will be far more familiar with Mellor's various pieces of iconic street design, without realising that they have anything to do with him.

Mellor was employed by engineering firm *Abacus* during the 1950s and 60s. During this period he designed the Abacus bus-shelter, of which over 140,000 have been installed. He also designed streetlights, public seating and a square post-box (the latter never took off). In 1965 he was commissioned by the government to re-design the humble traffic light. There are still over 25,000 of the Mellor-designed traffic lights in operation today.

In 1973 Mellor set up his cutlery business, manufacturing his own designs. David Mellor shops hold their own in several locations, including Sloane Square and Covent Garden.

Since 1990 Mellor's cutlery production has been based in the purpose built 'Round Building' in Hathersage.

Mellor was elected the youngest ever Royal Designer for Industry at the age of 32, has received honorary doctorates from both Sheffield universities, made an OBE in 1981 and a CBE in 2001. He was inducted into Sheffield's Walk of Fame in 2007.

Mi Amigo Flypast

On the 22nd February 2019 at 8.45am, the RAF and USAF carried out a fly past to commemorate the 75th anniversary of the Mi Amigo plane crash in Endcliffe Park. *BBC Breakfast* was broadcast live from Endcliffe Park for the fly past, and over 10,000 people turned up to watch.

Dakota ZA947 of the RAF's Battle of Britain Memorial Flight

MC-130J Commando II and CV-22 Osprey of the 352nd Special Operations Wing

KC-135 Stratotanker of the USAF's 100th Air Refueling Wing

Two Typhoons of the RAF's 41 Squadron

Four F-15E Strike Eagles of USAF 48th Fighter Wing

#RememberTheTen, #TonyGotAFlypast, #MiAmigo75th, #sheffieldflypast

The 10 Mi Amigo crew members who died are remembered by a monument at the site of the crash.

Lt Kriegshauser (pilot)
Lt Curtis (co-pilot)
Lt Humphrey (navigator)
Lt Hernandez (bomb-aimer)
Sgt Mayfield (radio operator)
Sgt Estabrooks (top-turret gunner)
Sgt Tuttle (lower turret gunner)
Sgt Robbins (rear-gunner)
Sgt Ambrosio (waist-gunner)
Sgt Williams (waist-gunner

Military

There wouldn't have been much for the Romans to fight over on the site of present-day Sheffield, but various coin and burial urn discoveries tell us that they were definitely here. We know too of a garrison stationed at nearby Templeborough.

The English Civil War saw Sheffield flip between Royalist and Parliamentarian control. This came to a head with a 10-day siege by Parliamentarian forces in August 1644. The Royalists surrendered and Sheffield Castle was destroyed.

Sheffield's central geographic location made it a good location for the construction of military barracks. In the 1790s the first barracks were built at Hillfoot to accommodate two cavalry troops. Hence the former *Old Light Horseman* pub (closed 1991) on the Penistone Road. A much larger barracks (to house 500 men, 250 horses and a military hospital) was built in 1848 in Hillsborough and was occupied until 1930. The parade ground of this has been roofed over and is now a Morrisons supermarket. The nearby *'New' Barrack Tavern* is still going strong.

Sheffield has more than played its part in recent conflicts, with large numbers answering the call to arms. The 1899–1902 Anglo-Boer War left its mark on the city with the Spion Kop at **Hillsborough Stadium** named after one of the battles in that conflict. **World War I** saw an enormous number of Sheffield's young men die on the front line, along with a **Zeppelin** raid on the city. World War II again saw large loss of life, this time with a significantly greater loss on the home front. Several bombing raids made it as far north as Sheffield, targeting the steel industry that was such an asset to the British war effort. The two nights of the Sheffield **Blitz** in December 1940 saw large scale loss of life and property. The **Mi Amigo** plane crash of 1944 saw further loss of Allied life (American) on Sheffield soil.

The steel industry played a pivotal role during the war years. During World War I it was an essential part of the war effort, producing enormous quantities of helmets, ammunition, guns, ships and later tanks. By the time of World War II you could add aeroplanes to the list. Many women stepped in to support the steel industry – the *Women of Steel* statue at Barker's Pool recognises their contribution.

As well as providing men, women and steel to the war effort, Sheffield also loaned its landscape, providing practice terrain and reservoirs for the successful **Dam Busters** raids.

Sheffield is also proud to have been on the side of three Royal Navy ships. The fourth **HMS Sheffield** will come with a billion-pound price tag and is due to start service during the 2020s.

Monopoly

GO	GO
OLD KENT ROAD	CLOWNE
COMMUNITY CHEST	COMMUNITY CHEST
WHITECHAPEL ROAD	THE WICKER
INCOME TAX	INCOME TAX
KINGS CROSS STATION	MIDLAND STATION
THE ANGEL ISLINGTON	THE PEAK DISTRICT
CHANCE	CHANCE
EUSTON ROAD	PEACE GARDENS
PENTONVILLE ROAD	WINTER GARDENS
JAIL	JAIL
PALL MALL	PONDS FORGE
ELECTRIC COMPANY	PUBLIC TRANSPORT
WHITEHALL	HILLSBOROUGH
NORTHUMBERLAND AVENUE	BRAMALL LANE
MARYLEBONE STATION	ROBIN HOOD AIRPORT
BOW STREET	HALLAM UNIVERSITY
COMMUNITY CHEST	COMMUNITY CHEST
MARLBOROUGH STREET	UNIVERSITY OF SHEFFIELD
VINE STREET	BOTANICAL GARDENS
FREE PARKING	FREE PARKING
STRAND	MOORE STREET
CHANCE	CHANCE
FLEET STREET	DIVISION STREET
TRAFALGAR SQUARE	THE OLD WEST GUN WORKS
FENCHURCH ST. STATION	SUPERTRAM
LEICESTER SQUARE	TOWN HALL
COVENTRY STREET	THE CRUCIBLE THEATRE
WATERWORKS	HEALTHCARE
PICCADILLY	VICTORIA STATION ROAD
GO TO JAIL	GO TO JAIL
REGENT STREET	FARGATE
OXFORD STREET	CLARKEHOUSE ROAD
COMMUNITY CHEST	COMMUNITY CHEST
BOND STREET	ST PAUL'S PLACE
LIVERPOOL ST. STATION	RIVER DON
CHANCE	CHANCE
PARK LANE	MEADOWHALL
BANK DEPOSIT	BANK DEPOSIT
MAYFAIR	SHEFFIELD CITY HALL

Mottos

- **All Saints Secondary School**
  Fortis in Fide - Strength in faith (Latin)
- **Birkdale School**
  Res Non Verba - Actions not Words (Latin)
- **Company of Cutlers in Hallamshire**
  Y Parvenir a Bonne Foi - To succeed through honest endeavour (French)
- **English Institute of Sport**
  Improving sporting performance through science, medicine, technology and engineering.
- **Fir Vale School Trust**
  Making dreams a reality
- **High Storrs School**
  Designed for Success
- **King Edward VII Secondary School**
  Fac recte, nil time - Do right, fear nothing (Latin)
- **Notre Dame High School**
  Ah! Qu'il est bon le bon dieu! – Ah! How good is the good God! (French)
- **Sheffield**
  Deo Adjuvante Labor Proficit - With God's help our labour is successful (Latin)
- **Sheffield Hallam University**
  Learn and Serve
- **Sheffield Wednesday**
  Consilio et Animis - By wisdom and courage (Latin)
- **Sheffield University**
  Rerum cognoscere causas - To discover the causes of things (Latin)

Mundella, Anthony John

> *I see a pretty state of things in your Municipality. Everything is mean, petty, and narrow in the extreme. What a contrast to Leeds!*

Letter to Robert Leader (1871).

Music and Culture

This is one area where Sheffield definitely punches above its weight.

Musically, Sheffield has produced both **Cockers** (not related), Pulp, Human League, **Def Leppard**, Reverend & The Makers, the Thompson Twins and the Arctic Monkeys to name but a few. Many of these have produced albums that have gone **Platinum**, both in England and abroad. As well as strong connections to these more well-known outfits, Sheffield has fingers in all of the different **Popular Music** pies, from electronic to folk.

The annual **Tramlines** festival brings the best of the rest to our city, the Botanical Gardens hosts open air concerts in the summer, we boast four orchestras and numerous choirs, morris-men and women jingle bells, hit sticks and play with swords, and the Sheffield **Carols** are sung in pubs across the city from November through to January.

Of course, a big part of the culture of Sheffield is expressed in its voice, both the **Dee Dah** dialect and the many curious **Local Phrases** that mystify visitors. There are **Poets** a-plenty, and numerous Sheffield authors putting that voice to paper **In Print**. Sheffield hosts the annual *Off The Shelf* literary festival which is one of the largest of its kind in the UK.

Sheffield has the Weston Park, Graves, Ruskin, Site and Millennium art galleries, along with a thriving theatrical scene – the Crucible, Lyceum and Studio theatres form the largest theatre complex in England outside of London.

We also have an eclectic mix of museums, from Weston Park Museum to the **National Videogame Museum** to the National Emergency Services Museum, with Kelham Island and Abbeydale Industrial Hamlet in the mix too.

Sheffield is proud to count among its own a fine crop of actors who have appeared **On Screen**, from Shaun **Bean** to Michael **Palin.** Sheffield has also been used as the backdrop for several **Films**, and **Doctor Who** has even paid us a visit. The International Documentary Festival is hosted in Sheffield and every year the Sheffield Adventure Film Festival (SHAFF) brings the best adventure, travel and extreme sports films to our door.

No surprise then that Sheffield was shortlisted for the first UK City of Culture in 2010.

National Football League System

Sheffield has a well-earned footballing pedigree, with Sheffield Football Club (dating from 1857) being officially recognised as the world's oldest football club, and both United and Wednesday having won their fair share of silverware over the years. While United and Wednesday play in the top couple of leagues, there are numerous other teams in the city that also take part in the Football League System. The system is layered in 'steps' with Step 1 being the Premiership, Step 2 being the Championship, and so on, with teams from each step promoted and relegated to the steps immediately above and below. Nationally, there are as many as 7,000 clubs participating somewhere in the pyramid.

Listed below are all those Sheffield teams that play within the National League System along with their home grounds. Both Handsworth and Sheffield Football Club currently have their home grounds outside of Sheffield itself.

STEP 1: English Football League - Premier League

- Sheffield United — *Bramall Lane*

STEP 2: English Football League - Championship

- Sheffield Wednesday — *Hillsborough Stadium*

STEP 3: English Football League - League One

STEP 4: English Football League - League Two

STEP 5: Northern Premier League – Premier Division

STEP 6: Northern Premier League – Division One South East

- Sheffield Football Club — *Coach & Horses, Dronfield*
- Stocksbridge Park Steels — *Bracken Moor*

STEP 7: Northern Counties East Football League - Premier Division

- Handsworth — *Sandy Lane, Worksop*

STEP 8: Northern Counties East Football League - Division One

Club	Ground
⚽ Hallam	*Sandygate Road*

STEP 9: Sheffield & Hallamshire County Senior Football League - Premier Division

Club	Ground
⚽ Burngreave	*Fir Vale Academy*
⚽ Ecclesfield Red Rose	*Chaucer School*
⚽ Frecheville Davys	*Davys Sports Club, Darnall*
⚽ Jubilee Sports	*Jubilee Sports Club, Hillsborough*
⚽ Oughtibridge War Memorial	*War Memorial Ground*
⚽ Stocksbridge Park Steels Reserves	*Bracken Moor*

STEP 10: Sheffield & Hallamshire County Senior Football League - Division One

Club	Ground
⚽ Handsworth Reserves	*Olivers Mount*
⚽ New Bohemians	*Hillsborough Arena*
⚽ Sheffield Medics	*Warminster Road*
⚽ Sheffield Union	*Warminster Road*

STEP 11: Sheffield & Hallamshire County Senior Football League - Division Two

Club	Ground
⚽ Caribbean Sports	*Caribbean Sports Club, Ecclesfield*
⚽ Sheffield Lane Top	*Civil Service Club, Ecclesfield*

National Videogame Museum

This was originally established as the National Videogame Arcade in Nottingham in 2015. In 2018 the NVA moved to Angel Street in Sheffield and was renamed the National Videogame Museum. The museum features playable exhibits from both contemporary and retro videogames – everything from BBC Micro, Sega and Gameboys to Xboxes and Playstations.

Nature Reserves

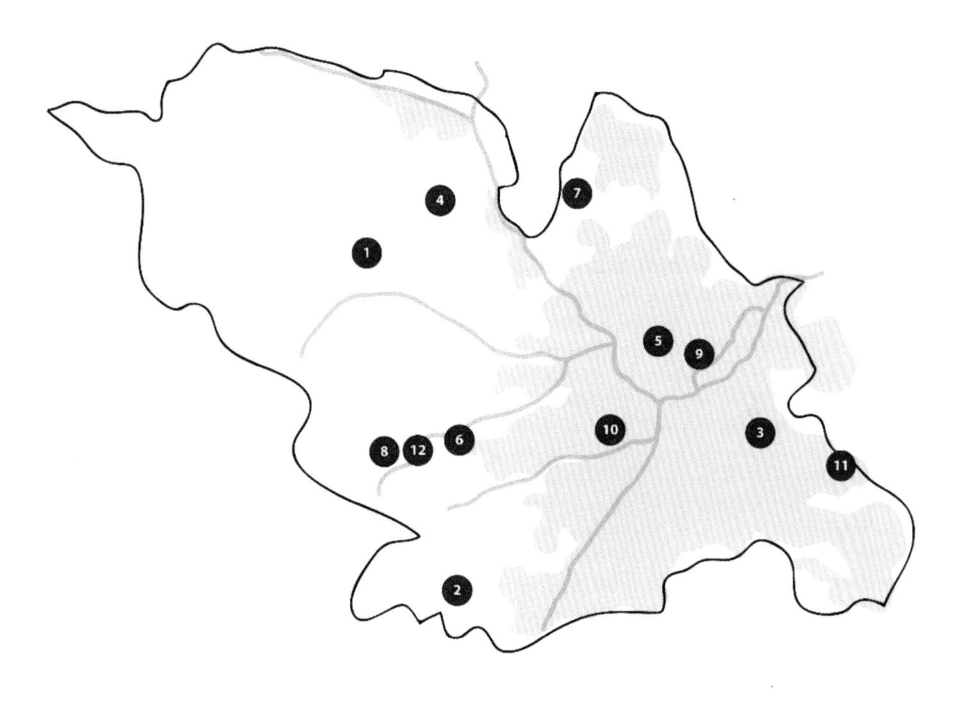

1.	Agden Bog	*Bog*
2.	Blacka Moor	*Moorland*
3.	Carbrook Ravine	*Woodland, wetland and wildflower meadow*
4.	Carr House Meadows	*Old English-style meadow*
5.	Crabtree Ponds	*Ponds*
6.	Fox Hagg	*Heathland and woodland*
7.	Greno Woods	*Ancient woodland*
8.	Hammond's Field	*Semi-improved wet pasture*
9.	Salmon Pastures	*Riverside*
10.	Sunnybank	*Woodland scrub*
11.	Woodhouse Washlands	*Grassland, scrub & floodplain grazing marsh*
12.	Wyming Brook	*Woodland and crags*

This list includes some real little gems - Sunnybank, hidden behind the petrol station at the ring-road end of Ecclesall Road; Crabtree Ponds, tucked away in Burngreave; and tiny Salmon Pastures by the river Don. At the other end of the scale, the expansive Greno Woods, Blacka Moor and Woodhouse Washlands will take some exploring.

Notable Trees

How on earth do you pick out individual trees from our 4.5 million? We've come up with 10 of the best, but realise there are 4,499,990 worthy contenders that didn't make the shortlist!

The Ancient Tree Inventory records the following six ancient trees within Sheffield. They define an 'ancient tree' as being in the final stage of its life, and old compared with others of its species. We've listed the tree, Ordnance Survey grid reference and girth.

- **Black Mulberry** SK4173086158 3m girth
  In private garden in Handsworth, over 400 years old
- **Hawthorn** SK4156382690 2.3m girth
  In woodland near Owlthorpe
- **Hawthorn** SK4170682699 2.2m girth
  In woodland near Owlthorpe
- **Pedunculate Oak** SK17309240 5.4m girth
  Woodland to the East of Howden Reservoir, over 600 years old, Tree of National Special Interest
- **Pedunculate Oak** SK3120084873 4.7m girth
  Field to the East of Whiteley Wood Road, Tree of National Special Interest
- **Sweet Chestnut** SK2341590459 5.5m girth
  On moorland between Dale Dyke and Strines Reservoirs, Tree of National Special Interest

Other notable trees recorded include:

- **Chelsea Road Elm** SK3372184643 2.8m girth
  Chelsea Road, shortlisted for 'Tree of the Year'
- **Ringinglow Yew** SK31228392 5.5m girth
  On private land off Ringinglow Road, mentioned in the Domesday book as part of the boundary between Mercia and Northumbria
- **Vernon Oak** SK3162680586 3m girth
  Street tree in Dore
- **White Willow** SK33548306 4.6m girth
  Hutcliffe Wood

On Screen

The list of television and film actors and actresses below is restricted to those born in Sheffield, ie born even if not entirely bred!

- Sean Bean
- Paul Bentley
- Paul Clayton
- Jessica Jane Clement
- Maurice Colbourne
- Thomas Craig
- David Crellin
- Basil Dignam
- Mark Dignam
- Graham Fellows
- Brian Glover
- Stuart Golland
- Ethel Griffies
- Patricia Haines
- Ryan Hawley
- Elizabeth Henstridge
- Robert Hudson
- Bobby Knutt
- Susan Littler
- Richard McCourt
- Julian Ovenden
- Michael Palin
- Judy Parfitt
- Tony Pitts
- Angela Pleasance
- Jessica Ransom
- Enzo Squillino Junior
- Dominic West

Orwell, George

> *It could justly claim to be called the ugliest town in the Old World: its inhabitants, who want it to be pre-eminent in everything, very likely make that claim for it … And the stench! If at rare moments you stop smelling sulphur it is because you have begun smelling gas.*
>
> The Road to Wigan Pier (1937).

Other Sheffields

It turns out that we are not alone. There are a bunch of other places in the world that have also decided to call themselves Sheffield.

England

- **Sheffield Bottom and Sheffield Lock**
  Sheffield Bottom is a small village in Berkshire, with a nearby lock on the Kennet and Avon Canal.

- **Sheffield, Cornwall**
  Originally built to house the workers of the nearby Sheffield Quarry, this is a tiny hamlet not far from Land's End.

- **Sheffield Park and Gardens**
  A landscaped garden in East Sussex, now owned by the National Trust. The gardens were designed by Capability Brown during the 18th Century.

America

- **Sheffield, Alabama, USA**
  A small town (population 10,000) that boasts the Muscle Shoals Sounds Studios where The Osmonds, Cher, Rolling Stones, Simon & Garfunkel, Arethra Franklin and many others recorded hit albums.

- **Sheffield, Illinois, USA**
  A village (population 1,000) founded by Joseph E. Sheffield (an American railroad magnate) and Henry Farnam in 1852. They flipped a coin to decide who to name it after.

- **Sheffield, Iowa, USA**
  Officially designated a city, but with a population of only just over 1,000, Sheffield was founded in 1876 and named after a friend of the founder.

- **Sheffield, Massachusetts, USA**
  The oldest town in Berkshire County, population 3,500.

- **Sheffield, Missouri, USA**
  Sheffield is a suburb of Kansas City. A post-office called 'Sheffield' opened in 1888 and the name has stuck.

- **Sheffield, Montana, USA**
  Today just a ranch, this has had several names since 1895 when the first post office was recorded. It finally settled on Sheffield in 1929, after the surname of a local rancher.

- **Sheffield, North Carolina, USA**
  A small community in the Clarksville township. Not much going on here.

- **Middleport, Ohio, USA**
  We can't completely claim this one, but the village of Middleport was orginally founded as Sheffield in the 1820s. It was also known as both Coalport and Salisbury at various times before settling on its current appellation.

- **Sheffield and Sheffield Lake, Ohio, USA**
  The former a small village, the latter a city of 10,000 inhabitants. Sheffield Lake is situated on the shore of Lake Erie, with Sheffield a few km to the south.

- **Sheffield, Pennsylvania, USA**
  A township of 1,000 inhabitants in Warren County Pennsylvania, originally settled in the 1830s by immigrants from New York.

- **Sheffield, South Dakota, USA**
  Nothing remains now, other than the name on a map. This was originally a small settlement, founded in 1910 and named after the hometown of the ancestors of the settlers.

- **Sheffield, Texas, USA**
  Founded in 1888, this is now a fairly non-descript small commune. The first postmaster, William Sheffield, gave his name to the community.

- **Sheffield, Vermont, USA**
  A small town of less than 1,000 inhabitants, founded in 1793.

- **Sheffield, Virginia, USA**
  Thomas Sheffield arrived in Virginia in 1619 and established a plantation here.

- **Sheffield Scientific School, Yale University**
  Named after the same Joseph E. Sheffield as the village in Illinois.

Canada

- **Sheffield, New Brunswick, Cananda**
  A parish and community created in 1786 and named after John Baker-Holroyd who was the 1st Earl of Sheffield at the time.

- **Sheffield, Ontaria, Canada**
  Established in 1809 by the Rev Cornell as 'Cornell' but renamed Sheffield on the opening of the first post office in 1832. Now a rurual community of a few hundred inhabitants.

Others

- **Sheffield, New Zealand**
  Named by John Jebson from Sheffield, England who was the first to work the lignite deposits in the area. Now a tiny farming settlement.

- **Sheffield, Tasmania**
  Known as the 'town of murals' due to large numbers of murals painted on the walls of buildings, Sheffield was originally founded in 1859 as 'Kentishbury'. Edward Curr from South Yorkshire renamed it in 1882 after his home town.

Palin, Michael

Born in 1943 in Ranmoor and educated at Birkdale School and Oxford, Michael Palin is one of Sheffield's greatest exports. His plaque on the Sheffield Walk of Fame refers to him as 'Comedian, Actor and Traveller.'

His career spans television and film comedy (both performance and writing) as well as more serious travel documentaries. Alongside this he has written fiction and non-fiction books for both adults and children. Amongst all of this he has managed to squeeze in a three-year stint as President of the Royal Geographical Society.

Palin won a BAFTA in 1989 (Best Supporting Actor in *A Fish Called Wanda*) and special BAFTA awards in 1992 and 1995. He was awarded a CBE in 2000 and a knighthood in 2019 for services to Culture, Geography and Travel. Even more importantly he was voted the greatest ever Yorkshireman in 2018.

Film Appearances

1971 *And Now for Something Completely Different*
1975 *Monty Python and the Holy Grail*
1977 *Jabberwocky*
1978 *All You Need Is Cash*
1979 *Monty Python's Life of Brian*
1981 *Time Bandits*
1982 *Monty Python Live at the Hollywood Bowl*
1982 *The Missionary*
1983 *Monty Python's The Meaning of Life*
1983 *The Crimson Permanent Assurance*
1984 *A Private Function*
1985 *Brazil*
1988 *A Fish Called Wanda*
1991 *American Friends*
1997 *Fierce Creatures*
2010 *Not the Messiah*

Classic Monty Python Sketches featuring Michael Palin

Architect's Sketch
Argument Clinic
Cheese Shop Sketch
Colin 'Bomber' Harris vs Colin 'Bomber' Harris
Dead Parrot Sketch
Dirty Hungarian Phrasebook
Fish Licence
Fish-Slapping Dance
Four Yorkshiremen
Funniest Joke in the World
Marriage Guidance Counsellor
The Mouse Problem
The Philosophers' Football Match
Seduced Milkmen
Self-Defence Against Fresh Fruit
The Spanish Inquisition
Upperclass Twit of the Year
Vocational Guidance Counsellor

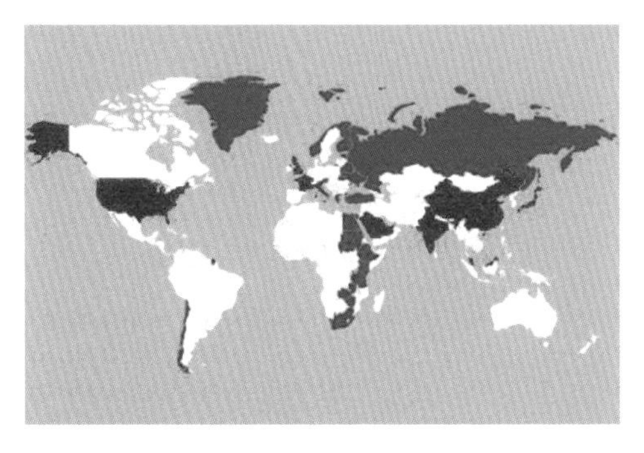

Around the World in 80 Days (1988)

Pole to Pole (1991)

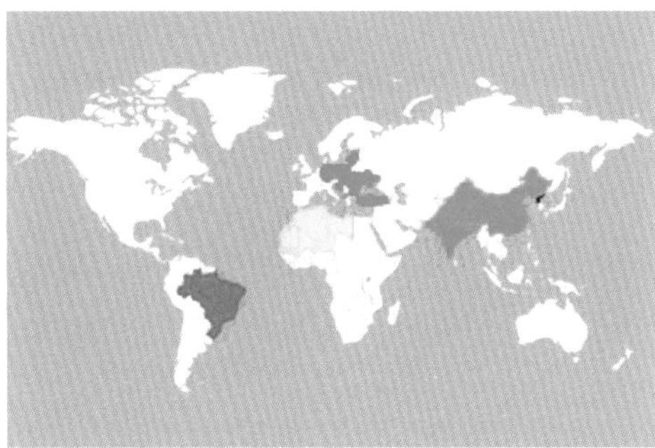

Sahara (2001-02)

Himalaya (2003-04)

New Europe (2006-07)

Brazil (2011-12)

North Korea (2018)

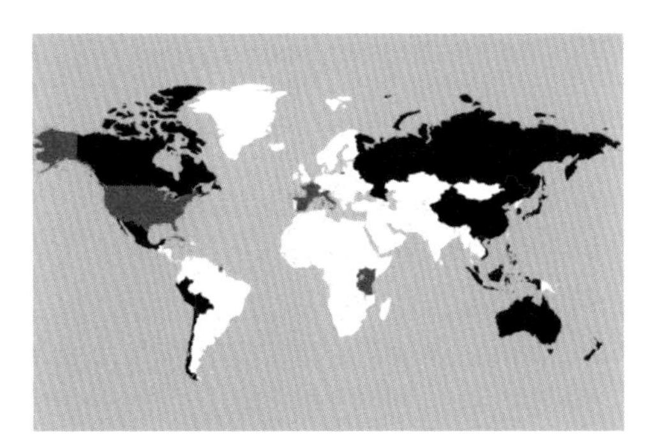

Full Circle (1996-97)

Hemingway Adventure (1999)

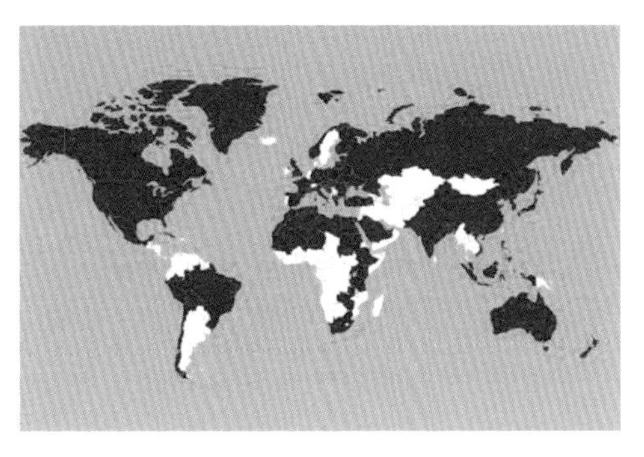

Combined

Castle parkrun

Three anti-clockwise laps of Manor Fields starting and finishing by the park entrance on City Road.

Ave Runners: 55
Fastest Male:
16:12 – Robert Smith
Fastest Female:
17:26 – Lizzie Brown
Fastest Age-Adjusted:
89.75% - Helen Eberlin

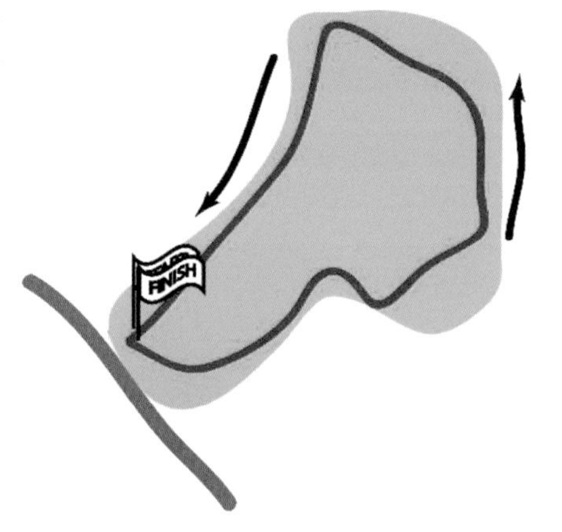

Concord parkrun

Starting and finishing at the golf club end of Concord Park, this course consists of two large anti-clockwise laps.

Ave Runners: 293
Max Runners: 414
Fastest Male:
15:42 – Mohammad Saleh
Fastest Female:
18:03 – Stephanie Burns
Fastest Age-Adjusted:
92.99% - Dot Kesterton

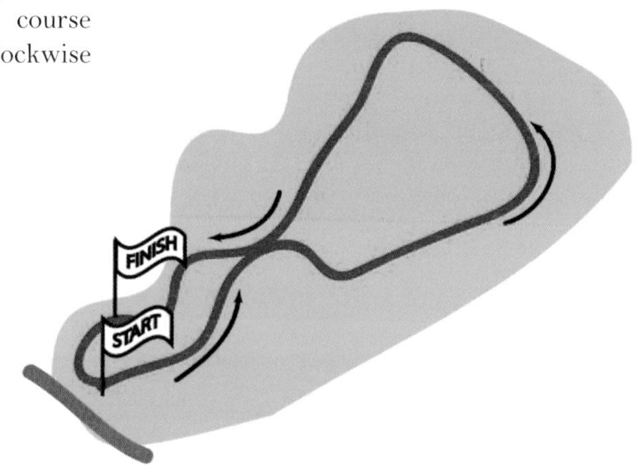

Endcliffe parkrun

The new route starts by the café, does one small loop towards Hunters Bar, and then runners do two large clockwise laps with the mantra 'turn left' wherever the route splits.

Ave Runners: 451
Max Runners: 884
Fastest Male:
15:23 – Paul Whitelam
Fastest Female:
16:39 – Rebecca Robinson
Fastest Age-Adjusted:
99.58% - Karin Hessenberg

Graves parkrun

Starting near the main car park, runners complete two anti-clockwise laps. The first lap includes a loop of the East Lake. The second lap cuts out this loop.

Ave Runners: 186
Max Runners: 446
Fastest Male:
16:19 – Joseph Newman-Billington
Fastest Female:
18:40 – Hattie Archer
Fastest Age-Adjusted:
90.48% - Yvonne Twelvetree

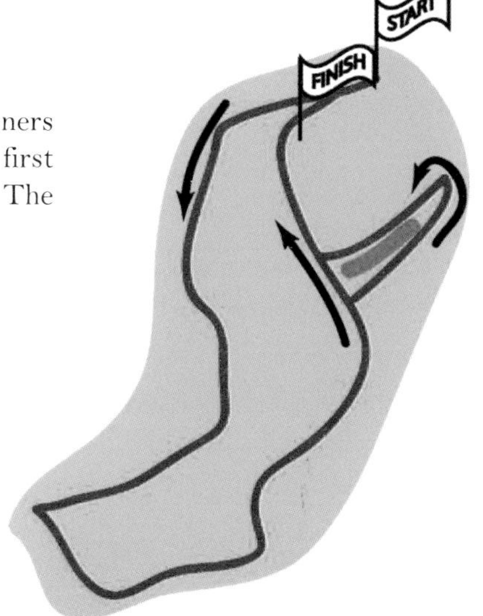

Hillsborough parkrun

Starting and finishing by the play area, this course consists of three identical clockwise laps.

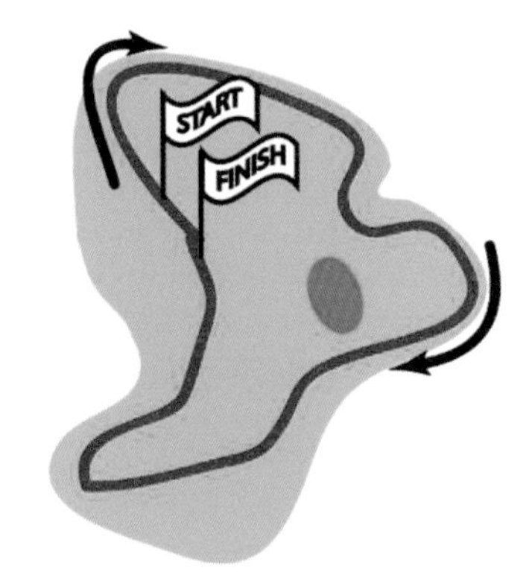

Ave Runners: 229
Max Runners: 750
Fastest Male:
15:50 – Mike Tanner
Fastest Female:
17:48 – Becky Rigby
Fastest Age-Adjusted:
92.31% - Thomas Thake

Millhouses parkrun

Three anti-clockwise laps, starting from near to the Abbey Lane car park end.

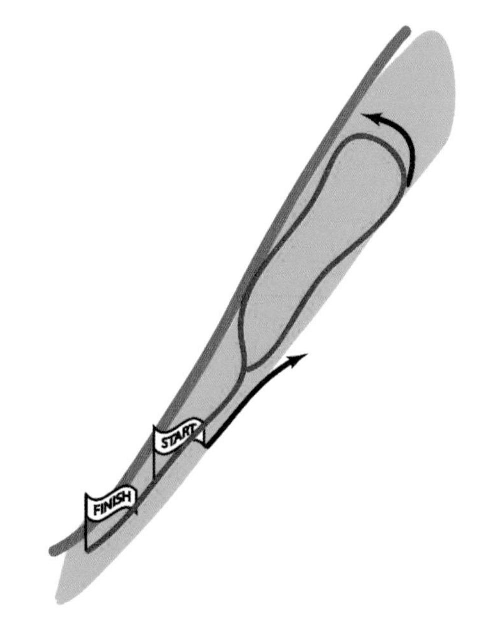

Ave Runners: 366
Fastest Male:
16:32 – Dominic Walton
Fastest Female:
18:08 – Sophie Wood
Fastest Age-Adjusted:
94.58% - Dot Kesterton

Parkin

Parkin is our version of gingerbread, although it could be argued of course that gingerbread is the rest of the country's version of our parkin! It is to be enjoyed all year round, but especially at Bonfire Night. Traditionally it was eaten on 'Parkin Sunday' which was the first Sunday in November.

You can find parkin in Lancashire too, although their version lacks treacle and therefore just isn't in the same league. If you aren't from Sheffield, chances are you haven't had parkin before and won't be able to get hold of it locally either. If you find yourself in this predicament, here's how to make the South Yorkshire version.

Ingredients

- 8oz self-raising flour,
- 8oz oatmeal,
- 8oz sugar,
- 2 teaspoons ginger
- 4oz margarine
- 4oz black treacle,
- 4oz golden syrup,
- 4oz lard,
- 2 eggs
- 1 cup of milk

Method

1. Mix together the flour, oatmeal, sugar and ginger and then mix in margarine.
2. Melt the treacle, syrup and lard together.
3. Add the treacle mixture to the flour mixture.
4. Whisk 2 eggs in 1 cup of milk and combine with the existing mixture.
5. Bake in a lined cake tin at 140C for approximately 1 hour.

Parkin Street

Named after a certain John Parkin, a file, knife and steel manufacturer who lived in Upperthorpe in the mid 19th Century.

Parks

City Parks (Visitor destinations in their own right)

- Concord Park
- Cholera Monument Grounds
- Endcliffe Park/Porter Valley Parks
- Ecclesall Woods
- Firth Park
- Graves Park & Animal Farm
- Hillsborough Park & Walled Garden
- Millhouses Park
- Norfolk Heritage Park
- Peace Gardens
- Rivelin Valley Park
- Sheffield Botanical Gardens
- Weston Park

District Parks (Serving a catchment area of up to 2km, containing a variety of landscape features and facilities)

- Bingham Park (Porter Valley Parks)
- Bolehill Recreation Ground
- Chapeltown Park
- Crookes Valley Park
- Devonshire Green
- Ecclesfield Park
- Greenhill Park
- Grenoside Recreation Ground
- Herdings Park
- High Hazels Park
- Manor Fields Park
- Meersbrook Park
- Mount Pleasant Park
- Oxley Park
- Parkwood Springs
- Parson Cross Park
- Richmond Park
- Rother Valley Country Park
- Stannington Park
- Tinsley Green Recreation Ground
- Whirlow Brook Park

Local Parks (Serving a catchment area of approximately 400m, generally have a play area and green space)

- Abbeyfield Park
- Angram Bank Recreation Ground
- Arbourthorne Recreation Ground and Pond
- Barbers Field
- Beaver Hill Recreation Ground
- Bowman Drive Recreation Ground (Lightwood)
- Brightside Recreation Ground
- Broadfield Road Open Space
- Burncross Recreation Ground
- Busk Meadow Park
- Carterhall Recreation Ground
- Chancet Wood
- Chelsea Park
- Colley Park
- Crookesmoor East Recreation Ground (Ponderosa)
- Darnall Neighbourhood Park
- Darnall Community Park
- Dore Recreation Ground
- Duchess Road Community Area

- Eastern Avenue/Arbourthorne Pond (also known as Arbourthorne Playing Field)
- Ellesmere Park
- Flockton Park
- Fox Glen Recreation Ground
- Foxhill Recreation Ground
- Frecheville Pond
- Glen Howe Park
- Green Oak Recreation Ground
- Halliwell Crescent/Wordsworth Avenue
- Handsworth Recreation Ground
- Heathlands Park
- Heeley Millennium Park
- Hollinsend Recreation Ground
- Jaunty Park
- Kettlebridge Doorstep Green
- Longley Park
- Lowfield Park
- Manor Sports Ground
- Mather Road Recreation Ground
- Middlewood Park & Playing Field
- Mosborough Country Park
- Mortomley Park
- Osgathorpe Park
- Phillimore Park
- Rolling Acres
- Ruskin Park
- Sky Edge Playing Field/Manor Oaks Road
- Sycamore Park
- Thorncliffe Recreation Ground
- Thorpe Hesley Recreation Ground
- Totley Hall Playing Field
- Tunwell Park (formerly Wooden Park)
- Waterthorpe Park
- Westwood Country Park
- Woodhouse Recreation Ground
- Woodthorpe Recreation Ground

Parks maintained by Bradfield Parish Council

- Ibbotson Memorial Field
- Coronation Park
- Dungworth Park and Pavilion
- Spider Park
- Stannington Park
- Storrs Park
- Sycamore Park
- Wadsley Park

Park Square

George Talbot (the 4th Earl of Shrewsbury) built himself a lodge a couple of miles out from the centre of Sheffield. This is what we know as the Manor Lodge. At the time it was built the lodge was in the middle of an enormous deer park that stretched out to present day Handsworth and Gleadless.

Park Square, Park Hill flats, Park and the Manor are all named after the Talbot estate. Today, the Manor Lodge still stands, and patches of the original parkland (eg Norfolk Park) still remain.

Parliamentary Constituencies

The current parliamentary constituencies have been in operation since 2010 following the most recent Boundary Commission. The periodic Boundary Commissions redefine constituency boundaries in response to changes in the size of the voting population so that each constituency contains a similar number of voters.

	Constituency	2019	2017	2015	2010
1	Penistone & Stocksbridge	Miriam Cates	Angela Smith	Angela Smith	Angela Smith
2	Sheffield Brightside & Hillsborough	Gill Furniss	Gill Furniss	Harry Harpham	David Blunkett
3	Sheffield Central	Paul Blomfield	Paul Blomfield	Paul Blomfield	Paul Blomfield
4	Sheffield Hallam	Olivia Blake	Jared O'Mara	Nick Clegg	Nick Clegg
5	Sheffield Heeley	Louise Haigh	Louise Haigh	Louise Haigh	Meg Munn
6	Sheffield South East	Clive Betts	Clive Betts	Clive Betts	Clive Betts

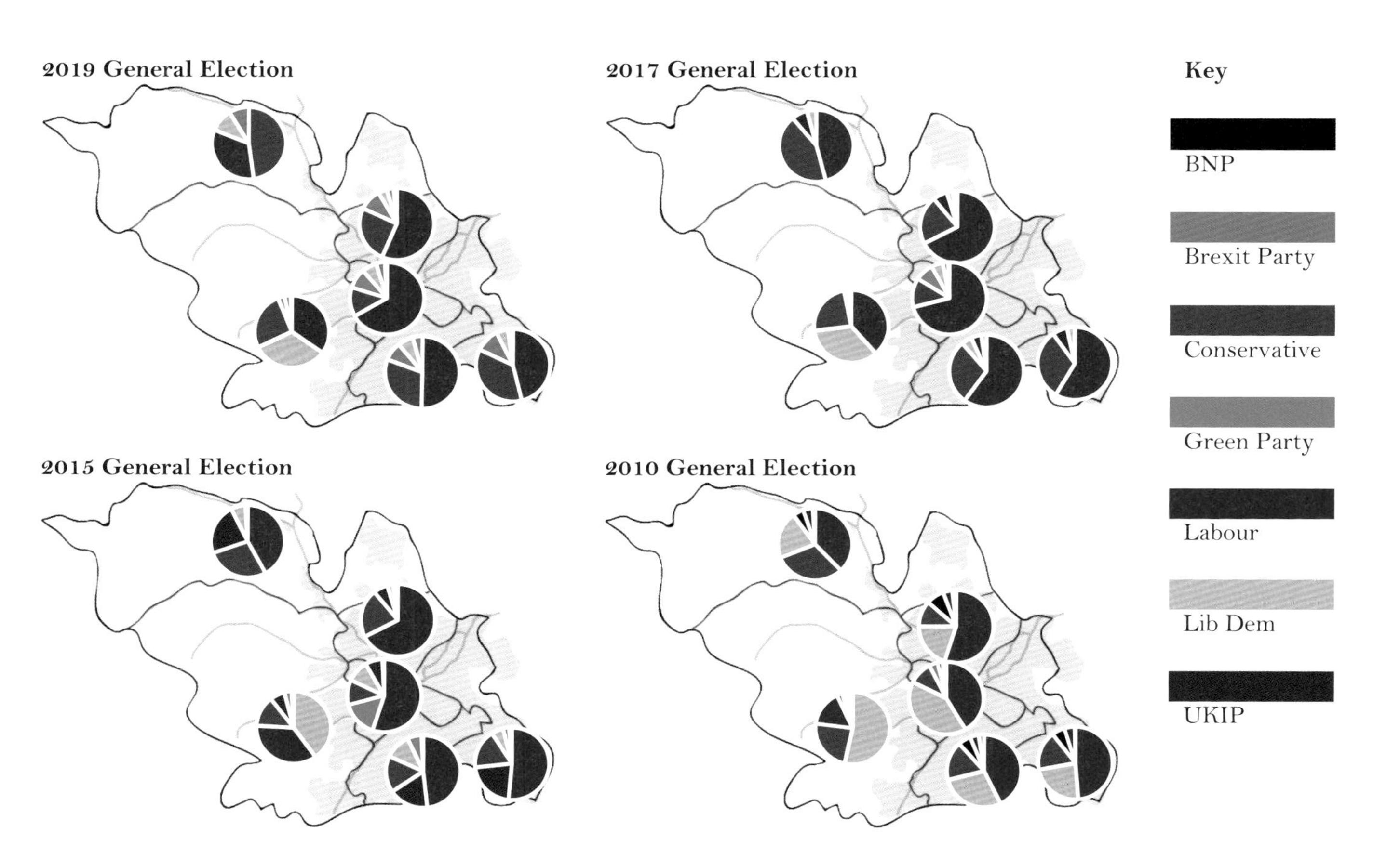
2019 General Election
2017 General Election
2015 General Election
2010 General Election
Key
BNP
Brexit Party
Conservative
Green Party
Labour
Lib Dem
UKIP

Peace Gardens

When St Paul's Church was demolished in the 1930's in order to extend the Town Hall, the St Paul's Gardens were laid out on the site. They quickly adopted the moniker 'Peace Gardens' on account of the Munich Agreement of 1938.

Plans to extend the Town Hall were shelved after the war and the gardens survived. They were formally renamed as the Peace Gardens in 1985. Removal of the remaining graveyard, remodelling of the gardens and construction of the present day water features took place in the late 1990s. Walk around the Peace Gardens and see if you can find: the memorials to Hiroshima and to those who died in the Spanish Civil War, a set of standard measures and the Bochum Bell.

Peat, Steve (Peaty)

Born: 17th June 1974

Education: Ecclesfield Comprehensive

Steve Peat is Britain's most successful downhill mountain biker. At one time he held the all-time world record for the number of international titles won.

Peat has ridden for the great professional teams, including Saracen, Team MBUK, GT Bikes, Orange Bikes and the Santa Cruz Syndicate. He was one of the 7 downhillers followed over the course of a year in the documentary film *Season.*

Originally a plumber before turning professional, Peat now part owns a clothing company and has also produced his own downhill mountain biking game.
Since 2011 he has organised the *Peaty's Steel City Downhill* (affectionately known as the 'biggest little race') that takes place in Grenoside Woods every summer.

Major wins

- Great Britain Downhill National Champion (8 wins)
- European Downhill Champion (3 wins)
- UCI Downhill World Cup (17 wins)
- UCI Downhill World Cup Overall (3 wins)
- UCI Downhill World Champion (1 win)
- World Championships representing Great Britain (1 gold, 4 silver medals)

People

Just where *do* you begin when summarising the contributions that particular individuals have made to making Sheffield great?

The history of Sheffield owes much to the scientific developments of individuals such as **Brierley**, Bessemer, Hadfield and Sorby, and to successful industrialists such as Mark Firth, John George Graves, and Ebenezer Elliot who also campaigned and put money behind more philanthropic ventures.

There are the creatives – artists such as Joe **Scarborough** and Pete McKee, **Poets**, authors (**In Print**), and a cast of individuals who have graced television and film with their talents **On Screen**.

Add to that list a wealth of musical talent who have contributed to the nation's rich and diverse range of **Popular Music.**

There are those that have contributed to local and national politics (famously or infamously!). Everyone in Sheffield can name at least one local former Deputy Prime Minister, but in recent times Roy Hattersley, Richard Caborn and David Blunkett also all have Sheffield roots. Venturing a little further into the past: prominent local G.H.B. Ward was an MP who campaigned extensively for open access for ramblers (Ward's piece on Lose Hill has its name as it was given to him by an earlier incarnation of the *Ramblers Association);* Frederick **Mappin** was an industrialist who was also the youngest ever Master Cutler and an MP; and Chartists Holberry and **Ironside** are both buried in Sheffield **General Cemetery**.

Then there are all those who have represented their county and country in one **Sport** or another– be it on the field, track, court or pitch.

Recent Sheffield greats have been inducted into the Sheffield Legends Walk of Fame and each have a plaque outside the town hall. These individuals are recognised for a whole variety of reasons, from sporting prowess to literary contributions to being the first British astronaut - Gordon **Banks**, Sean **Bean**, Grace **Clough**, Joe **Cocker**, Sebastian **Coe**, Derek **Dooley**, Margaret **Drabble**, Jessica **Ennis Hill**, Tony Foulds, Barry **Hancock**, Brendan **Ingle**, **Def Leppard**, Nick **Matthew**, David **Mellor**, Michael **Palin**, Steve **Peat**, Helen **Sharman**, Joe **Simpson**, Joe **Scarborough**, Michael **Vaughan** and Clinton **Woods**.

Platinum

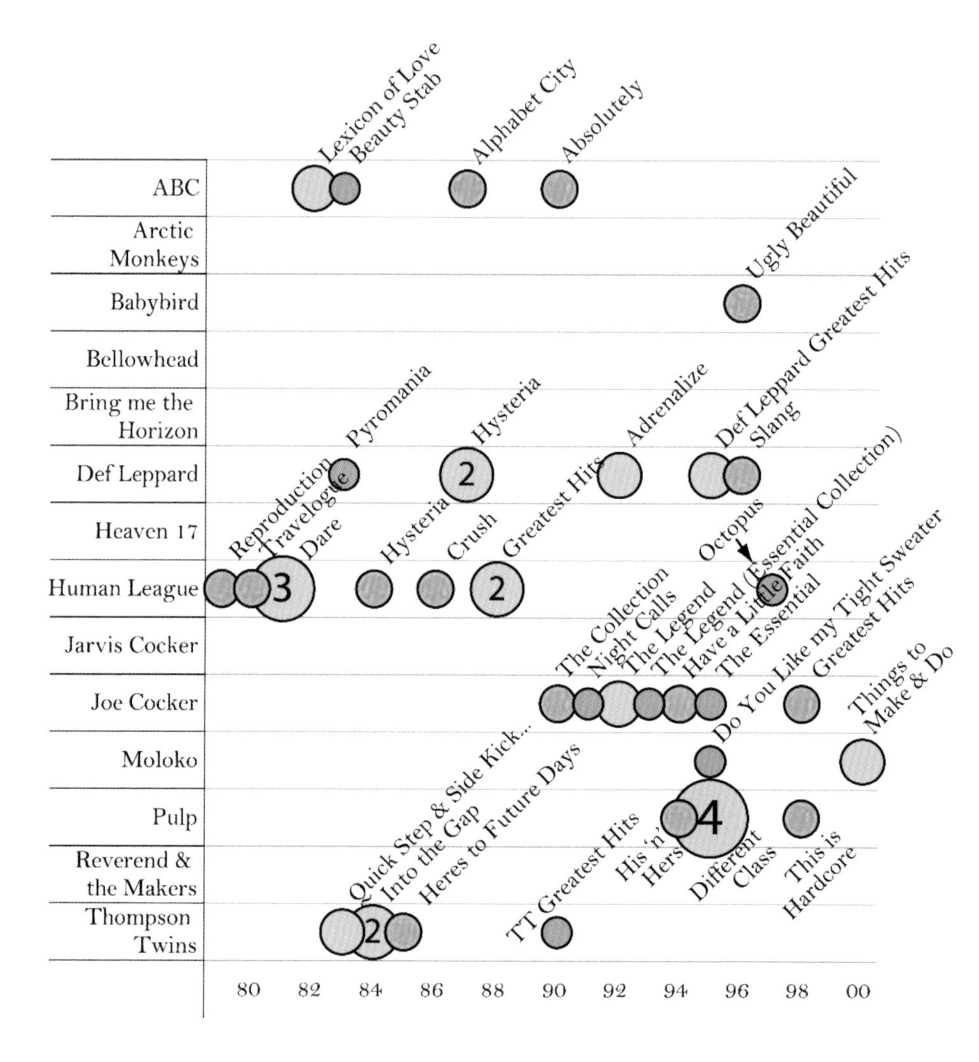

The British Phonographic Industry (BPI) certifies official music sales in Britain

All BPI silver certification and above for albums released by Sheffield groups or individuals is charted above. This obviously excludes certification awarded for these and/or other album sales in other countries, as well as certification awarded for singles.

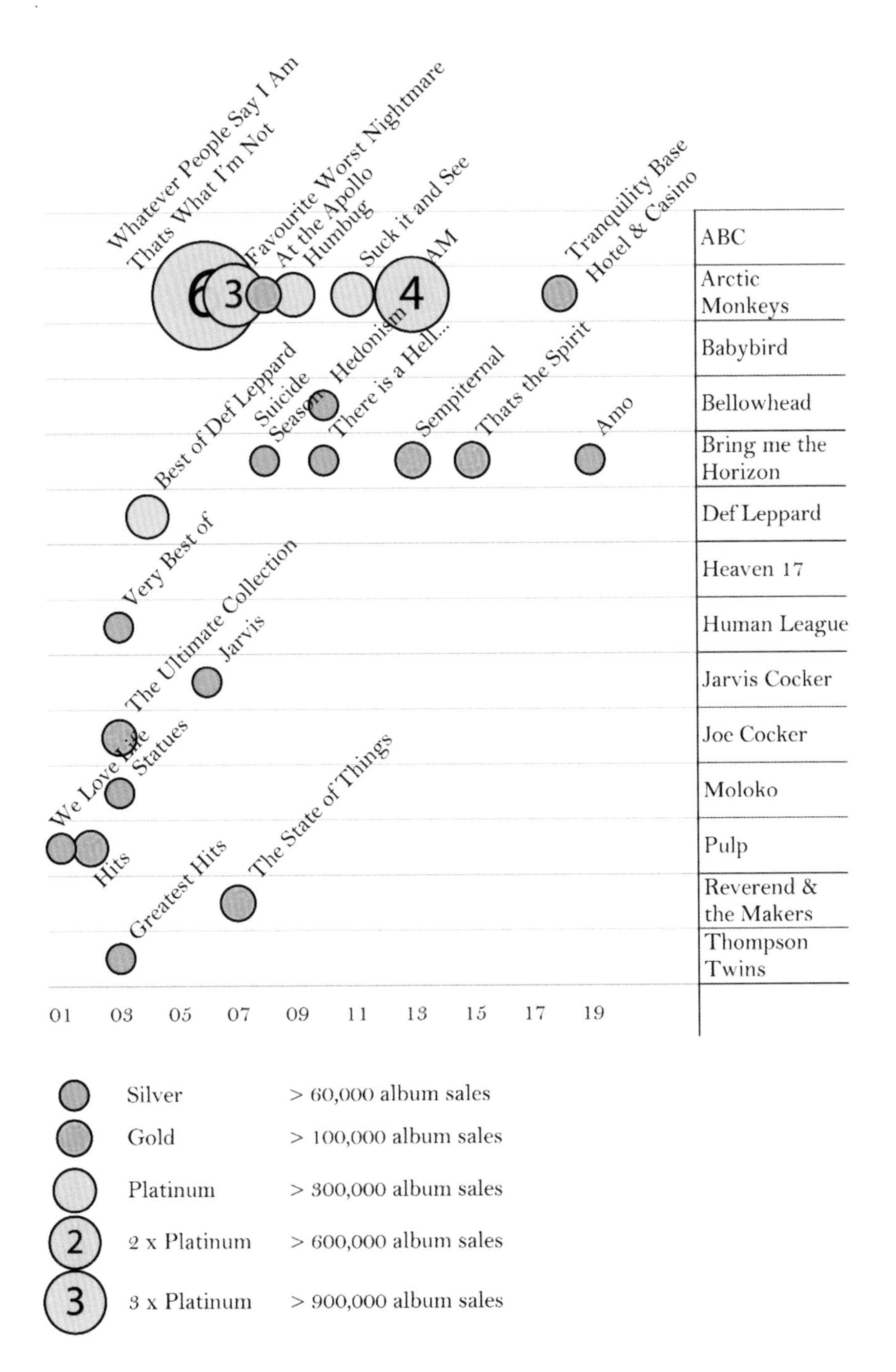
Whatever People Say I Am
Thats What I'm Not
Favourite Worst Nightmare
At the Apollo
Humbug
Suck it and See
AM
Tranquility Base
Hotel & Casino
6
3
4
Hedonism
Best of Def Leppard
Suicide Season
There is a Hell...
Sempiternal
Thats the Spirit
Amo
Very Best of
The Ultimate Collection
Jarvis
We Love Life
Statues
Hits
The State of Things
Greatest Hits
ABC
Arctic Monkeys
Babybird
Bellowhead
Bring me the Horizon
Def Leppard
Heaven 17
Human League
Jarvis Cocker
Joe Cocker
Moloko
Pulp
Reverend & the Makers
Thompson Twins
01
03
05
07
09
11
13
15
17
19
Silver
> 60,000 album sales
Gold
> 100,000 album sales
Platinum
> 300,000 album sales
2
2 x Platinum
> 600,000 album sales
3
3 x Platinum
> 900,000 album sales

Poets

- **Ebenezer Elliot (1781-1849)**
  A factory owner who campaigned to repeal the Corn Laws. John Betjeman's poem "An Edwardian Sunday, Broomhill, Sheffield" makes reference to the statue of Elliot that stands in Weston Park.
- **John Holland (1794-1872)**
  Edited the Sheffield Iris newspaper. Of Holland's poems, Montgomery wrote "they would be twice as good if they were as short again!"
- **Alice Kipling (1837-1910)**
  Born in Sheffield, mother of Rudyard Kipling
- **James Montgomery (1771-1854)**
  Twice arrested for sedition, also editor of the Sheffield Iris newspaper. A number of streets in Sheffield are named after Montgomery and there is a statue close by the cathedral commemorating him.

Ponds Forge

Today the Porter Brook and the River Sheaf meet underground somewhere beneath Sheffield Station, and then proceed to join the River Don. Before Sheffield took it over, this area was originally countryside with a number of ponds where the three rivers met. Hence the first iron forge built here in the 17th Century was known as *Ponds Forge.* The name was retained by all subsequent iron and steel works on the site, as well as the international swimming pool complex that was opened in 1991 for the World Student Games. There is an enormous anvil outside today's building – a tribute to times gone past perhaps, or maybe just too expensive to have moved!

Ponds Forge swimming pool is one of only 10 Olympic specification swimming pools in the UK and, with a depth of 5.85m, lays claim to the deepest diving pool in Europe.

The Old Queens Head pub on nearby Pond Hill is the oldest surviving domestic building in Sheffield. It is referred to as *The Hawle at the Poandes* in an inventory of the estate of George Talbot in 1582, but was built over a century earlier in 1475. Rumour has it that there is a tunnel from the site of the former Sheffield Castle that went via the Old Queens Head all the way to the Manor Lodge.

Popular Music

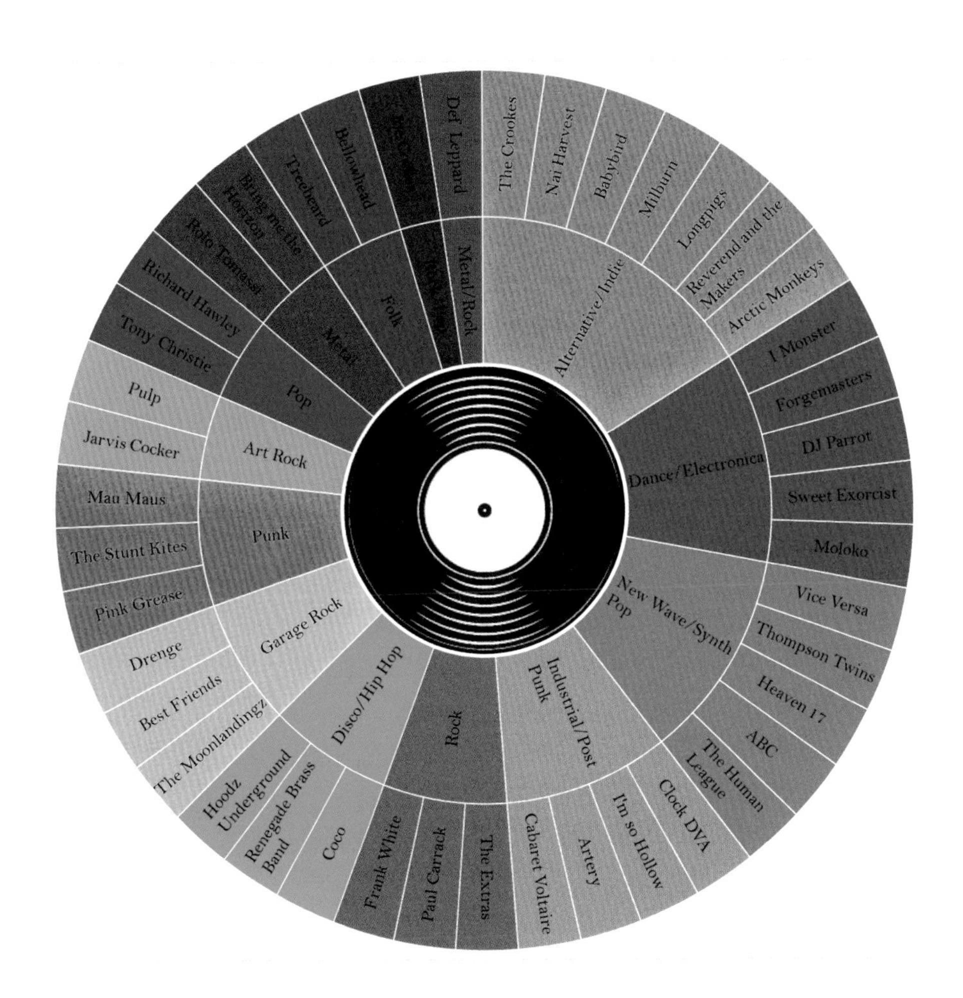

Population

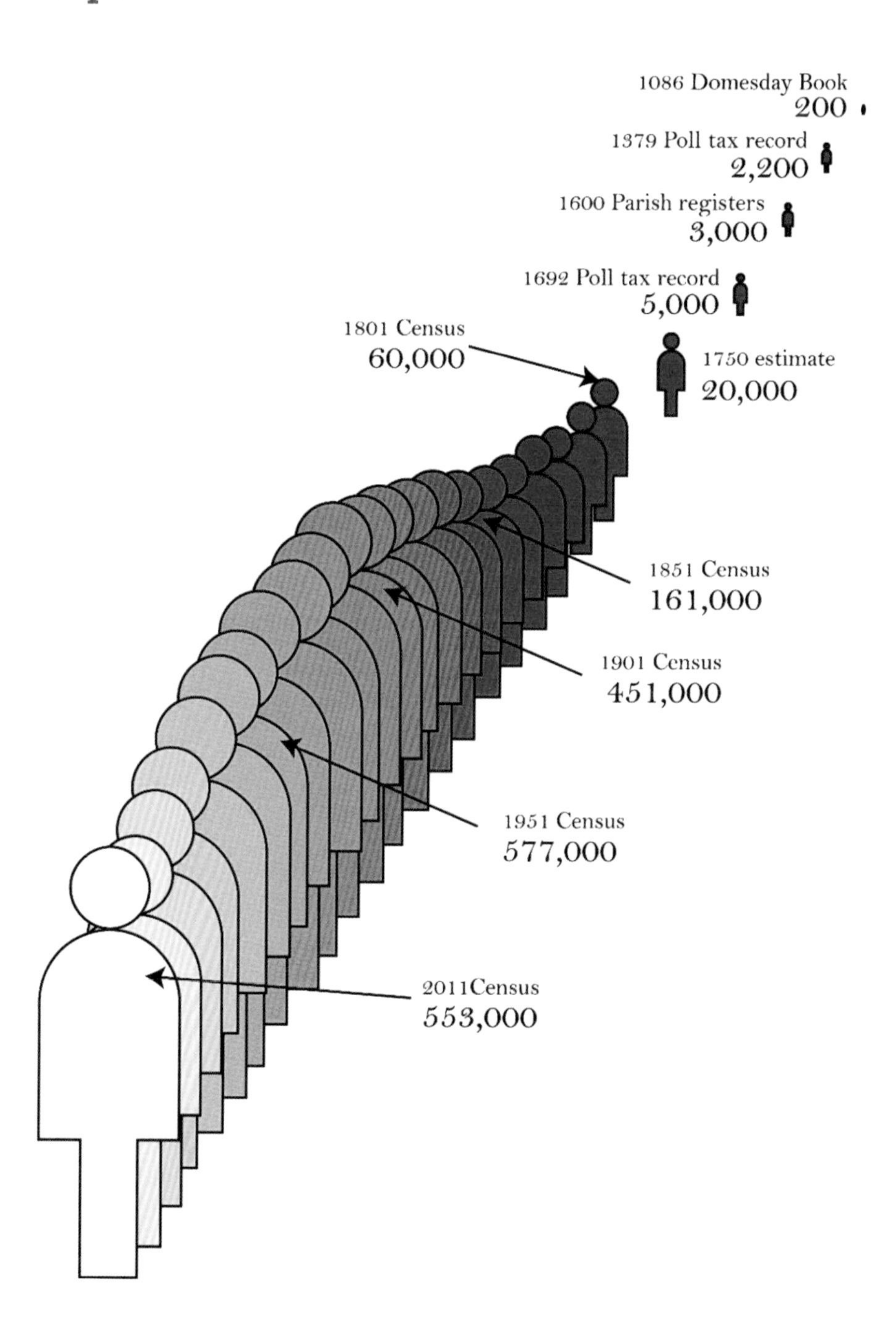
1086 Domesday Book
200
1379 Poll tax record
2,200
1600 Parish registers
3,000
1692 Poll tax record
5,000
1801 Census
60,000
1750 estimate
20,000
1851 Census
161,000
1901 Census
451,000
1951 Census
577,000
2011Census
553,000

Portsmouth

Destination	Road distance	Drive time	Public Transport
Aberdeen	390m	6h20	6h18
Bath	190m	3h00	3h06
Birmingham	93m	1h35	1h08
Brighton	229m	3h40	3h39
Bristol	180m	2h40	2h35
Cambridge	148m	2h20	2h53
Cardiff	206m	3h00	3h28
Dover	248m	3h45	3h12
Edinburgh	256m	4h20	3h32
Exeter	254m	3h55	3h49
Gatwick	205m	3h05	2h47
Glasgow	257m	4h00	4h27
Heathrow	171m	2h45	2h56
Holyhead	155m	2h50	4h07
Inverness	413m	7h00	8h05
Ipswich	198m	3h05	3h36
John O'Groats	531m	9h20	21h06
Liverpool	107m	2h00	1h56
London	167m	3h20	2h08
Manchester	40m	1h20	0h53
Northampton	103m	1h40	2h21
Norwich	160m	3h15	3h35
Oxford	140m	2h20	2h16
Penzance	363m	5h35	6h46
Portsmouth	**227m**	**3h30**	**4h33**
Scarborough	103m	1h55	2h19
St Davids	305m	5h10	7h22
Stranraer	266m	4h35	6h23
York	63m	1h05	1h04

Drive times are given under good traffic conditions. Public transport times are given from Sheffield railway station to the transport terminus in the destination concerned.

Postcodes

The postal area of Sheffield (S) covers a total of 45 Districts. Of these only 19 cover the Sheffield Local Authority area itself.

S	**6**	**3**	**AB**
Area	District	Sector	Unit

The final two letters of the unit do not use C, I, K, M, O or V, so as not to resemble digits or each other when hand-written. Within Sheffield each active postcode unit has an average of 20 properties associated with it.

✉ S1-11, 12*-13*, 14, 17, 20-21, 35*-36*	Sheffield
✉ S18	Dronfield
✉ S21, 25-26, 60-63, 65-66	Rotherham
✉ S32-33	Hope Valley
✉ S40-45	Chesterfield
✉ S64	Mexborough
✉ S70-75	Barnsley
✉ S80-81	Worksop

*postcode district lies partially within Sheffield Local Authority area.

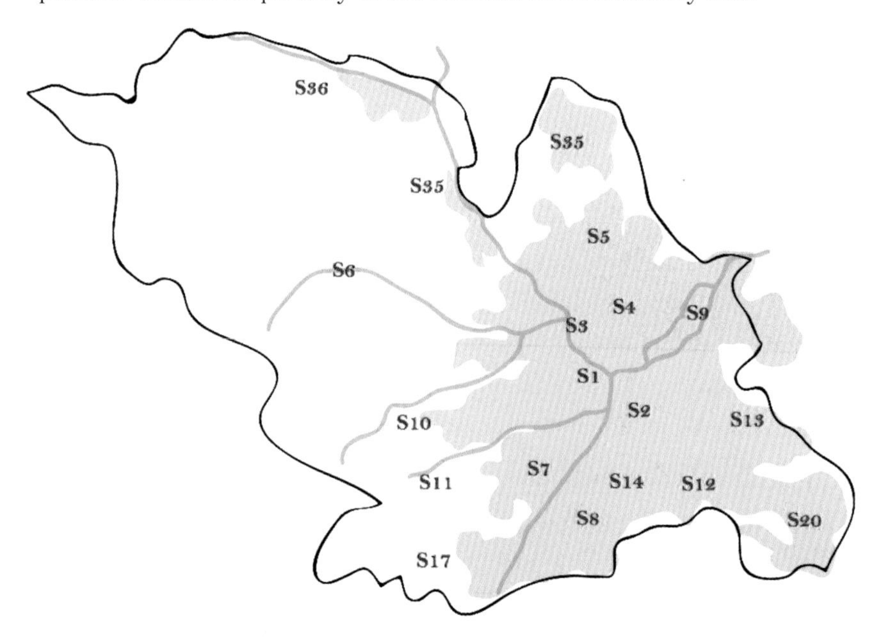

Additionally, there are non-geographic postcode districts:

🖂 S49	Chesterfield bulk users
🖂 S94	National office for the 2021 Census
🖂 S95-98	Sheffield bulk users
🖂 S99	Jobcentre plus

Properties per Postcode Sector

The size of each section of the tree map below is proportional to the number of properties in that postcode sector. For example, the sector S1 2 contains approximately 500 properties, whereas S6 1 contains just over 5000.

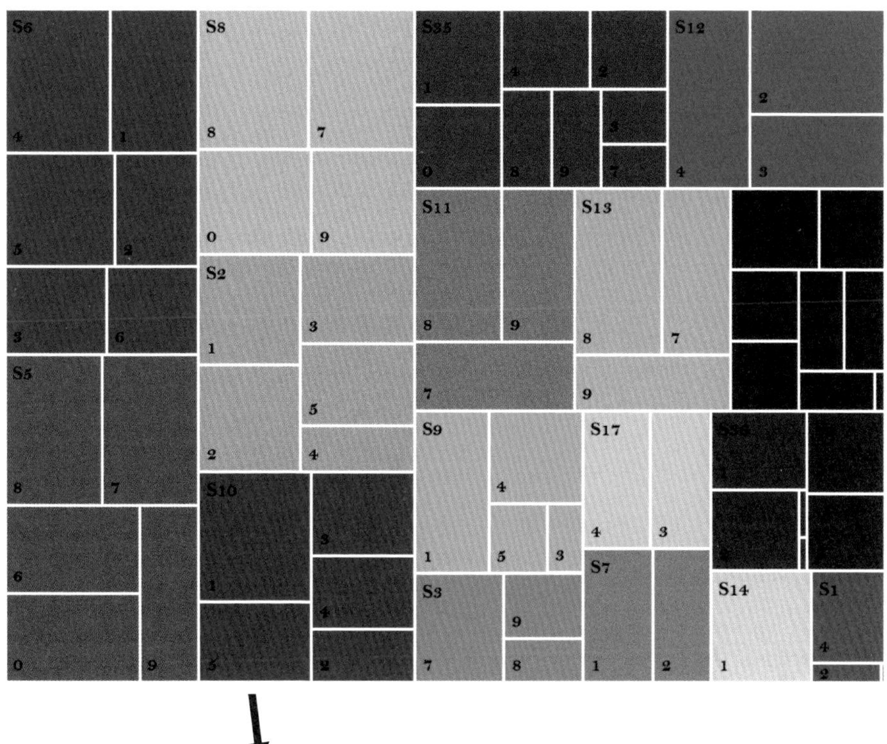

Active units in S10 5

AA, AB, AD, AE, AF, AY, BA, BB, BD, BE, BH, BJ, BL, BN, BP, BQ, BR, BS, BT, BU, BW, BX, BY, BZ, DA, DB, DD, DE, DF, DH, DJ, DL, DN, DP, DQ, DR, DS, DT, DU, DW, DY, EA, EB, ED, FA, FB, FD, FE, FF, FG, FH, FJ, FL, FN, FP, FQ, FR, FS, FT, FU, FW, FX, FY, FZ, GA, GB, GD, GF, GG, GH, GJ, GL, NA, NB, ND, NE, NF, NG, NH, NJ, NL, NN, NP, NQ, NR, NS, NT, NU, NW, NX, NY, NZ, PA, PB, PD, PE, PF, PG, PH, PJ, PL, PN, PP, PQ, PR, PS, PT, PU, PW, PX, PY, QA, QW, RA, RB, RD, RE, RF, RG, RH, RJ, RL, RN, RP, RQ, RR, RS, RT, RU, RW, RX, RY, RZ, SA, SB, SD, SE, SF, SG, SH, SJ, SK, SN, SP, SQ, SR, SS, ST, SU, SW, SX, SY, SZ, TA, TB, TD, TE, TF, TG, TH, TJ, TL, TN, TP, TQ, TR, TS, TT, TU, TX, TY, TZ, UA, UB, UD, UE, WR, WX, XZ,YS

Prehistoric and Ancient Sheffield

Humans have occupied the Sheffield area for thousands of years. Nearby Cresswell Crags have evidence of Neanderthal occupation from around 50,000 years ago and contain the most northerly cave paintings in Europe, dating from 15,000 years ago.

Closer to home you don't have to go far to see evidence of ancient occupation – you just need to know where to look. Most of the sites identified here contain one or more Ancient Scheduled Monuments on account of their historical significance.

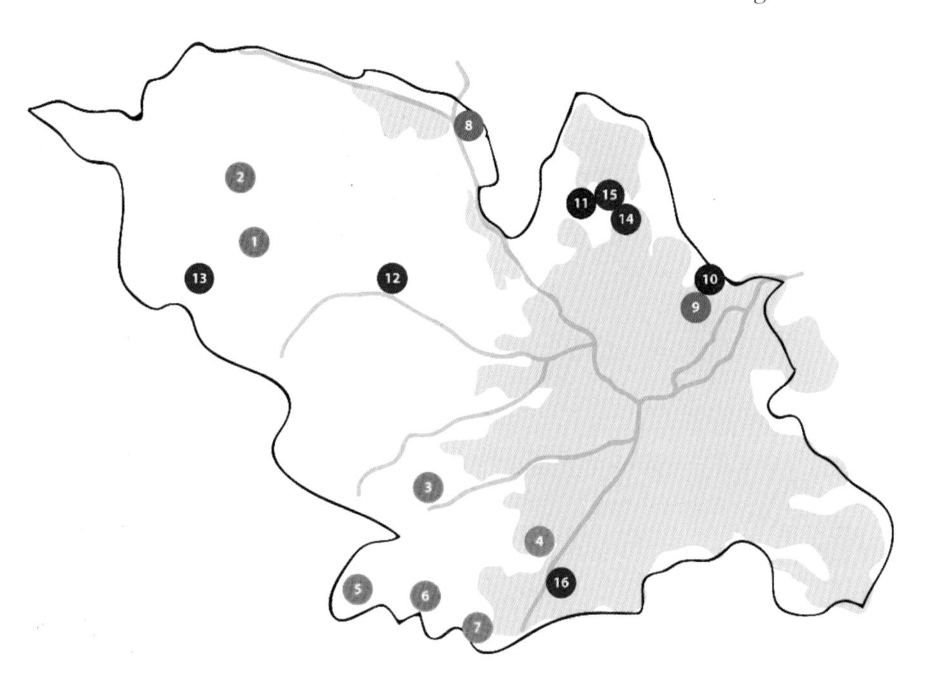

Bronze Age sites (2500BC – 800BC)

1. Four Ancient Scheduled Monuments lie in close proximity to the junction of Penistone Road and Mortimer Road: the impressive 400m long Bar Dyke earthworks consisting of a ditch and a parallel mound of earth; the Cowell Flat pre-historic field system covering an area 300m x 200m with evidence of 5 field divisions and the remains of a dwelling house; a ring cairn (circular earthen bank 25m in diameter); and a cairnfield of several small cairns that are likely to contain burial remains.
2. The Ewden Beck site is of national significance. There is a cross-dyke – a ditch up to 2m deep and 3m wide – extending for 1200m. The cross-dyke cuts through a burial site of over 100 barrows, and there is also a ring cairn with upright stones in the centre.

3. Stone Circle on Ash Cabin Flat, overlooking Wyming Brook.
4. Cup and Ring carving on a rock in Ecclesall Woods. This is the only known pre-historic rock carving in the Sheffield area.
5. Another location where you can tick off several sites in one visit: Carl Wark is a fortified millstone grit outcrop inhabited until the end of the iron age, and then again after the Roman occupation; the Winyards Nick and Toads Mouth prehistoric field systems have cairns (covered by heather) that mark field boundaries, and there is evidence of ancient fields having been cleared of stones which were then used to create raised field boundaries. Between Winyards Nick and the Hathersage Road there is a ring cairn and also a large 7m long cairn that almost certainly contains burial remains.
6. Two ring cairns at Ciceley Low, the largest of which is 30m in diameter.
7. Two cairnfields (most likely burial cairns), a ring cairn and banks suggesting ancient fields.

Iron Age (800BC – 43AD)

8. Quern workings at Wharncliffe rocks. A 'quern' was a round stone used in pairs to hand grind various other materials. Querns were hewn from Wharncliffe Crags throughout the Iron Age and Roman occupation. There are estimated to be 8000 querns around the rocks, many overgrown with heather. The name Wharncliffe derives from 'Quern Cliff.'
9. Wincobank Iron Age hill fort. Used as a World War II anti-aircraft gun site.

Romano Britain (43AD – 410AD)

10. Roman Ridge. There are two surviving sections either side of Jenkin Road of this 27km long ridge that stretched from Wincobank to Mexborough. No-one is quite sure exactly when this was built (consensus is between 1000BC and 1000AD), by whom or for what purpose (theories include as a defensive barrier or a boundary marker).
11. There are two known areas of terraced fields and enclosure walls from the Romano-British era: Handlands settlement, covering an area of approximately 300m x 200m in Greno Woods; and a similar site in nearby Wheata Woods.

Medieval (400AD – 1400AD)

12. High Bradfield contains not one, but two sites of motte and bailey castles dating from the 12th Century.
13. Base of a wayside cross on Bradfield Moor, marked as 'New Cross' on maps. The base of the cross remains, with the sizable inset hole indicating that the cross would have been large enough to be visible for miles.
14. Standing Cross in the churchyard of St Mary's Ecclesfield – a good example of a simple cross, most likely in its original position.
15. Willow Garth moated site and fishpond - a moated island close to the site of Ecclesfield Priory. The moat is 10m wide and intact almost all the way round.
16. Partially excavated remains of Beauchief Abbey and three fishponds.

Professions

Blue bars represent Sheffield employment by sector. Orange bars represent the national employment picture were Britain to have the same population as Sheffield.

Pubs

There are over 500 pubs and bars in Sheffield – from city centre bars to cosy village pubs with everything in between. Every month the Sheffield branch of CAMRA awards a 'Pub of the Month'. If you are looking for some inspiration or want to try somewhere different, the list below of all the pubs that have won more than one award since 2010 seems to be a good place to start...

□ Pub of the Month ■ Pub of the Year

Pub	2010	2011	2012	2013	2014	2015	2016	2017	2018	2019	2020
Kelham Island Tavern	■	■		■	■	■	■	■	■		
Gardeners Rest, Neepsend		□								■	
Shakespeare's, City Centre			■			□		□			
Red Deer, City Centre			□	□		□				□	
Harlequin, City Centre		□		□			□		□		
Rutland Arms, City Centre		□		□					□		
Wisewood Inn, Loxley								□			□
Old Queen's Head, City Centre								□		□	
Bath Hotel, City Centre							□			□	
Commercial, Chapeltown	□									□	
Ale House, Millhouses									□	□	
Dog & Partridge, City Centre					□					□	
Blake, Walkley			□							□	
Devonshire Cat, City Centre						□			□		
Beer Engine, Sharrow							□		□		
Wellington, Shalesmoor		□							□		
Fat Cat, Kelham Island	□								□		
White Lion, Heeley							□		□		
Sheaf View, Heeley						□			□		
Broadfield, Abbeydale Road				□				□			
Closed Shop, Commonside					□		□				
Three Tuns, City Centre					□		□				
Mount Pleasant, Norton Lees				□		□					

Railways

There are a surprising number of former railway lines and stations in Sheffield, with much of the infrastructure still in evidence.

- Sheffield & Rotherham Railway Company
- North Midland Railway
- Sheffield, Ashton-under-Lyme and Manchester Railway
- Manchester, Sheffield and Lincolnshire Railway
- South Yorkshire Railway
- Midland Railway
- Sheffield District Railway

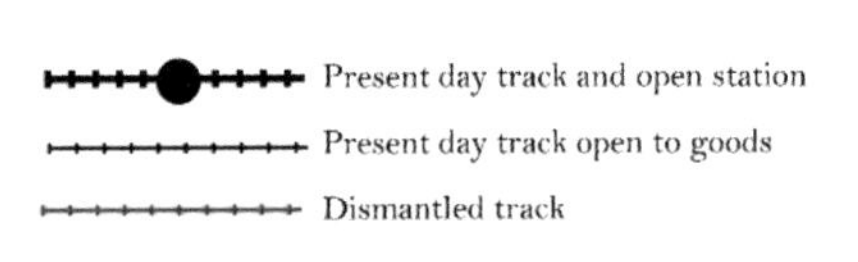

Station now a private residence

Remains of station visible

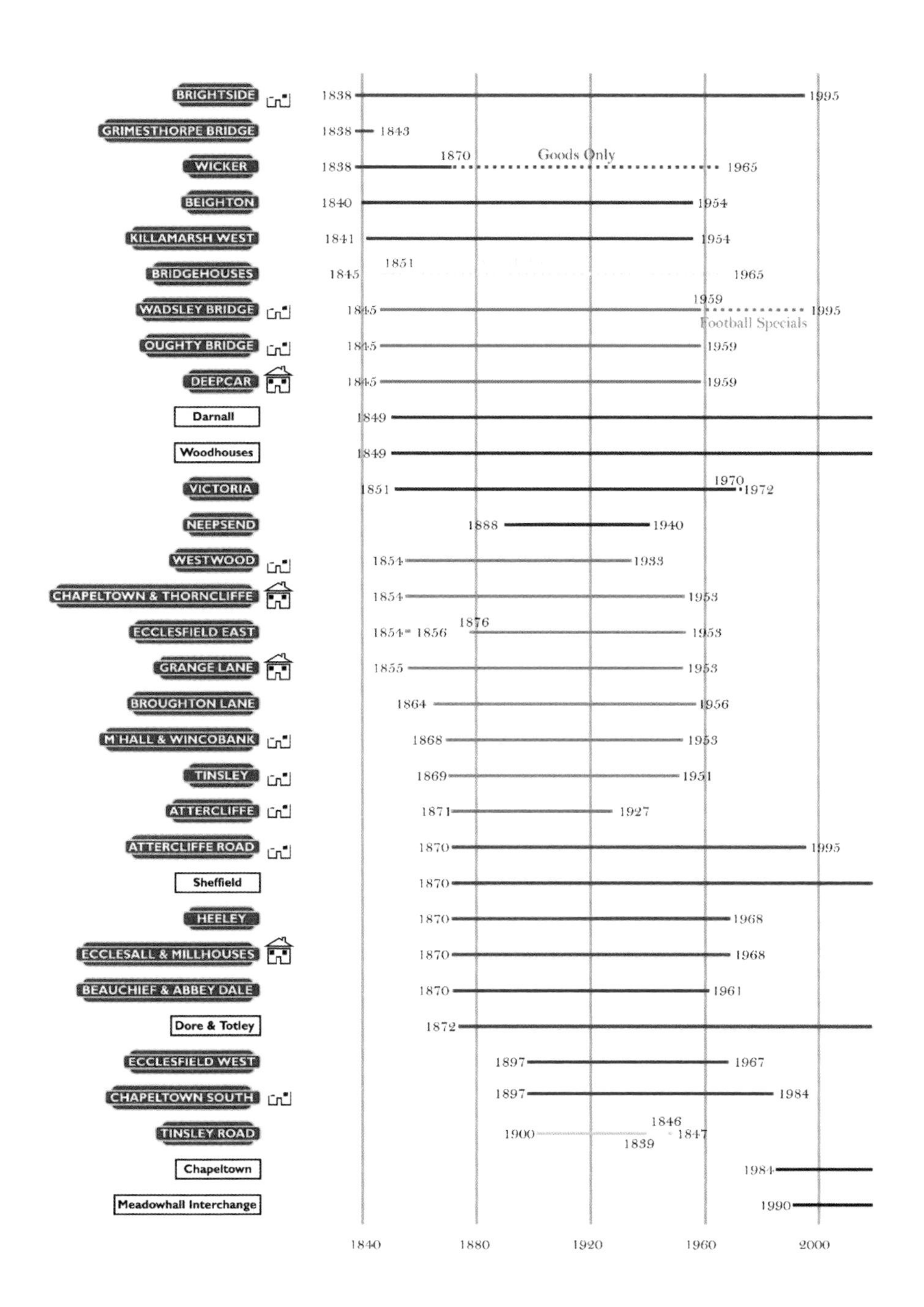

BRIGHTSIDE
1838
1995
GRIMESTHORPE BRIDGE
1838
1843
WICKER
1838
1870
Goods Only
1965
BEIGHTON
1840
1954
KILLAMARSH WEST
1841
1954
BRIDGEHOUSES
1845
1851
1965
WADSLEY BRIDGE
1845
1959
1995
Football Specials
OUGHTY BRIDGE
1845
1959
DEEPCAR
1845
1959
Darnall
1849
Woodhouses
1849
VICTORIA
1851
1970
1972
NEEPSEND
1888
1940
WESTWOOD
1854
1933
CHAPELTOWN & THORNCLIFFE
1854
1953
ECCLESFIELD EAST
1854
1856
1876
1953
GRANGE LANE
1855
1953
BROUGHTON LANE
1864
1956
M'HALL & WINCOBANK
1868
1953
TINSLEY
1869
1951
ATTERCLIFFE
1871
1927
ATTERCLIFFE ROAD
1870
1995
Sheffield
1870
HEELEY
1870
1968
ECCLESALL & MILLHOUSES
1870
1968
BEAUCHIEF & ABBEY DALE
1870
1961
Dore & Totley
1872
ECCLESFIELD WEST
1897
1967
CHAPELTOWN SOUTH
1897
1984
TINSLEY ROAD
1900
1839
1846
1847
Chapeltown
1984
Meadowhall Interchange
1990
1840
1880
1920
1960
2000

Rawson, Mary Anne

1801-1887

Hear the word 'Rawson' in the same breath as Sheffield and you may well think of the Rawson Spring pub in Hillsborough that occupies what was once the Hillsborough Baths, or possibly even the actual Rawson Spring that used to supply Hillsborough Barracks with water.

This Rawson, however, was a 19th Century anti-slavery campaigner. Mary Rawson was born into a wealthy family in Wincobank, and chose to use her position of privilege to persuade and influence others in a quest to end slavery. At the age of just 24 she founded the Sheffield Female Anti-Slavery Society to campaign for the end to slavery in the British Empire. Once this was achieved in 1833, she turned her campaigning to a demand for a universal end to slavery.

Rawson corresponded with many of the (more well-known) male abolitionists at the time and was visited by both Lord Shaftesbury and William Wilberforce

Rawson's philanthropy extended to setting up a school for local children in the grounds of Wincobank Hall, where she lived all her life. After she died, the school continued for a number of years thanks to the endowment she left it.

Sadly Wincobank Hall is no more – the area has since been re-developed as the Flowers Estate.

Read all about it!

Today, Sheffield has one daily newspaper – *The Star* – and one weekly paper – *The Sheffield Telegraph.* The *Green 'Un* was printed up until 2013 and was one of the last local sports papers in the country to remain in print (it is now published online). All three are published by Sheffield Newspapers Ltd.

The graphic overleaf charts the history of the main Sheffield newspapers. In addition to those illustrated, there were a number of small independent weekly or daily papers published at various times from the 1850s until the 1890s, but none stood the test of time, and *The Star* and *The Sheffield Telegraph* eventually emerged from the melee.

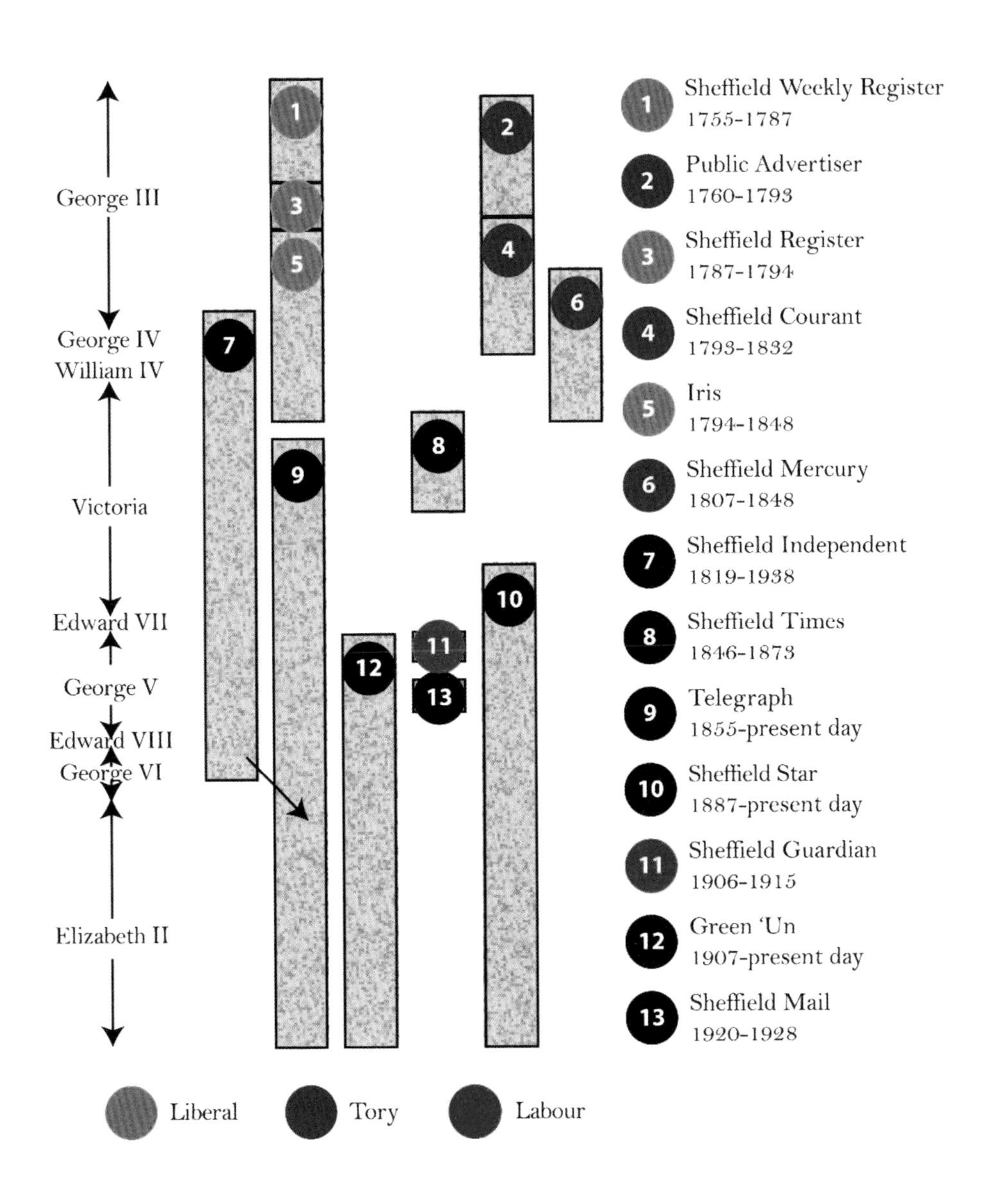
George III
George IV
William IV
Victoria
Edward VII
George V
Edward VIII
George VI
Elizabeth II
1
2
3
4
5
6
7
8
9
10
11
12
13
1 Sheffield Weekly Register 1755-1787
2 Public Advertiser 1760-1793
3 Sheffield Register 1787-1794
4 Sheffield Courant 1793-1832
5 Iris 1794-1848
6 Sheffield Mercury 1807-1848
7 Sheffield Independent 1819-1938
8 Sheffield Times 1846-1873
9 Telegraph 1855-present day
10 Sheffield Star 1887-present day
11 Sheffield Guardian 1906-1915
12 Green 'Un 1907-present day
13 Sheffield Mail 1920-1928
Liberal
Tory
Labour

Both *The Star* and the *Sheffield Telegraph* have changed their names several times, before settling on their current titles. *The Star*, in particular, seems to have been very confused over it's identify. The *Sheffield Telegraph* had a short period (1986-89) when it was not in print.

The Star
The Star (1938-present)
Telegraph & Star (1937-38)
Yorkshire Telegraph & Star (1898-1937)
Evening Telegraph & Star and Sheffield Daily Times (1888-97)
Sheffield Evening Telegraph (1887-88)

Sheffield Telegraph
Sheffield Telegraph (1942- 86 and 89-present)
Telegraph & Independent (1939-42)
Sheffield Telegraph & Daily Independent (1938-39)
Sheffield Telegraph (1934-38)
Sheffield Daily Telegraph (1855-1934)

Reade, Charles

Hillsborough, though built on one of the loveliest sites in England, is perhaps the most hideous town in creation. All the ups and downs and back slums. Not one of its wriggling, broken-backed streets has handsome shops in an unbroken row. Houses seem to have battled in the air, and stuck wherever they tumbled down dead out of the melee. But worst of all, the city is pock-marked with public-houses, and bristles with high round chimneys… More than one crystal stream runs sparkling down the valleys and enters the town; but they soon get defiled, and creep through it heavily charged with dyes, clogged with putridity, and bubbling with poisonous gases, till at last they turn to mere ink, stink, and malaria, and people the churchyards as they craw.

Put Yourself in His Place (1870)

Reservoirs

In the 1700s most of Sheffield's water supply was obtained in a relatively ad hoc way from rivers, springs and wells. Barker's Pool was the city's first reservoir. Being built at the highest point of the city centre, water could be released to run in channels, cleaning the streets as it flowed. In 1742 the Old Great Dam was built in Crookesmoor (this survives as the boating lake in Crookesmoor Park), from where water was pumped to a cistern on Division Street, before being carted around the city in casks. Over time several nearby smaller reservoirs (New Dam, Godfrey Dam, Butchers Dam, Pisgah Dam, Ralph Dam, and Misfortune Dam) were constructed on Crookesmoor to supply the ever-growing population. Pisgah Dam was the largest of these, holding over twice as much water as the boating lake. Pisgah Dam has been renamed Hadfield Dam and remains today, covered over by a housing estate and playing fields just behind School Road in Crookes. There is also a giveaway 'Reservoir Road'.

Following the Cholera epidemic of 1832 the first of the Redmires reservoirs was constructed (it should have been two, but they ran out of money) to supply the Crookesmoor reservoirs. The other two reservoirs at Redmires followed over the next 20 years, along with the lower Rivelin Dams.

In the Loxley Valley, Dale Dyke reservoir was constructed in the early 1860s to supply drinking water to the city, and then breached in 1864 while it was being filled for the first time causing the Great Sheffield Flood.

Agden and Strines reservoirs were constructed at a similar time, being completed in 1869.

Dale Dyke was reconstructed in 1875, and Dam Flask reservoir completed in 1896, covering the remains of Dam Flask village that had been destroyed in the Dale Dyke disaster.

One valley further north, Underbank reservoir was completed in 1904, followed not long afterwards by Broomhead and More Hall reservoirs.

In 1903 an underground tunnel over 4 miles long was built to connect Ladybower reservoir to the Rivelin Dams. The Rivelin Dams were originally built as 'compensation reservoirs' to guarantee a continuous flow of water along the River Rivelin. The Ladybower pipe ensured that the Rivelin Dams always had a sufficient supply of water without having to drain the water supply for the city from the Redmires Reservoirs. The tunnel is an impressive feat of engineering with a drop of just 6 feet over its entire length. There is a similar tunnel running from Dam Flask to the Rivelin Dams.

Rivers

Sheffield is defined by its rivers - they have shaped both our landscape and our history.

The River Sheaf, along with the Limb and Meersbrook, originally formed part of the boundary between the Anglo-Saxon kingdoms of Mercia and Northumbria, and now gives its name to our city. The River Rivelin has powered our industry for three or more centuries. The River Don has provided transport connections, and both the River Loxley and the River Don were witness to England's greatest manmade flooding disaster when Dale Dyke reservoir ruptured in 1864.

Today the rivers and brooks give the city green arteries that radiate outwards, providing opportunities for both recreation and wildlife.

Catchment areas (km^2)

≋ **Blackburn Brook**	**41.0**
≋ **Car Brook**	**7.1**
≋ **Ewden Beck**	**27.3**
≋ **Little Don**	**45.8**
≋ **River Don**	**63.2**
Confluence with Little Don to confluence with Loxley	*31.0*
Confluence with Loxley to confluence with Car Brook	*24.1*
Confluence with Car Brook to confluence with Rother	*8.1*
≋ **River Loxley**	**75.8**
Agden reservoir to confluence with Don	*13.9*
Hobson Moss source to Agden reservoir	*12.5*
Strines Dike	*19.7*
River Rivelin	*29.7*
≋ **River Rother***	**83.0**
≋ **River Sheaf**	**69.8**
Porter	*17.1*
All other tributaries	*52.7*

*a large amount of this catchment area lies outside of Sheffield.

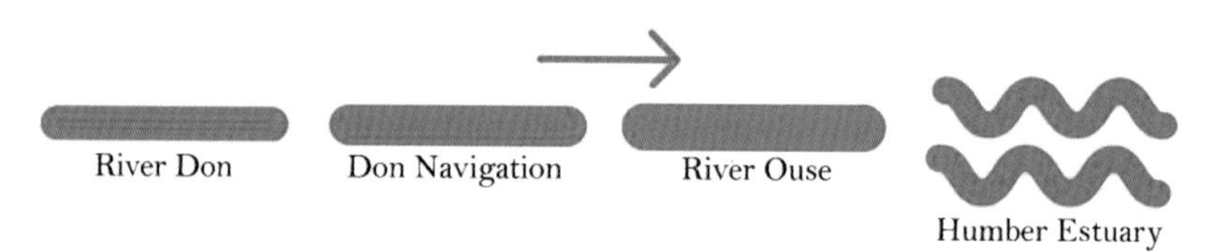

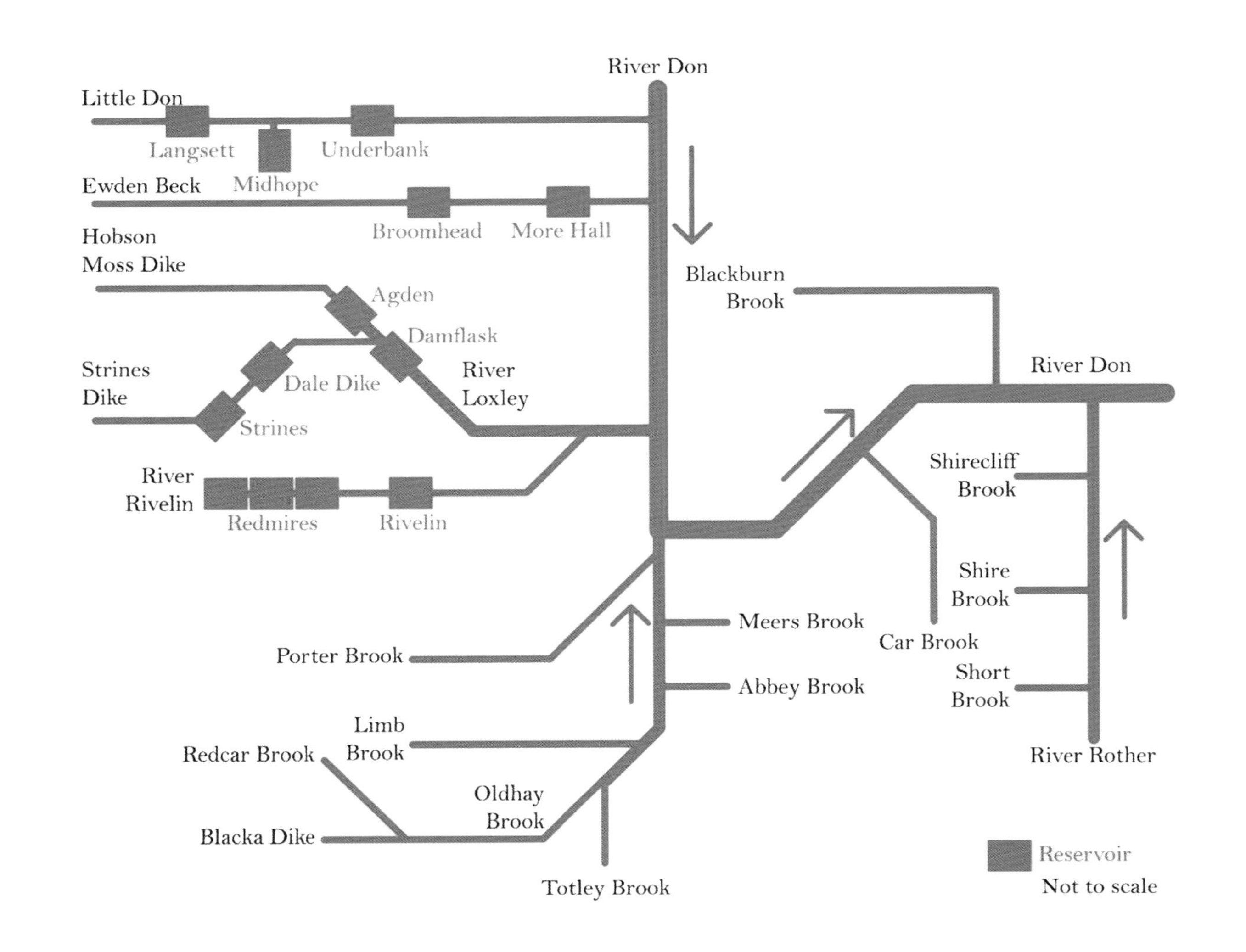
River Don
Little Don
Langsett
Midhope
Underbank
Ewden Beck
Broomhead
More Hall
Hobson Moss Dike
Agden
Damflask
Blackburn Brook
River Don
Strines Dike
Dale Dike
Strines
River Loxley
River Rivelin
Redmires
Rivelin
Shirecliff Brook
Shire Brook
Meers Brook
Car Brook
Porter Brook
Abbey Brook
Short Brook
Limb Brook
Redcar Brook
River Rother
Oldhay Brook
Blacka Dike
Totley Brook
Reservoir
Not to scale

Robin Hood – the case for Sheffield

'Robin of Loxley!' Wait a moment, surely Loxley is in Sheffield, not Nottingham. This is one strand of a growing amount of evidence emerging that can be used to make a case for Robin Hood originally coming from Sheffield rather than Nottingham. It all makes sense, you know it does...

- Loxley was once part of the Sherwood Forest.
- The turnpike from the Sheriff of Nottingham's castle to Guy of Gisbourne's castle in York ran through Loxley.
- Robin Hood was known as 'Robin of Loxley.'
- There are records that someone called Robert Locksley of Bradfield Parish killed his father and befriended a 'Little John'.
- A grave claiming to be that of Little John is to be found in Hathersage Church graveyard.
- Richard II gave a pardon on 22nd May 1382 to a 'Robert Dore of Wadsley, otherwise known as Robert Hode.'
- Robert Dore was recorded as having been born in a cottage at Little Haggas Croft, close by Rodney Hill.
- There is a Robin Hood's Cave on Stanage Edge.
- There are Robin Hood's Wells near Loxley and Ecclesfield.
- There was a former Robin Hood pub in Stannington.
- Featherbed Moss (overlooking Derwent Dams) was formerly known as Robin Hood's Moss.

Sark Road

One of four streets (Sark Road, Alderney Road, Jersey Road and Guernsey Road) in S2 all named after the Channel Islands. Other groups of 'themed' roads in Sheffield include:

Battles (S10): Bosworth, Flodden, Marston, Newbury

Birds (S2): Curlew, Heron, Mount, Kestrel, Magpie, Osprey, Partridge, Plover, Quail, Starling, Swift, Wren

Castles belonging to the McCullough Family (S10): Barholm, Cardoness

Dales (S7): Coverdale, Dovedale, Fossdale, Swaledale

Dales (S12): Camdale, Ribblesdale, Teesdale

Derbyshire place names (s12): Bretton, Burgbage, Hayfield, Longstone, Stanage, Thornbridge, Wardlow, Youlgreave

East Riding Villages (S6): Bessingby, Carnaby, Speeton

Duke of Norfolk titles and seats (S1,2,4): Arundel, Earl Marshall, Fitzalan, Fitzwalter, Maltravers, Norfolk, Stafford, Surrey

Lakes (S8): Arnside, Buttermere, Crummock, Coniston, Grasmere, Keswick, Langdale, Rydale, Thirlmere, Troutbeck, Windermere

Legend of Hereward the Wake (S8): Bourne, Crowland, Hereward

Literary Figures (S5): Adlington, Barrie, Buchanan, Chaucer. Dryden, Lytton, Meynell, Morgan, Palgrave, Wordsworth

Lords of the Manor of Ecclesfield (S5): Dunninc, Godric

Flowers (S19): Aster, Daisy, Jasmine, Lilac, Primrose, Rose, Violet

Groves (S10); Broomgrove, Clarkegrove, Eastgrove, Southgrove

'Mouth' (S7): Barmouth, Falmouth, Lynmouth, Plymouth

Lawyers (S9): Brett, Chelmsford, Jessel, Palmer, Roundel, Selborne, Westbury

Robin Hood (S6): Friar, Robin Hood

Rugby Stadia (S19): Arms Park, Auckland, Dunedin, Murrayfield, Twickenham and the not so well known Stonegravels

Trees (S9): Alder, Chestnut, Larch, Maple, Willow

Types of Oak (s6): Durmast, Golden Oak, Holme Oak, Oak Apple, Red Oak, Scarlet Oak

Yorkshire place names (S20): Ardsley, Athersley, Barnsdale, Blaxton, Broadlands, Darfield, Deanhead, Grassington, Kingswood, Melton, Moorthorpe, Ravenfield, Redbrook, Royston, Rylstone, Threshfield, Wooldale

Scarborough, Joe

Born: 1938

Education: Marlcliffe School

On leaving school at 16, Scarborough worked first in a pea factory and then in the Thorpe Hesley coal mine. To make time for his newly found passion for painting he took on a variety of more occasional labouring jobs before eventually being in a position where he was able to concentrate solely on his painting.

His pictures are instantly recognisable – busy, humorous scenes illustrating everyday life in Sheffield. His prints adorn many walls in Sheffield and original Scarborough's command auction prices in the £1000's both here and in America.

His work can be seen in public collections in the Sheffield Museums and at Sheffield Hallam University, including the 30 foot long *Sheffield Through the Ages*. Today, Scarborough lives in his narrow boat on Victoria Quays. He was inducted into the Sheffield Walk of Fame in 2008.

Secondary Schools

- **All Saints Catholic High School**
  Opened in 1976 on the site of the former St Paul's School, merging with the De La Salle Grammar School (Pitsmoor) at the same time.
- **Birkdale School**
  Private boys' school for ages 4-18 opened in 1904.
- **The Birley Academy**
  Opened in 1986. Formerly known as the Thornbridge Secondary School.
- **Bradfield School**
  Opened 1957
- **Chaucer Business and Enterprise College**
  Chaucer originally opened in 1964 as the third comprehensive school in the city. Rebuilt and renamed in 2006.
- **Ecclesfield Secondary School**
  Ecclesfield Grammar School opened in 1931, and later merged with Hunshelf Secondary Modern in 1967 to become Ecclesfield Comprehensive School.
- **Fir Vale School**
  Opened in 1998 by Queen Elizabeth II on the site of the former Earl Marshal School.
- **Firth Park Academy**
  Opened in 1920, became a Grammar school in 1937 and then a comprehensive in 1969. Former pupils are known as Firparnians.
- **Forge Valley School**
  Formed in 2011 as the merger of Myers Grove and Wisewood schools.
- **Handsworth Grange**
  Opened in 1988 on the site of the former Brook School, merging with Beaver Hill Secondary at the same time.
- **High Storrs School**
  Originally the Central Higher School which opened in the city centre in 1880, High Storrs opened on its current site in 1933.
- **Hinde House School**
  Opened in 1964, Hinde House was the first state-funded all through primary and secondary school in the country.
- **King Ecgbert School**
  Originally a technical school, King Ecgbert became a comprehensive in 1969. Notable alumni include Joe Root and Jessica Ennis.
- **King Edward VII School**
  Opened in 1905 as a merger between the Royal Grammar and the Wesley College, themselves dating from 1603 and 1838 respectively.
- **Meadowhead School**
  Formed when Jordanthorpe Comprehensive and Rowlinson School merged in 1987. The Rowlinson site became Norton College.

- **Mercia School**
  Opened in 2018 on the site of the former Abbeydale Grange School.
- **Newfield School**
  Opened in 1958.
- **Notre Dame Catholic High School**
  Opened on the current site in 1948 when the original city centre school (opened in 1855) merged with the Oakbrook School.
- **Oasis Academy Don Valley**
  Opened in 2015 – a through school for ages 4-16.
- **Outwood Academy City**
  Originally opened as the City Pupil Teacher Centre, became the City Grammar School in 1941 and the City School in 1969.
- **Parkwood School**
  Opened in 2000, formerly known as Herries School.
- **Sheffield High School for Girls**
  Private school for girls, ages 4-18. Opened 1878. Notable alumni include Margaret Drabble.
- **Sheffield Park Academy**
  Opened in 2006 on the site of the former Waltheof School.
- **Sheffield Springs Academy**
  Hurlfield and Ashleigh Schools merged in 1960 to form Myrtle Springs, which in turn re-opened as Sheffield Springs School in 2006.
- **Silverdale School**
  Opened in 1957. Notable alumni include Michael Vaughan.
- **Stocksbridge High School**
  Opened in 1927. Produced 2 members of the Arctic Monkeys.
- **Tapton School**
  Opened in 1960, taking senior pupils away from Nethergreen, Springfield County and Crookes Endowed schools. Notable alumni include Sebastian Coe and Jared O'Mara.
- **UTC Sheffield City Centre**
  Opened 2013, catering for ages 13-19.
- **UTC Olympic Legacy Park**
  Opened 2016, catering for ages 13-19.
- **Westbourne School**
  Co-educational private school for ages 3-16, opened 1885.
- **Westfield School**
  Eckington County School opened in 1930, became Eckington Grammar in 1945, and Westfield Comprehensive in 1957. Notable alumni include Neil Warnock.
- **Yewlands**
- Opened 1957, formerly Yew Lane School.

Sharman, Helen

Born: 30th May 1963

Education: Grenoside Junior and Infant School, Jordanthorpe Comprehensive, University of Sheffield, Birkbeck College London.

Helen Sharman beat over 13,000 applicants to become the first British Astronaut as part of Project Juno, a joint Soviet-British venture. She was the second woman to visit a space station, and the 15th woman in space.

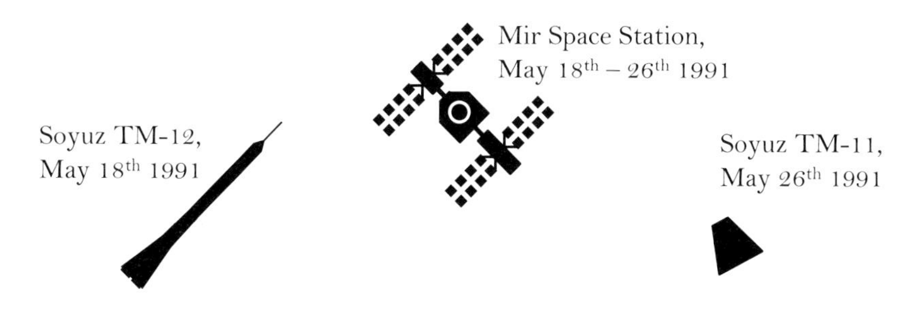

Nickname: *Girl from Mars* – Helen Sharman was employed as a chemist by Mars (confectioners) before her career as an astronaut.

Autobiography: *Seize the Moment*, 1993.

Honours:

- Officer of the Order of the British Empire (OBE), 1992
- Companion of the Order of St Michael and St George (CMG) for services to Science and Technology Outreach, 2018
- 11 Honorary Degrees
- Sheffield Walk of Fame, 2006

Things named after Helen Sharman:

- 1 School in the Netherlands
- 2 Houses in British secondary schools
- 1 school science block
- 1 road in Stafford
- 1 block of student flats in Sheffield.

Sheffield List

The Sheffield list is the oldest and most commonly used classification of woodworking tools.

Straight	Curved	Spoon	Bent-Back	Description	Profile
1		21		Straight chisel	
2		22		Skew chisel	
3	12	24	33	Flattest gouge	
4	13	25	34	Gouge	
5	14	26	35	Gouge	
6	15	27	36	Gouge	
7	16	28	37	Gouge	
8	17	29	38	Gouge	
9	18	30		Semi-circular gouge	
10	19	31		U-gouge	
11	20	32		Tall u-gouge	
39	40	43		60 Degree v-gouge	
41	42	44		45 Degree v-gouge	
45	46			90 Degree v-gouge	

The words 'straight', 'bent', 'spoon' and 'bent back' refer to the shape of the gouge lengthways. The 'description' describes the gouging profile.

For example, a number 3 would be the flattest gouge with a straight shape. A number 12 would be the flattest gouge with a bent shape.

There is no radius given for the curvature of each gouge – this varies from manufacturer to manufacturer. However, for any particular manufacturer the profile of the gouge would flatten as the number decreases.

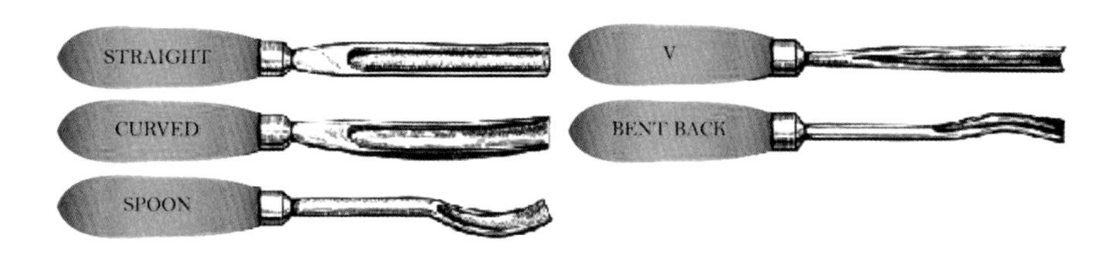

Sheffield Mayday Traditions

Traditions of Maypole dancing and May Kings and Queens were alive and well in Sheffield, even up to the end of the last century, but are harder to find today. Having said that, you can usually track a maypole down at the annual *Highland Fling* that takes place in Graves Park on May bank holiday weekend.

Every year a small group of hardy morris men and women from Sheffield's City Morris and Pecsaetan Morris groups congregate at the top of Sidlings Hollow overlooking the Loxley Valley at approximately 5.31am on the morning of 1st May, to dance, sing and generally welcome in the summer on our behalf.

Hal-an-tow, jolly rumble O
We were up long before the day O
To welcome in the summer,
To welcome in the May O
The summer is a-coming in
And winter's gone away O

Sheffield Meridian

Sheffield is located at a latitude and longitude of

53°22'58.69"N, 1°27'57.24"W.

The Sheffield Meridian is the great circle that passes through Sheffield and both poles. It lies 97km to the West of the Prime (Greenwich) Meridian.

If Sheffield had its own time-zone (and perhaps it should!) it would be 5 minutes 52 seconds behind Greenwich Mean Time.

The distance to the equator along the Sheffield Meridian is 5936km. The distance to the North Pole along the Sheffield Meridian is 4071km.

Other places lying on or close to the Sheffield Meridian:

- Muckle Roe (Shetland Islands)
- South Shields
- Knaresborough
- Derby
- Coventry
- Nantes (France)
- Biarritz (France)
- Ougadougou (Burkino Faso)
- Kumasi (Ghana)

Places lying at a similar latitude to Sheffield:

- Petropavlovsk Kamchatskiy (Russia)
- Novokuznetsk (Russia)
- Samara (Russia)
- Bydgoszez (Poland)
- Bremen (Germany)
- Groningen (Netherlands)
- Gainsborough
- Stockport
- Liverpool
- Dublin
- Churchill Falls (Newfoundland)
- Edmonton (Alberta)

Silver

Different metals react to varying degrees with food, affecting its taste to a greater or a lesser extent. Silver, whilst more expensive than steel, made higher quality cutlery because it reacted less with food (gold cutlery was even more desirable for the same reason).

In 1743 Thomas Boulsover accidentally discovered that a thin layer of silver fused to copper could be worked to create 'silver' cutlery much more cheaply. This combination became known as 'Sheffield Plate.' Although Boulsover had a successful career, like many others of his time he failed to take out a patent which meant others could copy his technique and that he never fully profited from his discovery.

There are two memorials to Boulsover, one in Tudor Square and one next to the path by Wire Mill Dam.

Until the late 18th Century, all silver in the UK was assayed (quality assured) in London. Both Birmingham and Sheffield successfully petitioned parliament about this and in 1773 were awarded the right to open assay offices in each of the two cities. Sheffield hallmarked its first piece of silver on 20th September of the same year. The Sheffield hallmark was a crown.

Sheffield's hallmark changed to the White Rose of York in 1975, and in 2008 the assay office made its most recent move to Beulah Street in Hillsborough – look out for it next time you use the Hillsborough Leisure Centre.

The only UK silver assay offices today are in London, Dublin, Edinburgh, Birmingham and Sheffield.

Sheffield Silver Hallmarks

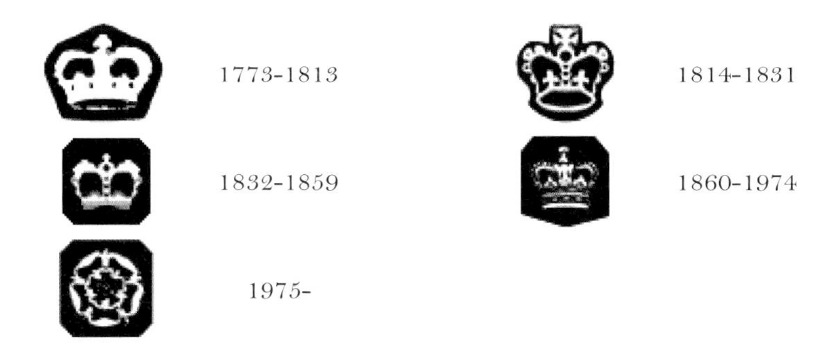

Simpson, Joe

Born: 9th August 1960

Education: Various

We all know Joe Simpson for *Touching the Void*, his book (and then subsequent film) that described the attempt that he and his climbing partner Simon Yates made to climb the Peruvian mountain Siula Grande in 1985.

The expedition was attempting the unclimbed west face of the 6,344m peak. On the descent Simpson injured his foot, meaning that Yates was forced to lower him down the mountain by rope in small stages. During the descent, Yates lowered Simpson over an unseen crevasse edge. Yates made the difficult decision to cut the rope to avoid them both being pulled off the mountain. Simpson survived the fall and managed to drag himself down to base camp 4 days later.

Following surgery to fix his injuries, Simpson was told that he would never climb again, and that even walking would be difficult. Only two years later, Simpson was climbing again.

Since the accident Simpson has written a number of books (*Touching the Void* has sold over 2 million copies) and does motivational speaking. Although he didn't grow up in Sheffield, Joe Simpson has spent a large portion of his life climbing and living in Sheffield. He was inducted into the Sheffield Walk of Fame in 2008.

Ski Village

Open from 1988 - 2012, the Sheffield Ski Village was the largest artificial ski complex in the whole of Europe. There was a total of 8 slopes, including moguls and a half pipe, as well as a downhill mountain bike trail. Numerous British Winter Olympians came to Sheffield to train.

The site has been plagued by vandalism and arson since it closed, but there are plans for redevelopment, and the city may yet have world-class artificial ski facilities again.

Snowfall

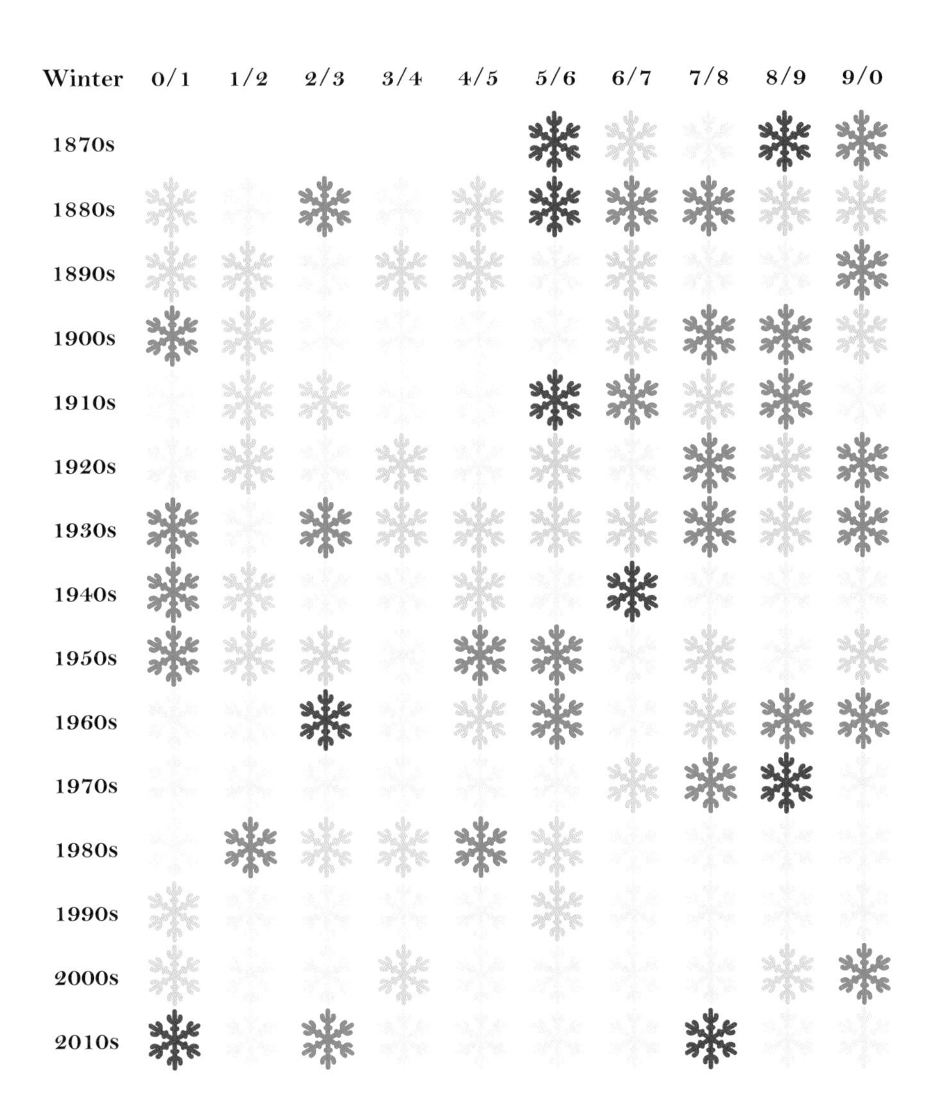

Winter
0/1
1/2
2/3
3/4
4/5
5/6
6/7
7/8
8/9
9/0
1870s
1880s
1890s
1900s
1910s
1920s
1930s
1940s
1950s
1960s
1970s
1980s
1990s
2000s
2010s

Little/no snowfall
Average snowfall
Above average snowfall
Heavy snowfall

Sport

Sheffield is much more than just two football teams. Look more closely and you quickly discover the prodigious talent that the city has produced across a hugely diverse range of sports and disciplines.

On the football field Derek **Dooley** holds a special place in the hearts of both blades and owls and we have a World Cup winner in the form of Gordon **Banks**, on the cricket field Sheffield has produced Michael **Vaughan**, on the dirt trail Steve **Peat**, in track and field Sebastian **Coe** and Jess **Ennis-Hill**, on the squash court Nick **Matthews**, in the ring Brendan **Ingle** and Clinton **Woods**, and on the water Grace **Clough**.

For those of us who have not quite made it yet as professional sportsmen and women there is plenty on offer.

For the runners we have **Parks**-a-plenty and literally miles and miles of trails and footpaths, there are the six weekly **parkruns**, a city half marathon and the Percy Pud 10km, not forgetting the new kid on the block - the Round Sheffield Run – or the numerous fell races such as the **Hallam Chase** for those who prefer off-road.

For the cyclists, there is (mainly!) lovely smooth tarmac courtesy of Amey, enough hills for even the most sadistic roadies and plenty of local cycling competitions. Alongside this, the mass participation Sky Ride events allow everyone an opportunity to cycle on closed roads.

For the climbers there are five indoor climbing walls, including the Depot which is the biggest bouldering centre in the UK. And if that wasn't enough, we are blessed with **Stanage Edge** on our doorstep that is arguably the best climbing crag in the country.

There are boxing gyms, rowing on Dam Flask, 10 **Golf** courses, international swimming and diving venues at **Ponds Forge**, a growing mountain biking scene, and all manner of active sports teams keeping the city healthy.

And once you've tired of taking part, there is plenty of sport to watch – you can join the 23,000 and 30,000 respectively who watch Wednesday and United at home each week, watch the Eagles play Championship rugby, see World Championship snooker at the Crucible, international swimming and diving at Ponds Forge, the World Bouldering Championships at the Cliffhanger Festival, and stand at the roadside to watch lycra-clad Tour de France riders pay us an occasional visit (**Yellow Jersey**)!

Stanage Edge

Known the world over among the climbing community, Stanage Edge is a Millstone Grit escarpment running north to south for three miles before continuing slightly less dramatically further south as Burbage Rocks, Froggatt Edge, Curbar Edge, Baslow Edge and Birchen Edge.

Although never more than 25m high, Stanage makes up for any lack of vertical stature with both its grippiness and the sheer number and variety of routes – over 1,700 in total!

From the Plantation area south, Stanage Edge lies entirely in Derbyshire, the northern section forming the boundary between South Yorkshire and Derbyshire. Technically therefore, Sheffield lays claim to some of the top of Stanage Edge with Derbyshire taking the rest. Fortunately, there isn't any sort of standoff between us and our Derbyshire cousins over Stanage and it is there to be enjoyed by everyone, right on our doorstep and an important part of Sheffield's great outdoor playground.

North to South Best Routes

Route	Difficulty/Grade		Length
Stanage End			
The Vice	E1	5b	10m
Surgeon's Saunter	HVS	5b	20m
Marble Wall			
Terrazza Crack	HVS	5a	10m
Nectar	E5	6b	15m
Meysner's Link up	E3	5c	20m
Goosey Goosey Gander	E5	6a	15m
Right Hand Tower	HVS	5a	15m
High Neb			
Kelly's Overhang	HVS	5b	15m
Quietus	E2	6a	15m
Old Friends	E4	6a	15m

Plantation (Derbyshire)

	Route	Grade	Tech	Length
*	Archangel	E3	5b	20m
*	Goliath's Groove	HVS	5a	20m
*	Ulysses Bow	E6	6b	20m
*	White Wand	E5	6a	20m
*	Not to be Taken Away	E2	6a	5m
*	Tower Face	HVS	5a	25m
*	The Strangler	E4	5c	15m

Popular End (Derbyshire)

	Route	Grade	Tech	Length
*	Millsom's Minion	E1	5b	20m
*	Calvary	E4	6a	20m
*	Left Unconquerable	E1	5b	15m
*	Right Unconquerable	HVS	5a	15m
*	BAWs Crawl	HVS	5a	10m
*	Off with his Head	E4	6b	15m
*	Heaven Crack	VD		10m
*	Dark Continent	E1	5c	20m
*	Congo Corner	HVS	5b	20m
*	Congo Corner Direct (The Link)	E1	5b	20m
*	Mississippi Buttress Direct	VS	4c	20m
*	The Asp	E3	6a	15m
*	Wuthering	E1	5b	20m
*	RH Cave Innominate/Harding's Finish	HVS	5a	20m
*	Ellis's Eliminate	VS	4c	20m
*	Robin Hood's RH Buttress Direct	HS	4a	20m
*	Whillan's Pendulum / Black Magic	HVS	5b	20m
*	Hargreave's Original Route	VS	4c	20m
*	April Crack	HS	4b	20m
*	Christmas Crack	HS	4a	20m
*	Hollybush Crack	VD		20m
*	Queersville	HVS	5a	20m
*	Flying Buttress	VD		25m
*	Flying Buttress Direct	E1	5b	25m
*	Censor	E3	5c	15m
*	Dangler	E2	5c	15m
*	Tippler Direct	E2	6a	15m
*	Tippler	E1	5b	20m
*	The Chameleon	E4	6a	15m
*	Eliminator	HVS	5b	15m
*	Manchester Buttress	HS	4b	15m

Steel (how to make the shiny stuff)

The steel-making process consists of two stages. The first is to remove the natural impurities from iron ore via oxidisation. The silicon, phosphorous, sulphur and carbon that occur naturally within iron ore have the effect of weakening the resulting iron. The removal of the impurities creates a carbon steel. The second stage is to add the appropriate amounts of other metals and elements to create the specific variety of steel required.

Main Chemical Processes

$$2C + O_2 \rightarrow 2CO$$

$$Si + O_2 \rightarrow SiO_2$$

$$2Mn + O_2 \rightarrow 2MnO$$

$$4P + 5O_2 \rightarrow 2P_2O_5$$

Henry Bessemer revolutionised the oxidisation process when he patented the Bessemer process in the 1850s. This involved melting the iron ore in a special vessel (a Bessemer converter) and blowing air through the molten ore. The oxygen in the air oxidised the impurities which formed a slag that could then be siphoned off. Carbon monoxide was also created and burned off. The remaining liquid formed carbon steel. By using his process Bessemer was able to undercut his competitors. In turn, seeing the cost benefits of his process, Bessemer's rivals were only too happy to pay Bessemer a fee for the use of his patented method – Bessemer became far richer from licensing his patent than from producing steel himself.

More recently, the Bessemer process has been refined, with pure oxygen being blown through the molten ore instead of air, and additional chemical agents added to lower the impurity levels.

Types of Steel

Carbon Steels

Described as low carbon (up to 0.3% carbon), medium carbon (0.3-0.6% carbon) or high carbon (more than 0.6% carbon) steel. Low carbon steel is used to make flat sheets, wire and vehicle bodywork. The very lowest carbon steel is referred to as 'wrought iron'. Medium carbon is used in the construction of buildings and bridges. High carbon steel is used for large machine parts and industrial castings. Very high carbon steel is referred to as 'cast iron'.

Alloy Steels

Varying amounts of manganese, silicon, nickel, titanium, copper, chromium, and aluminium are added to produce the desired properties. Alloy steels are used for a variety of applications, depending on the property of the resultant steel, for example pipes, car parts, transformers and electric motors.

Stainless steels

Invented in Sheffield by Harry Brearley in 1913, stainless steel generally contains 10-20% chromium along with a quantity of nickel. It is 200 times less corrosive than carbon steel and therefore well-suited for items such as kitchen utensils.

Tool Steels

These steels contain varying amounts of tungsten, molybdenum, cobalt and vanadium. These alloys are heat resistant and durable, and are used to make cutting and drilling equipment.

Sunrise

The shortest day (winter solstice) occurs on either Dec 21st or 22nd when the length of daylight in Sheffield is 7 hours 29 minutes. However, the evenings start getting lighter 8 days earlier (earliest sunset is 3:46pm GMT), and the mornings continue to get darker for another 9 days (latest sunrise is 8.21am GMT).

The longest day (summer solstice) is June 20th or 21st when daylight in Sheffield lasts 17 hours and 1 minute. The earliest sunrise is 3 days earlier at 4:36am BST and the latest sunset is 9.38pm BST 4 days later.

At the equinoxes (spring and autumn), the length of daylight is exactly 12 hours. The spring equinox occurs between March 19th and 21st depending on the year. The autumn equinox occurs between September 20th and September 24th, again depending on the year.

By way of contrast, a little further south in London they have a longer 'shortest day' of 7 hours and 49 minutes, but a shorter 'longest day' of 16 hours 38 minutes. We will leave you to do the maths, but we reckon this might mean that Sheffield gets more daylight than London over the course of the year!

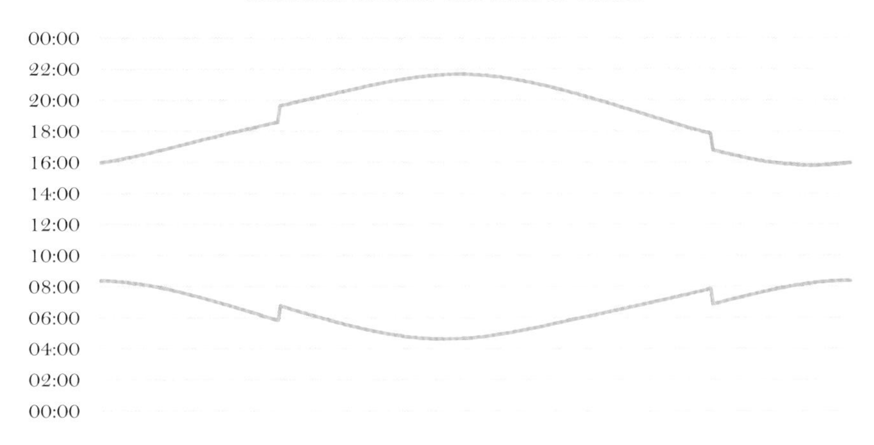

Sheffield Supergun

On 11th April 1990 customs officials seized 8 large metal tubes, bound from Forgemasters in Sheffield to Iraq. These were destined to form what would have been the largest gun in the world at the time (over 40m long). Simultaneously, similar seizures of other supergun components were made across Europe. At the time Forgemasters understood that the tubes had been ordered for use by a petrochemical company.

The development of an Iraqi gun capable of launching satellites into space to secure a military advantage was known as Project Babylon. Canadian rocket engineer Dr Gerald Bull worked with the Iraqi's on Project Babylon. He was assassinated the day before the discovery of the rocket parts – no-one is sure which international security forces carried out the assassination.

Charges were made in relation to the supergun affair (but not against Forgemasters) and then mysteriously dropped.

Supertram

Sheffield Supertram signals operate concurrently with traffic signals as follows.

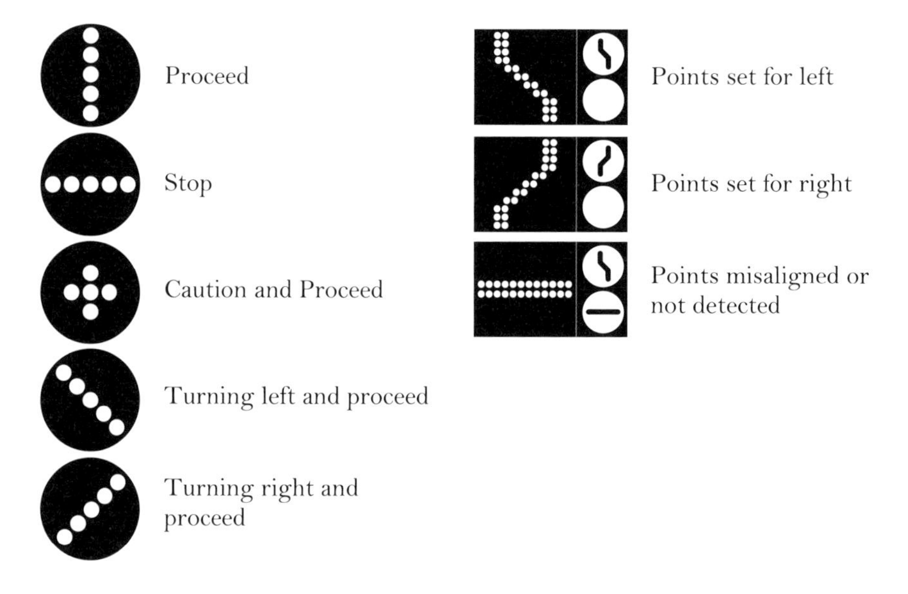

There are 50 tram stops on the Sheffield Supertram network.

Standard dimensions for Supertram stops

- Length: 26.5m
- Depth: 3m with a 1:20 slope
- Height: 37.5cm

Meadowhall and Netherthorpe Road tram stops have 'island' platforms.

With the exception of Halfway, Herdings Park, Malin Bridge and Middlewood all tram stops have two platforms.

City Hall, Granville Road/The Sheffield College, Leppings Lane, Manor Top/Elm Tree, Park Grange and West Street tram stops have staggered platforms.

Multi-operator tickets valid on Supertram (Jan 2020)

Ticket type	Valid on:	Valid for:	Price
DayRider	Supertram and Stagecoach buses in Sheffield	Unlimited travel on day of issue	£3.00
South and West Yorkshire Dayrider (Stagecoach)	Stagecoach buses and Supertram in South and West Yorkshire	1 day	£4.00
MegaRider	Supertram and Stagecoach buses in Sheffield	1 week	£10.00
South and West Yorkshire Goldrider (Stagecoach)	Stagecoach buses and Supertram in South and West Yorkshire	1 week	£15.00
Monthly MegaRider	Supertram and Stagecoach buses in Sheffield	1 month	£39.50
TravelMaster, South Yorkshire (SYPTE)	Local buses, trains and Supertram in South Yorkshire	1 day	£6.00
		Book of five 1-day tickets	£28.50
		1 week	£20.75
		1 month	£77.25
		3 months	£227.00
		1 year	£775.00
TravelMaster, Sheffield zone (SYPTE)	Local buses, trains and Supertram in Sheffield (local authority area)	1 week	£18.60
		1 month	£69.25
		3 months	£203.00
		1 year	£688.00
South Yorkshire Day Tripper (SYPTE)	Local buses, trains and Supertram in South Yorkshire	1 day (not valid on trains before 09.30 Mon–Fri)	£5.00
Railmaster (SYPTE)	Trains and Supertram in South Yorkshire	1 month	£56.50
South Yorkshire Peak Explorer (SYPTE)	All buses and Supertram in South Yorkshire, buses running between South Yorkshire and the northern Peak District	1 day	£8.00

Surnames

Top 50 surnames in Sheffield from the 1840s and in 2020. The bars on each side are drawn to the same scale. In 2020 there were just over 3,000 Smiths, 600 Allens and 400 Greaves. In 1840 22% of Sheffielders possessed one of the surnames on the list. In 2020 it was just 7%.

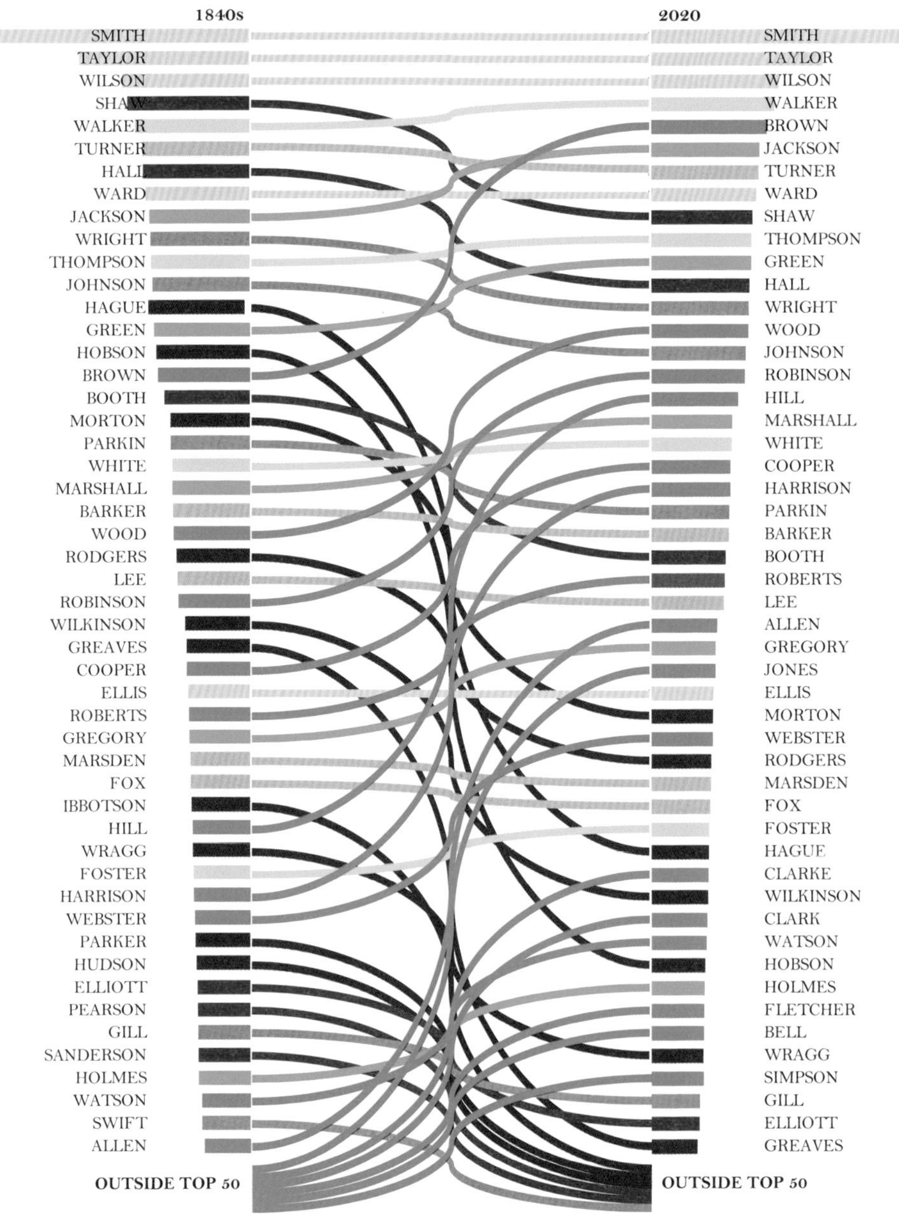

Talbots

The Talbot family inherited land in Sheffield when John Talbot (1st Earl of Shrewsbury) married into the Furnival family in the early 15th Century. Francis Talbot (4th Earl of Shrewsbury and Baron of Furnival) later adopted Sheffield as his place of residence and made the castle (built earlier by Thomas de Furnival) his home. In 1516 Francis built a manor house on the castle estate on a hill a couple of miles from Sheffield (we know this as the Manor). In 1520 he added a private family chapel to the parish church in Sheffield. This remains today as the Shrewsbury Chapel which forms part of Sheffield cathedral, and is also where the 4th Earl's remains were placed when he died in 1538.

George Talbot, 6th Earl of Shrewsbury (two generations later) was appointed 'keeper' of Mary Queen of Scots. He moved Mary between a number of locations on his estate, with Mary spending the period from 1570-1584 in Sheffield Manor Lodge before being moved to Wingfield Manor and then subsequently tried and executed for treason in 1587.

George Talbot is the only Talbot to have held the title of Earl Marshall (a hereditary office of state ranking below the Lord High Constable and above the Lord High Admiral) – 14 Dukes of Norfolk have held this title since and continue to do so today.

George Talbot moved in moneyed circles – his second wife was Bess of Hardwick (of Hardwick Hall), who in turn was the widow of Sir William Cavendish (of Chatsworth).

George Talbot is also buried in the Shrewsbury Chapel.

Francis and George may be no more, but the line of Talbots is very much alive and well. The 22nd Earl of Shrewsbury goes by the name of Charles Henry John Benedict Crofton Chetwynd Chetwynd-Talbot, and holds the additional titles of 22nd Earl of Waterford, 7th Earl Talbot and Lord High Steward of Ireland.

In 1606, the Howard family (who held the titles of Earl of Arundel and Duke of Norfolk at the time) inherited large parts of what is now Sheffield from the Talbots when Thomas Howard married Alathea Talbot.

Tallest Buildings

Tallest buildings in Sheffield through time. All these buildings are still standing.

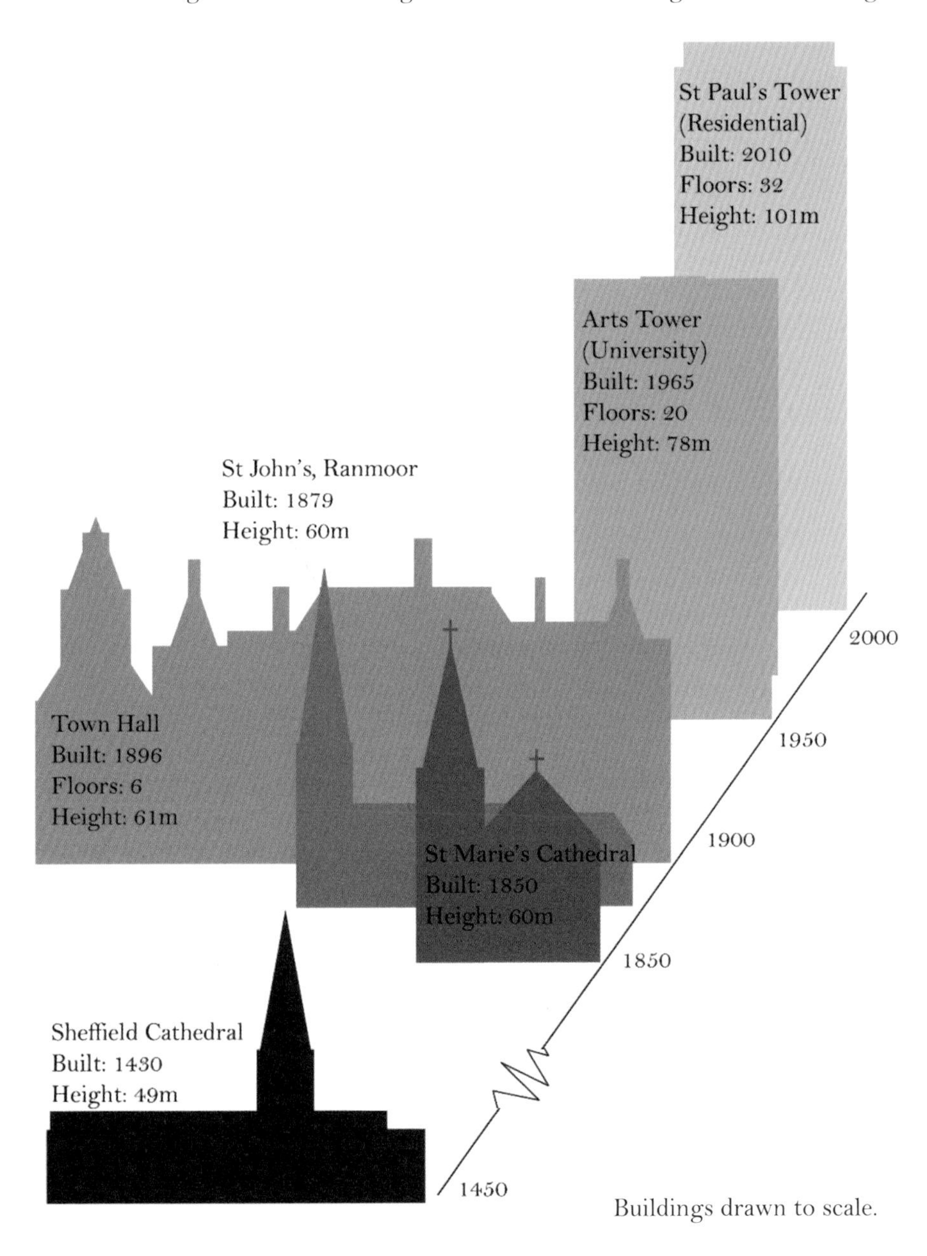

Buildings drawn to scale.

Timeline

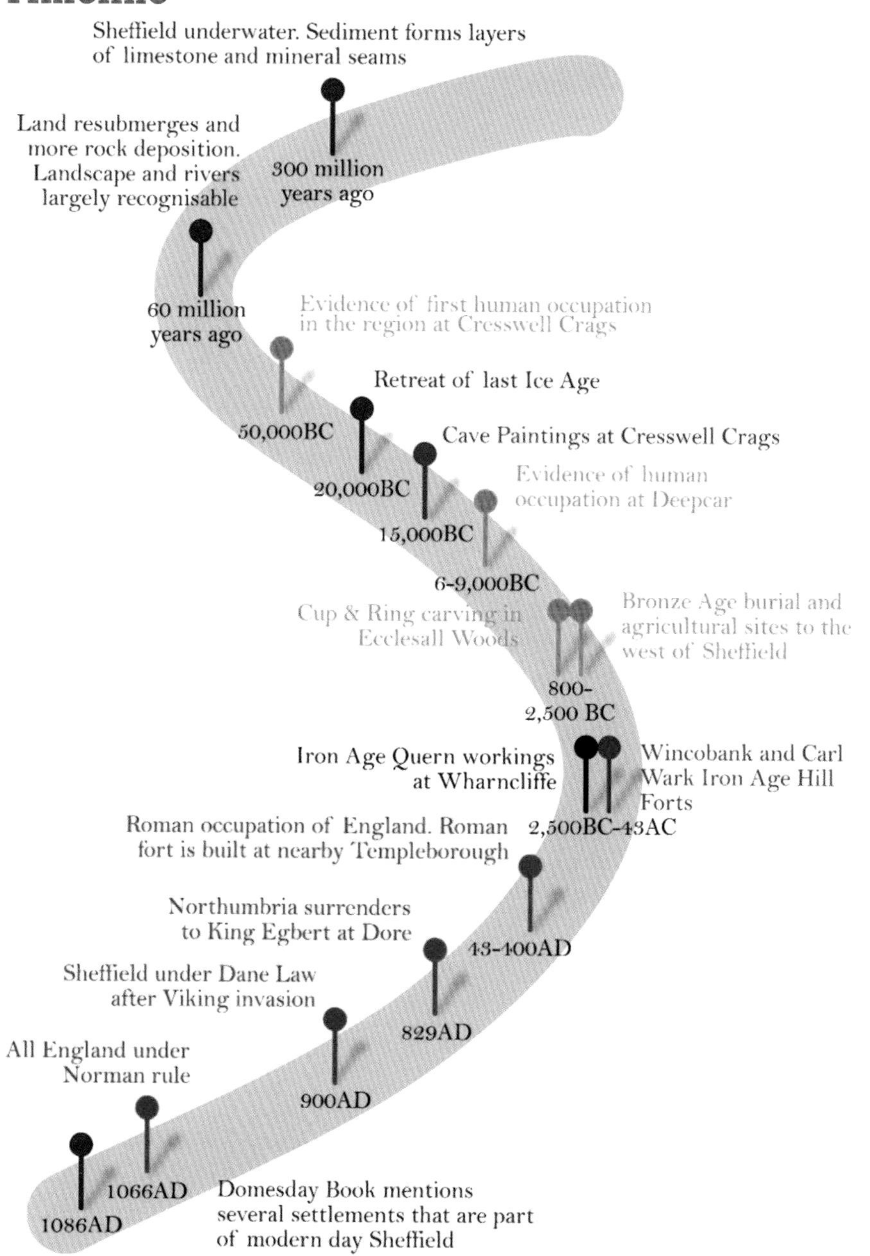
Sheffield underwater. Sediment forms layers of limestone and mineral seams
300 million years ago
Land resubmerges and more rock deposition. Landscape and rivers largely recognisable
60 million years ago
Evidence of first human occupation in the region at Cresswell Crags
50,000BC
Retreat of last Ice Age
20,000BC
Cave Paintings at Cresswell Crags
15,000BC
Evidence of human occupation at Deepcar
6-9,000BC
Cup & Ring carving in Ecclesall Woods
Bronze Age burial and agricultural sites to the west of Sheffield
800-2,500 BC
Iron Age Quern workings at Wharncliffe
Wincobank and Carl Wark Iron Age Hill Forts
2,500BC-43AC
Roman occupation of England. Roman fort is built at nearby Templeborough
43-400AD
Northumbria surrenders to King Egbert at Dore
829AD
Sheffield under Dane Law after Viking invasion
900AD
All England under Norman rule
1066AD
1086AD
Domesday Book mentions several settlements that are part of modern day Sheffield

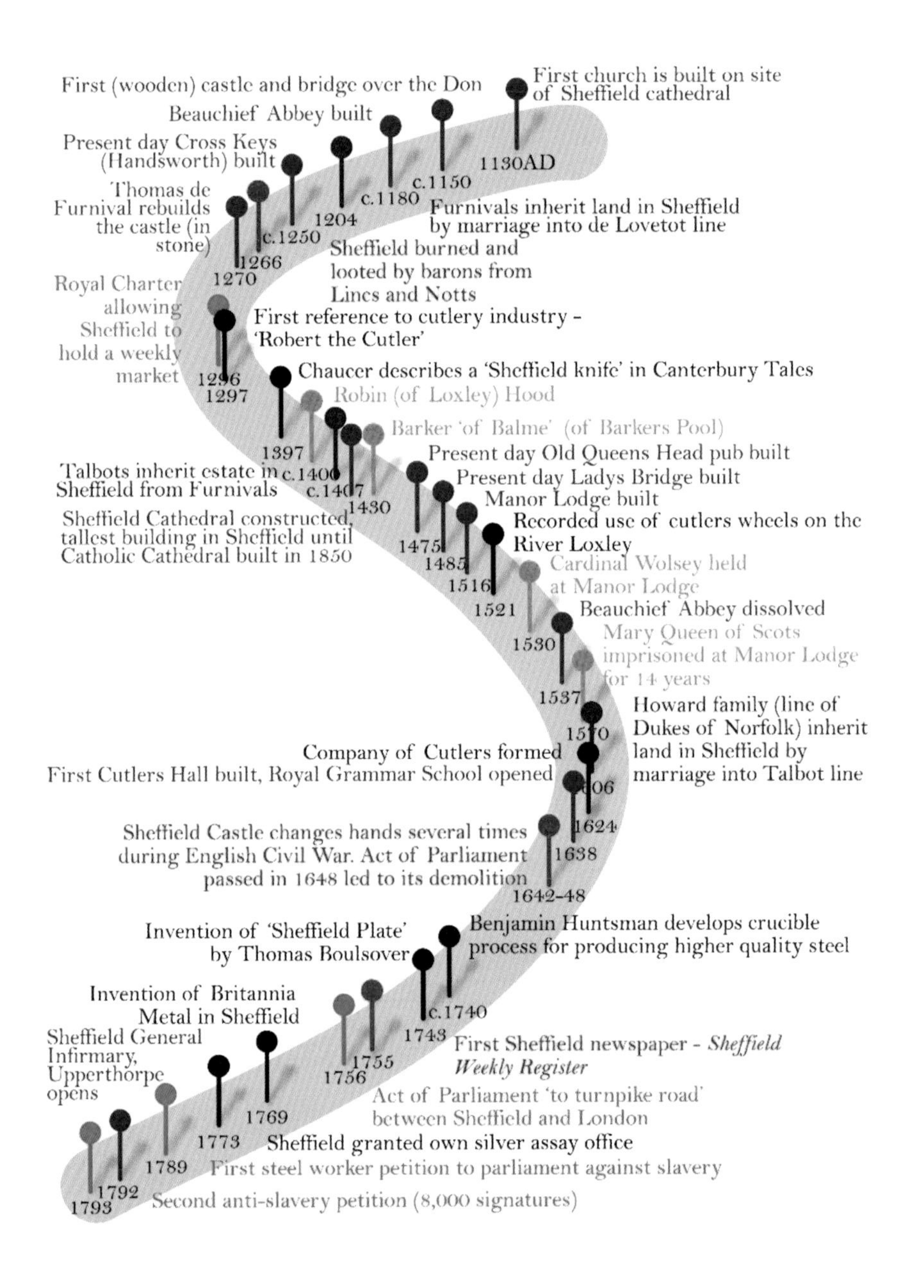
First church is built on site of Sheffield cathedral
1130AD
First (wooden) castle and bridge over the Don
c.1150
Beauchief Abbey built
c.1180
Present day Cross Keys (Handsworth) built
1204
Furnivals inherit land in Sheffield by marriage into de Lovetot line
c.1250
Sheffield burned and looted by barons from Lincs and Notts
1266
Thomas de Furnival rebuilds the castle (in stone)
1270
Royal Charter allowing Sheffield to hold a weekly market
1296
First reference to cutlery industry - 'Robert the Cutler'
1297
Chaucer describes a 'Sheffield knife' in Canterbury Tales
1397
Robin (of Loxley) Hood
c.1400
Talbots inherit estate in Sheffield from Furnivals
c.1407
Barker 'of Balme' (of Barkers Pool)
1430
Sheffield Cathedral constructed, tallest building in Sheffield until Catholic Cathedral built in 1850
Present day Old Queens Head pub built
1475
Present day Ladys Bridge built
1485
Manor Lodge built
1516
Recorded use of cutlers wheels on the River Loxley
1521
Cardinal Wolsey held at Manor Lodge
1530
Beauchief Abbey dissolved
1537
Mary Queen of Scots imprisoned at Manor Lodge for 14 years
1570
Howard family (line of Dukes of Norfolk) inherit land in Sheffield by marriage into Talbot line
1606
Company of Cutlers formed
1624
First Cutlers Hall built, Royal Grammar School opened
1638
Sheffield Castle changes hands several times during English Civil War. Act of Parliament passed in 1648 led to its demolition
1642-48
Benjamin Huntsman develops crucible process for producing higher quality steel
c.1740
Invention of 'Sheffield Plate' by Thomas Boulsover
1743
First Sheffield newspaper - *Sheffield Weekly Register*
1755
Act of Parliament 'to turnpike road' between Sheffield and London
1756
Invention of Britannia Metal in Sheffield
1769
Sheffield granted own silver assay office
1773
Sheffield General Infirmary, Upperthorpe opens
1789
First steel worker petition to parliament against slavery
1792
Second anti-slavery petition (8,000 signatures)
1793

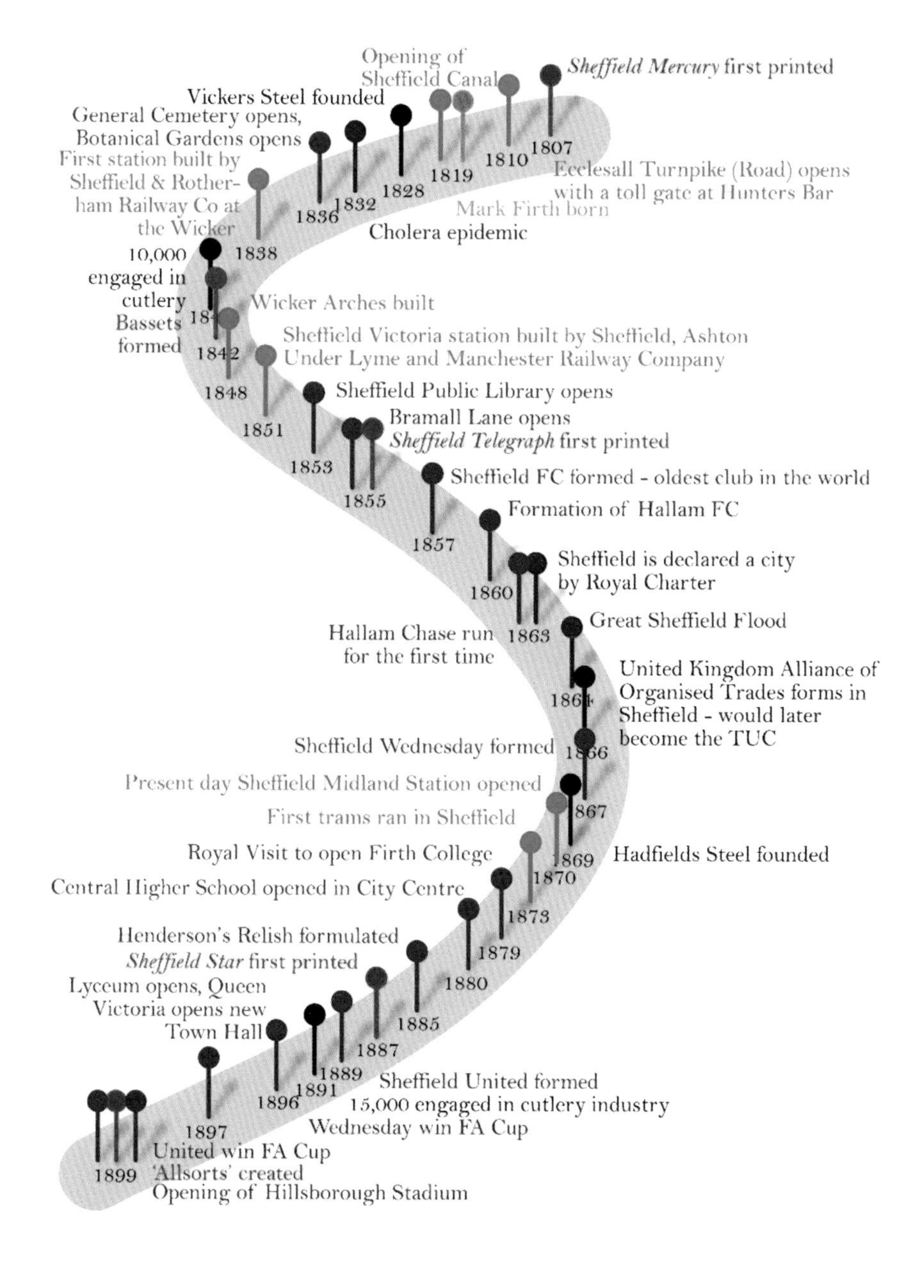

Sheffield Mercury first printed
1807
Ecclesall Turnpike (Road) opens with a toll gate at Hunters Bar
1810
Mark Firth born
Opening of Sheffield Canal
1819
Cholera epidemic
Vickers Steel founded
1828
General Cemetery opens, Botanical Gardens opens
1832
1836
First station built by Sheffield & Rotherham Railway Co at the Wicker
1838
10,000 engaged in cutlery
Bassets formed
Wicker Arches built
1842
Sheffield Victoria station built by Sheffield, Ashton Under Lyme and Manchester Railway Company
1848
1851
Sheffield Public Library opens
1853
Bramall Lane opens
Sheffield Telegraph first printed
1855
Sheffield FC formed - oldest club in the world
1857
Formation of Hallam FC
1860
Sheffield is declared a city by Royal Charter
1863
Hallam Chase run for the first time
Great Sheffield Flood
1864
United Kingdom Alliance of Organised Trades forms in Sheffield - would later become the TUC
Sheffield Wednesday formed
1866
Present day Sheffield Midland Station opened
867
First trams ran in Sheffield
869
Hadfields Steel founded
Royal Visit to open Firth College
1870
Central Higher School opened in City Centre
1873
1879
Henderson's Relish formulated
Sheffield Star first printed
1880
Lyceum opens, Queen Victoria opens new Town Hall
1885
1887
1889
1891
Sheffield United formed
15,000 engaged in cutlery industry
1896
Wednesday win FA Cup
1897
United win FA Cup
1899
'Allsorts' created
Opening of Hillsborough Stadium

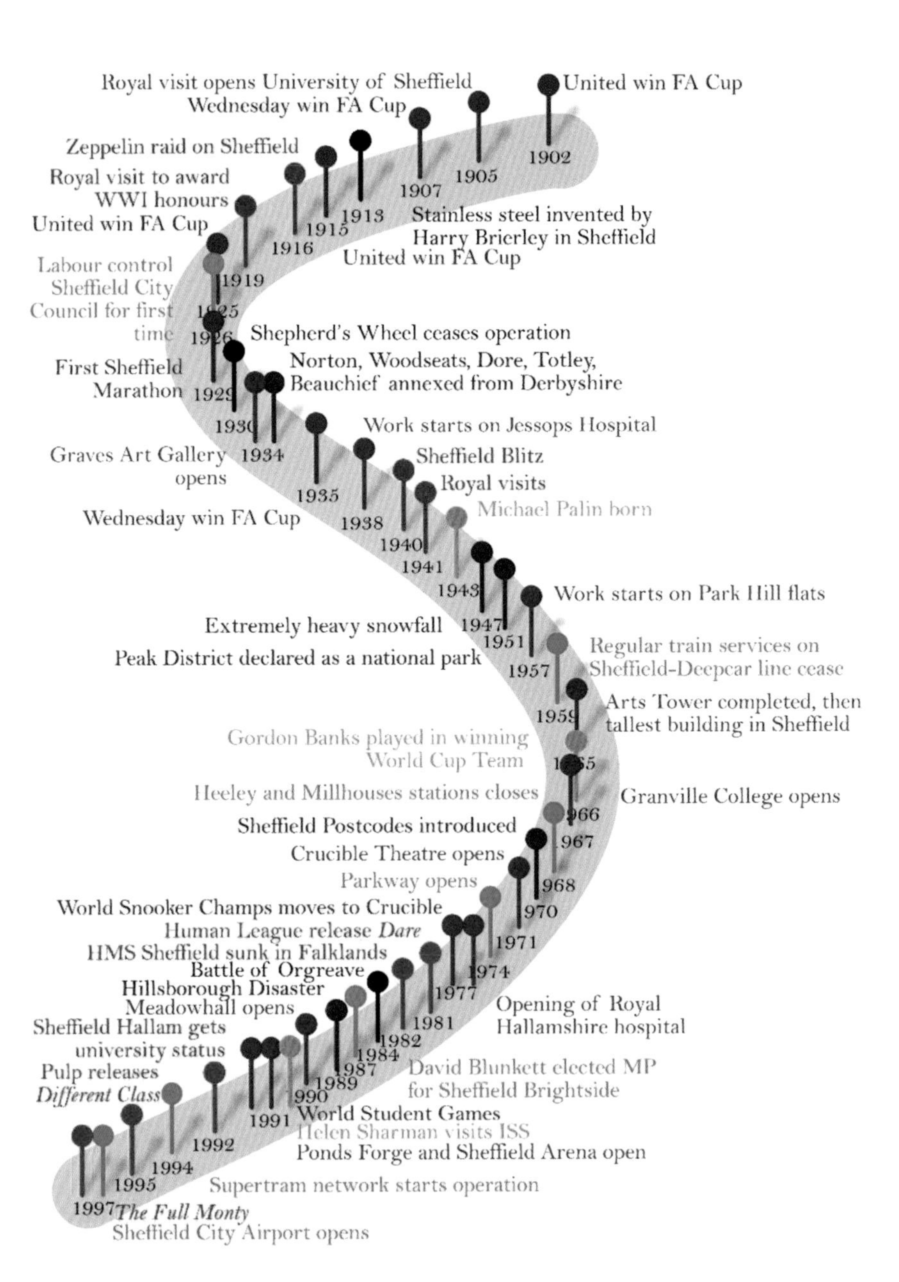
Royal visit opens University of Sheffield
Wednesday win FA Cup
United win FA Cup
1902
1905
1907
Zeppelin raid on Sheffield
Royal visit to award WWI honours
United win FA Cup
1913
1915
1916
Stainless steel invented by Harry Brierley in Sheffield
United win FA Cup
Labour control Sheffield City Council for first time
1919
1925
1926
Shepherd's Wheel ceases operation
First Sheffield Marathon
Norton, Woodseats, Dore, Totley, Beauchief annexed from Derbyshire
1929
1930
1934
Work starts on Jessops Hospital
Graves Art Gallery opens
Sheffield Blitz
Royal visits
Michael Palin born
Wednesday win FA Cup
1935
1938
1940
1941
1943
Work starts on Park Hill flats
Extremely heavy snowfall
1947
1951
Peak District declared as a national park
1957
Regular train services on Sheffield-Deepcar line cease
Arts Tower completed, then tallest building in Sheffield
1959
Gordon Banks played in winning World Cup Team
Heeley and Millhouses stations closes
Granville College opens
Sheffield Postcodes introduced
Crucible Theatre opens
Parkway opens
World Snooker Champs moves to Crucible
Human League release *Dare*
HMS Sheffield sunk in Falklands
Battle of Orgreave
Hillsborough Disaster
Meadowhall opens
Sheffield Hallam gets university status
Pulp releases *Different Class*
1968
1970
1971
1974
1977
Opening of Royal Hallamshire hospital
1981
1982
1984
1987
1989
David Blunkett elected MP for Sheffield Brightside
1991
World Student Games
Helen Sharman visits ISS
Ponds Forge and Sheffield Arena open
1992
1994
1995
Supertram network starts operation
1997
The Full Monty
Sheffield City Airport opens

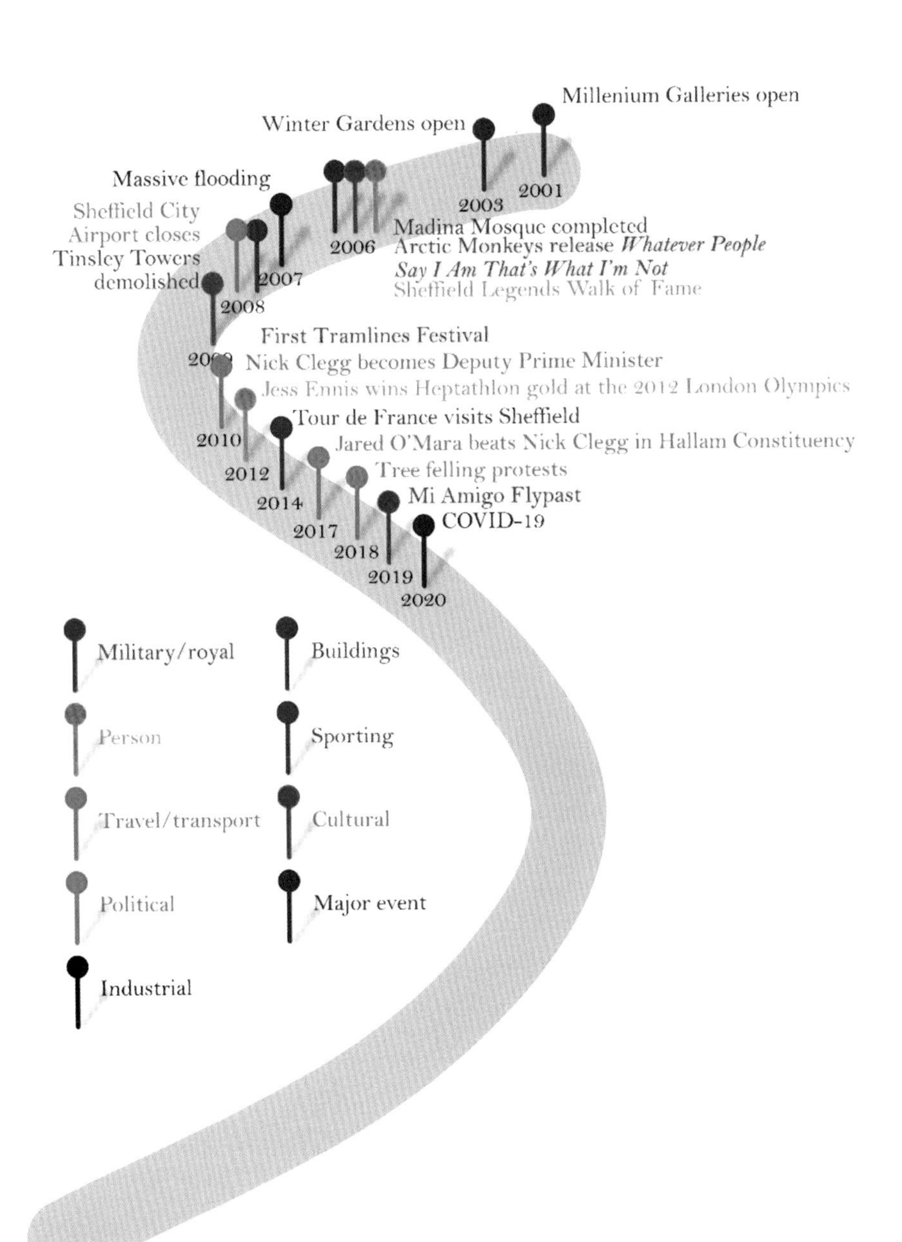
Millenium Galleries open
Winter Gardens open
2001
2003
Massive flooding
Sheffield City
Airport closes
Tinsley Towers
demolished
2006
2007
2008
Madina Mosque completed
Arctic Monkeys release *Whatever People Say I Am That's What I'm Not*
Sheffield Legends Walk of Fame
First Tramlines Festival
Nick Clegg becomes Deputy Prime Minister
Jess Ennis wins Heptathlon gold at the 2012 London Olympics
Tour de France visits Sheffield
Jared O'Mara beats Nick Clegg in Hallam Constituency
Tree felling protests
Mi Amigo Flypast
COVID-19
2010
2012
2014
2017
2018
2019
2020
Military/royal
Buildings
Person
Sporting
Travel/transport
Cultural
Political
Major event
Industrial

Tinsley Towers

The once iconic Tinsley Towers were officially cooling towers numbers 6 and 7 of the Blackburn Meadows Power Station.

Coal – fired power station opened 1921 on the Blackburn Meadows site

Towers 6 and 7 built in 1937-38 to replace earlier square towers

M1 motorway built around cooling towers in the 1960s

Power station decommissioned in 1980

Towers 6 and 7 left standing due to proximity to the M1 motorway

Towers 6 and 7 demolished by controlled explosion at 3am on 24th August 2008

76m tall – only the Arts tower and St Paul's tower are taller

The two towers weighed 2,000 and 3,000 tonnes each

The closest tower was just 17m from the M1 southbound carriageway

When operating, each tower could handle over a million gallons per hour

The Tinsley Viaduct, carrying the M1 over the Don Valley was the first two-tier road bridge built in the United Kingdom.

The viaduct is just over 1km long and was built using steel (it would have been rude not to!) box girders for a total cost of £6m. Three disasters involving similarly constructed bridges led to a temporary partial closing of the viaduct and a programme of strengthening work in the 1970s. Further major strengthening in 2006 came with a bill of £85 million (cheap in comparison to the estimated £1.4 billion disruption to the national economy of closing the M1 in order to rebuild the viaduct completely). The viaduct carries over 110,000 vehicles daily.

Traffic

Sheffield has approximately 1,200 miles of road (currently being resurfaced and maintained by Amey, along with 2,000 miles of pavement, almost 70,000 streetlights and nearly 30,000 road signs). There are just shy of 500 traffic signals keeping us moving.

The number travelled by vehicle on Sheffield's roads each year is approximately 1.7 billion miles, which works out at around 4,000 miles per vehicle.

Road	Vehicles per 24- hour period
M1	110,000
A630 (Parkway)	69,000
A61 Ring Road (St Mary's Gate)	50,000
A61 Penistone Road (Hillsborough)	40,000
A625 Ecclesall Road	25,000
B6053 Eckington Way	21,000
A6135 Barnsley Road (Firth Park)	21,000
A6109 Attercliffe Road	20,000
A6101 Rivelin Valley Road	18,000
A621 Abbeydale Road	16,000
A6109 Brightside Road	9,000
B6070 City Road	7,000
Denby Street (off Bramall Lane)	1,200
Townhead Road (Dore)	1,000
Jepson Road (Firth Park)	650
Ringstead Crescent (Sandygate)	250

Tramlines Music Festival

Tramlines is an annual three-day music festival held every summer since 2009. Initially events were held in various venues around the city centre, but in more recent years, the main stage has moved to Hillsborough Park. Hugely popular, Tramlines has won the 'Best Metropolitan Festival' award twice, in 2012 and in 2019.

Headline acts

2009 21°C

- Reverend and the Makers
- The La's Little Boots
- Pixie Lott

2010 20°C

- Echo and the Bunnymen
- Mystry Jets
- Simian Mobile Disco

2011 18°C

- Ash
- Ms. Dynamite
- Futureheads

2012 23°C

- Alt-J
- Theme Park
- The White Album

2013 29°C

- Alt-J
- The Selecter
- Toddla T Sound

2014 27°C

- Public Enemy
- Katy B
- The Cribs

2015 18°C

- Wu Tang Clan
- Basement Jaxx
- The Charlatans

2016 24°C

- Dizzee Rascal
- Catfish and the Bottlemen
- Kelis

2017 20°C

- Libertines
- Primal Scream
- Metronomy

2018 22°C

- Stereophonics
- Noel Gallagher's High Flying Band
- Craig David's TS5

2019 21°C

- Two Door Cinema Club
- Courteneers
- Nile Rodgers & Chic

2020

- Cancelled due to CV-19

Tree Canopy Cover

Tree canopy cover in each ward given as a percentage.

Triangulation (Trig) Points

In 1935 the Ordnance Survey started a more accurate mapping of the British Isles. To do this they established a network of 6,500 triangulation points to be sited on prominent geographic features and to be used as the basis for the national map. Brigadier Martin Hotine designed the standard pillar (often referred to as a *Hotine* Pillar) on which surveyors would have placed their theodolites to take bearings of neighbouring triangulation points. The survey started in 1935 produced the OSGB36 datum which is still used today, although modern surveying methods make the trig points redundant.

Within the Sheffield authority area there are 25 trig point sites, most of which still possess their Hotine Pillar.

It probably won't surprise you to know that there is a community of 'trig point baggers' who collect trig point visits along with the associated views.

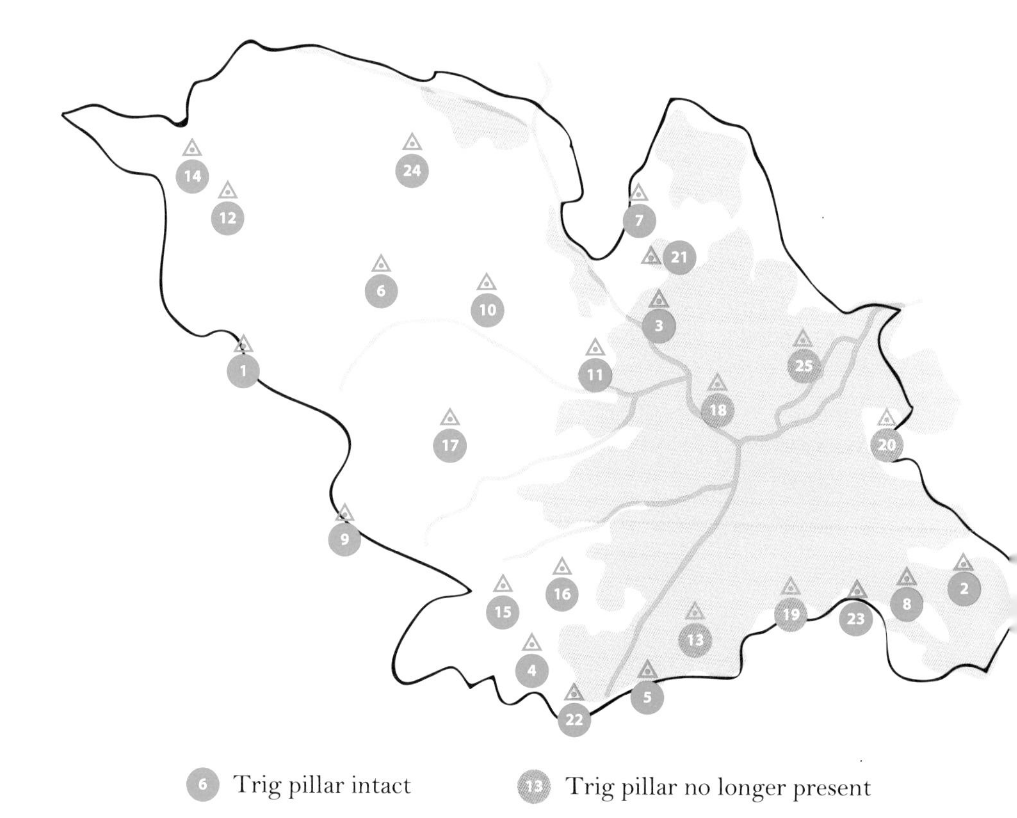

Key	Name	Height	OS Ref	What.Three.Words
1	Back Tor	538m	SK197909	actor.cried.populate
2	Beighton	93m	SK430838	straw.keep.aside
3	Birley Edge	157m	SK330922	enjoyable.united.social
4	Blacka Plantation	295m	SK289812	tested.chest.sticky
5	Bradway	203m	SK330805	aside.quarrel.prices
6	Emlin Ridge	385m	SK239933	overheat.decreased.mimics
7	Greno Knoll	307m	SK323956	marked.aims.frame
8	Hackenthorpe	132m	SK412833	result.novel.motor
9	High Neb	458m	SK228853	drip.hotel.pool
10	Kirk Edge	396m	SK277929	hero.cure.steep
11	Loxley Common	239m	SK309906	shadow.paint.mice
12	Margery	546m	SK189956	decoder.wrist.ideas
13	Meadow Head	191m	SK343822	clay.sports.neat
14	Outer Edge	542m	SK177969	though.tipping.surfaces
15	Ox Stones	420m	SK280831	votes.invent.odds
16	Ringinglow	321m	SK299836	noises.unit.fakes
17	Rod Moor	384m	SK262884	ladder.fork.only
18	Shirecliffe Gunsite	175m	SK349896	eaten.gosh.swear
19	The Herdings	218m	SK374830	jeeps.palms.before
20	Tinsley Park	95m	SK403883	school.monks.loves
21	Top End	250m	SK327936	scales.daily.flown
22	Totley	234m	SK303796	words.barn.baked
23	Whitelane End	210m	SK396829	after.swift.clocks
24	Whitwell Moor	359m	SK249972	trouble.articulated.archduke
25	Wincobank Hill	161m	SK377910	season.member.guard

Trippet

Trippet is an old Sheffield family name. Records show a John 'Trypet' in 1379 and a (presumably) different John 'Trippet' was Master Cutler in 1694.

Trippet Lane was originally 'Red Croft,' and was renamed as Trippet Lane in the late 18th Century.

Tup

The Old Tup is a local Christmas-time tradition dating from the mid-nineteenth Century. Groups of men would go from door to door carrying a hobby horse's head (usually that of a goat or horse) mounted on a pole with the pole-holder covered in sack-cloth. They would then perform a play that usually involved Beelzebub, a butcher and someone dressed in drag, and often involved the killing of Old Tup.

Originally very much a working class tradition that largely died out during the twentieth Century, there are still some committed middle class exponents who play at being their working class predecessors and keep the tradition alive at Christmas each year.

Tunnels

There is more going on underneath Sheffield than you might give credit for.

Numerous old mine workings riddle the ground underneath the city. Shafts were sunk over 300 yards deep to reach the coal seam with workings travelling over a mile underground from the shaft in some cases.

Under the city centre the Porter and Sheaf are guided through impressive closed culverts. You can read about the Megatron in earlier pages.

At a length of 5.7km, Totley rail tunnel is the fourth longest mainline rail tunnel in England. At the time of its construction in 1893 it was the second longest. Only the Severn tunnel and the two Channel tunnels are longer. The tunnel incorporates a huge natural chamber half-way along that was discovered during its construction.

There is another (lost) railway tunnel, in use up until 1948 and almost a quarter of a mile long, that runs under Spital hill, from Brunswick Road to the site of the new Tesco superstore.

And what of the claims that there was a tunnel dug from the site of Sheffield Castle to Manor Lodge, via the Old Queen's Head at Ponds Forge...the jury is still out.

Twenty Six Point Two

1929 -1931 Sheffield Independent Marathon

The first marathon to take place in Sheffield started at Barkers Pool, finishing at Niagra Sports Ground. There were 48 entrants, of which only 16 finished!

1946 – 1961 Doncaster to Sheffield Marathon

This started on Chequer Road in Doncaster, and finished at Sheffield Station, with a visit to Rotherham en route.

1982 - 1990 Sheffield Marathon and Half Marathon

Both started by Sheffield Wednesday football stadium and finished in Hillsborough Park (for some presumably well-thought out reason, the half marathon finished in Tinsley Park in 1982 and 1983).

1991 – 2003 Sheffield Marathon and Half Marathon

The start and finish moved to Don Valley Stadium, although in 1993 the race started from Bramall Lane. In the last year of running, the route altered to what would become the new half marathon route through the City Centre, with the full marathon heading out into Orgreave.

2004 – 2014 Sheffield Half Marathon

Increasing numbers participated, despite the route (large parts of which ran through industrial parts of the city) not being universally popular. In 2014, the race was officially cancelled at the last minute due to a failure to place water around the course for runners, but the runners literally voted with their feet and ran the race anyway.

2015 – present day Sheffield Half Marathon

With the closing of Don Valley Stadium the course moved to a city centre start, running out and up to Ringinglow before a largely downhill return to the city centre. Not a course for fast times, but great for runners and spectators alike.

Twin Towns

Sheffield has established numerous connections with towns and cities all over the world.

The map below shows all those towns and cities formally linked to Sheffield through the Sheffield International Linking Committee. Those marked with * have a less formal 'friendship agreement' with Sheffield.

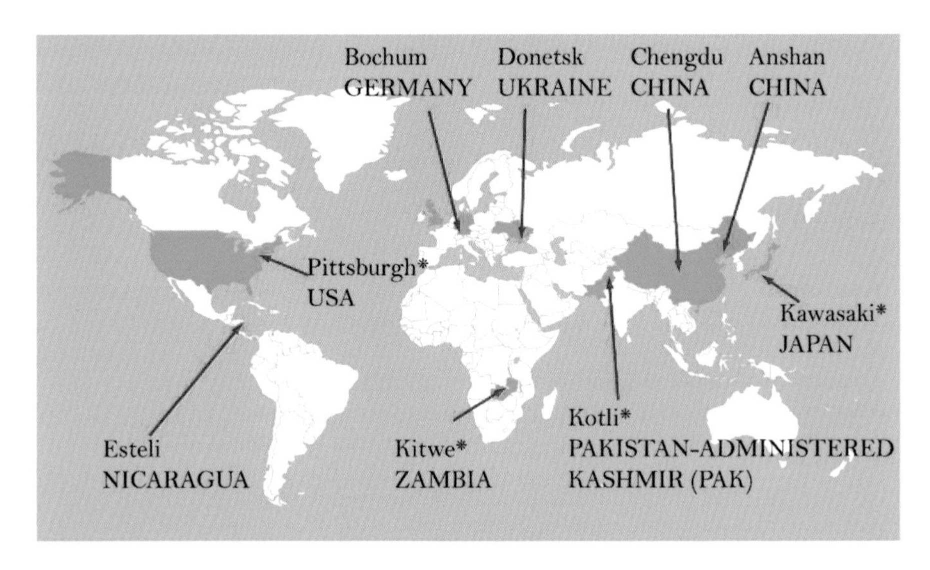

Sheffield
Population: 518,000
Rank: 4th City
Famous for: Steel
Known as: Steel City
Motto: *With God's help our labour is successful.*

Bochum
Population: 365,000
Rank: 16th City
Famous for: Cultural capital of the Ruhr, largest mining museum in the world
Also twinned with: Donetsk

Anshan
Population: 1,400,000
Rank: 60th City
Famous for: Steel, Talcum powder
Also twinned with: Clermont-Ferrand

Chengdu
Population: 14,800,000
Rank: 4th City
Famous for: Pandas
Known as: Hibiscus City/Brocade City/Turtle City
Motto: *Fast city, slow life.*
Also twinned with: Montpellier, Phoenix, Perth

Donetsk
Population: 900,000
Rank: 5th City
Famous for: Steel
Also twinned with: Bochum, Moscow, Pittsburgh, Vilnius

Esteli
Population: 120,000
Rank: 8th City
Known as: Diamond of Segovia
Motto: *Estelí, lover of the present, builder of the future*
Also twinned with: Stavanger

Kawasaki
Population: 1,500,000
Rank: 8th City
Famous for: Heavy industry
Also twinned with: Baltimore, Salzburg

Kitwe
Population: 530,000
Rank: 2nd City
Famous for: Mining
Motto: *Let's build us a city!*
Also twinned with: Detroit

Kotli
Population: 46,000
Rank: N/A
Famous for: Waterfalls

Pittsburgh
Population: 2,300,000
Rank: 27th City
Famous for: Steel
Known as: City of Bridges (446)
Motto: *Benigno Numini - With the Benevolent Deity*
Also twinned with: Bilbao, Donetsk, Skopje, Sofia, Zagreb

A6102, Norton, Sheffield, UK

Hackenthorpe, Sheffield, UK

Bochum, Germany

Donetsk, Ukraine

Under Your Feet

Throughout history, there has been extensive exploitation of the abundant mineral riches sitting underneath Sheffield. The rapid growth of Sheffield during the industrial revolution in particular owes much to the ability to mine local coal, ganister and clay to support the burgeoning steel industry. Ganister is a type of sandstone that was used to make heat-resistant bricks that lined the furnaces used in the production of steel. Fireclay was mined for the same purpose.

While little remains of the more recent large coal mining infrastructure, many of the old coal, ganister and fireclay mine workings can still be located, often buried within woodland.

Limestone has also been mined in the area – although not quite originating from Sheffield, the limestone used to build the Palace of Westminster was sourced from a quarry at Green Moor, a mile to the north of Stocksbridge.

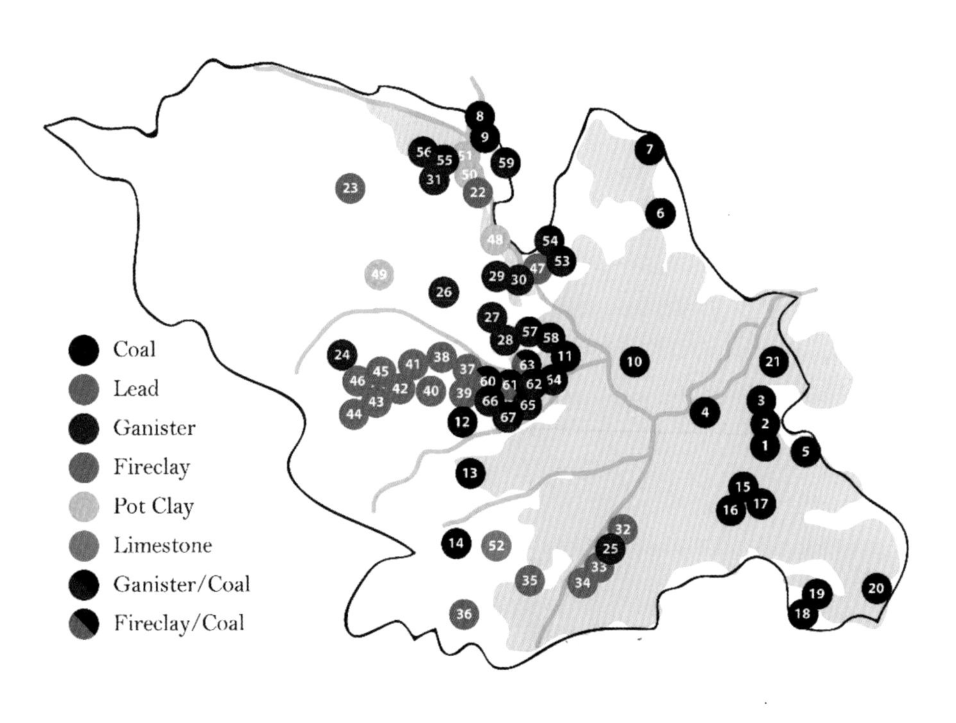

Coal

1. Bramley Hall Colliery
2. Handsworth Colliery
3. High Hazel Colliery
4. Nunnery Colliery
5. Orgreave Colliery
6. Smithy Wood Colliery
7. Thorncliffe Colliery
8. Wharncliffe Deepcar Mine
9. Lowood Deepcar Mine
10. Parkwood Springs Mine
11. Wisewood Mine
12. Hopwood Pit
13. Lodge Moor Pit
14. Barber Fields Drift Mine
15. Birley Colliery
16. Birleyvale Colliery
17. Birleymoor Colliery
18. Moorside Mine
19. Swallow Mine
20. Holbrook Mine
21. Tinsley Park Colliery

Lead

22. Bitholmes Mine
23. Broomhead Mine (submerged under Broomhead Reservoir)

Ganister

24. Gibraltar Mine
25. Beauchief Mine
26. Spitwinter Mine
27. Stubbin Pit Mine
28. Langhouse Mine
29. Hagg Stones Mine
30. Hope Mine
31. Hollinsbusk Mine

Fireclay

32. Marriot Wood Mine
33. Hutcliffe Wood Mine
34. Abbey Mine
35. Moss Mine
36. Strawberry Lee Mine
37. Storrs Mine
38. Storrs Bridge Mine
39. Griffs Mine
40. Hilltop Mine
41. Dungworth Pit
42. Hall Broom No 2 Mine
43. Hall Broom No 1 Mine
44. Crawshaw Mine
45. Ughill Mine
46. Wheatshire Mine
47. Don Vale Mine

Pot Clay

48. Usher Wood Mine
49. Edgemount Mine
50. Bitholmes Wood Mine
51. Bitholmes Mine

Limestone

52. Whirlow Quarry

Mixed

53. Beeley Wood No 1 Ganister/Coal
54. Beeley Wood No 2 Ganister/Coal
55. Ramsdens Ganister/Coal
56. Townend Ganister/Coal
57. Wadsley Common Ganister/Coal
58. Wadsley Park Ganister/Coal
59. Wharncliffe Lowoods Ganister/Coal
60. Acorn Hill Pits No1 & 2 Fireclay/Coal
61. Little Matlock Fireclay/Coal
62. Broadhead Flatts Ganister/Coal
63. Low Matlock Fireclay/Coal
64. Broadhead Ganister/Coal and Cockle Shelf Ganister/Coal
65. Hollins Pit Ganister/Coal
66. Stannington Wood Ganister/Coal
67. Minerva Pit Ganister/Coal

University Graduation

It is a bit of an urban myth that Sheffield has a higher 'staying on rate' – the proportion of Sheffield graduates who remain in the city after graduating - than anywhere else. Maybe not surprising, given what Sheffield has to offer, but it does mean that there are a lot of people living in Sheffield who have worn one of these gowns!

University of Sheffield Graduation Regalia

Bachelors Degrees*

Postgrad Diplomas, PGCE*

Masters Degrees*

Doctorates

*Hood lining is the colour of the faculty. In this case lemon yellow signifies the Faculty of Social Sciences

Higher Doctorates*

Sheffield Hallam University Graduation Regalia

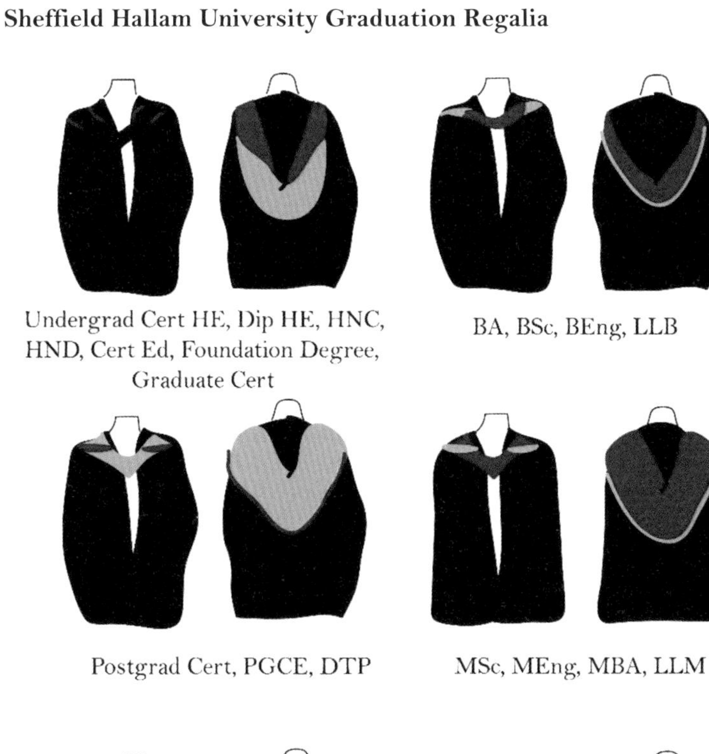

Undergrad Cert HE, Dip HE, HNC, HND, Cert Ed, Foundation Degree, Graduate Cert

BA, BSc, BEng, LLB

Postgrad Cert, PGCE, DTP

MSc, MEng, MBA, LLM

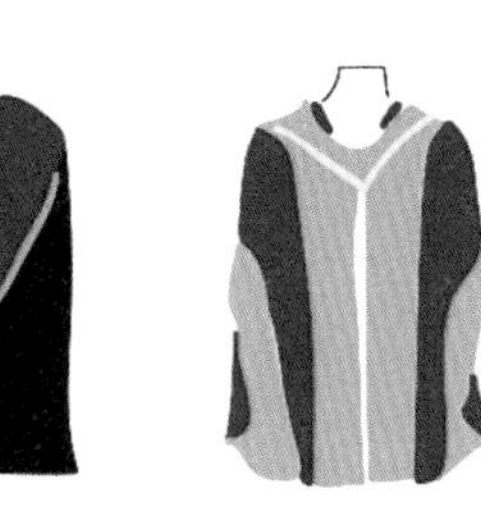

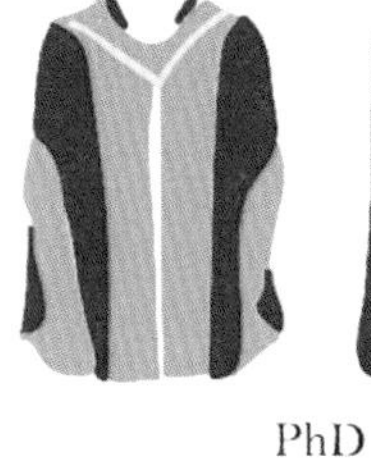

MPhil

PhD

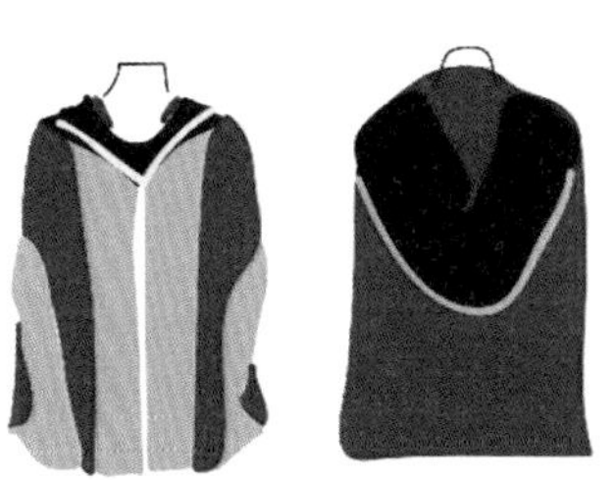

EdD, DBA

Vdiff

Welcome to the mysterious world of climbing grades!

The first thing to say is that there are many different ways of grading climbs which only serves to complicate things. The second is that however you do it, there is always going to be a measure of subjectivity when grading a climb.

Lets starting with the British Trad Grade. This comes in two parts. The Technical Grade (for example 4a, 6c) provides a measure of the technical difficulty of the climb. Generally, this describes the 'hardest' move on the climb, but it is worth noting that there could be any number of 5b moves on a 5b climb. The adjectival part (eg VDiff, VS) is a measure of the overall difficulty of the climb. For example, this takes into account the length of the climb, how exposed the climb is and the nature of the rock.

In an effort to simplify things, the French came up with Sport Grades which attempt to provide a single grade that captures both the technical demands and the overall difficulty of a climb. Because the Sport Grade is not *just* a technical indicator, a Sport Grade 4a is not generally the same as a British Trad Grade 4a.

The International Climbing and Mountaineering Federation (UIAA) grades and the Norwegian grading systems both also ascribe a single value to a climb. The Norwegians originally used the UIAA grades, but because our Scandinavian friends thought that a grade 6 was the hardest that anyone could climb, the Norwegian system tends to assign lower grades to climbs than the UIAA.

The American system is actually part of a more comprehensive grading system that classifies hikes, walks, scrambles as well as rock climbing. Grade 1 is walking, grades 2 and 3 are scrambling, grade 4 is simple climbing, and grade 5 is subdivided to cope with the range of challenges presented by rock climbing routes.

The Australian scale (often referred to as the Ewbank Scale) again assigns a single number to a climb, taking into account *technical difficulty, exposure, length, quality of rock, protection and other smaller factors.* A Ewbank score of 1 indicates that you can walk up the rock (without using hands). The hardest climbs in Australia have a Ewbank score of 35.

- Beginner
- Experienced
- Advanced
- Expert
- Elite

Colour bands indicate equivalent overall difficulty across different climbing types taking account of protection and environment. More at **rockfax.com**

Sport Grade	British Trad Grade (for well protected routes)	UIAA	USA	Norway	Au
1	Mod Moderate	I	5.1	3	4
2	Diff Difficult	II	5.2		6
2+	VDiff Very Difficult	III	5.3	4	
3a		III+	5.4		8
3b	HVD Hard Very Difficult	IV-		4+	10
3c	Sev Severe	IV	5.5		12
4a	HS Hard Severe	IV+	5.6	5-	
4b	VS Very Severe (UK tech 4a / UK tech 4c)	V-	5.7	5	14
4c		V	5.8		15
5a	HVS Hard Very Severe (4c / 5b)	V+		5+	16
5b		VI-	5.9		17
5c	E1 (5a / 5c)	VI	5.10a	6-	18
6a	E2 (5b / 6a)	VI+	5.10b	6	19
6a+		VII-			20
6b	E3 (5c / 6a)	VII	5.10c	6+	21
6b+			5.10d, 5.11a	7-	22
6c	E4 (6a / 6b)	VII+	5.11b		23
6c+		VIII-	5.11c	7	24
7a	E5 (6a / 6c)	VIII	5.11d	7+	25
7a+		VIII+	5.12a		
7b	E6 (6b / 6c)		5.12b	8-	26
7b+		IX-	5.12c	8	27
7c		IX	5.12d	8+	28
7c+	E7 (6c / 7a)	IX+	5.13a		29
8a	E8 (6c / 7a)		5.13b	9-	30
8a+		X-	5.13c	9	31
8b	E9 (7a / 7b)	X	5.13d		32
8b+		X+	5.14a	9+	33
8c	E10 (7a / 7b)	XI-	5.14b	10-	34
8c+		XI	5.14c		
9a	E11 (7a / 7b)		5.14d	10	35
9a+		XI+	5.15a	10+	36
9b		XII-	5.15b		37
9b+		XII	5.15c	11-	38

Free poster from Rockfax.com © Rockfax 2000, 2002, 2008, 2014, 2016, 2020

Graphic courtesy of Rockfax.

Vaughan, Michael

Born: 29th October 1974

Education: Silverdale

Michael Vaughan moved to Sheffield from Manchester when he was 9 years old. It was while he was at secondary school that he was talent spotted by the Yorkshire side for whom he went on to play for his entire career, from 1993 – 2009.

Vaughan played his first test match in 1999, becoming the 600th player to represent England in test cricket. He went on to captain the team from 2003 – 08, during which time England won 26 test matches (a record during a single captaincy).

Victory over Australia in the Ashes in 2005 was the highlight of his captaincy – this was the first Ashes win for England since 1987. That year, the England cricket team won the *Sports Personality Team of the Year Award*, Vaughan was awarded an honorary doctorate from Sheffield Hallam University, given the Freedom of the City of Sheffield and made an OBE. He was inducted into the Sheffield Walk of Fame in 2009.

Career Statistics

	Test Matches	One Day Internationals	First Class Cricket	Limited Overs
Matches	82	86	268	196
Runs scored	5,716	1,982	16,295	5,256
Average	41.44	27.15	36.95	30.03
Centuries	18	0	42	3
Fifties	18	16	68	30
Top Score	197	90*	197	125*
Balls bowled	978	796	9,342	2,585
Wickets	6	16	114	62
Bowling Average	93.50	40.56	46.00	31.53
Catches	44	25	118	63

Vickers (1828-2003)

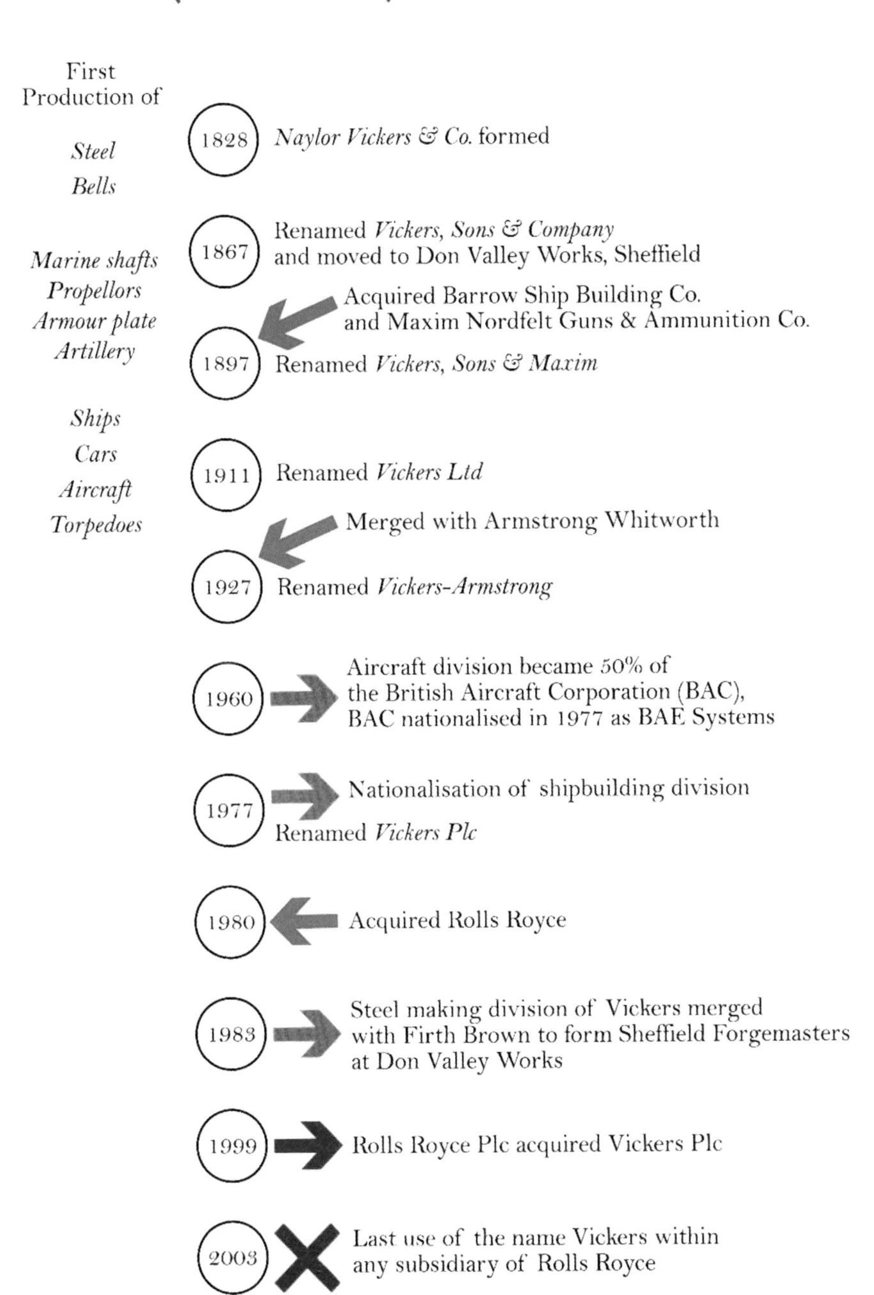

Villains

Frank Fearn (d.1782): Clubbed a local man to death on his way to High Bradfield. Following his hanging, Fearn's body was hung in a gibbet on Loxley Common until the bones fell through the gibbet fifteen years later!

Spence Broughton (1746-1792): Highwayman, arrested and then executed after his attack on the Rotherham & Sheffield Mail. Broughton's body was returned to the crime scene on Attercliffe Common and hung in a gibbet for 36 years. The address of Attercliffe's Noose & Gibbet pub is Broughton Lane.

Mary Thorpe (d.1800): Only female criminal from Sheffield recorded as being executed – hanged for the murder of a child born out of wedlock.

Charles Peace (1832-1879): Notorious burglar and member of the Guttapercha Gang in Sheffield, Peace committed two murders (one of which was of a policeman) and was eventually hanged in Armley Gaol.

George Mooney: Leader of the infamous Mooney Gang that operated in Sheffield in the years immediately preceding and following the First World War. Mooney made his money running illegal pitch and toss games on Skye Edge, taking advantage of the gambling epidemic that arose as a result of munitions workers earning higher wages during the war years.

Sam Garvin: A seasoned criminal who was second to George Mooney before forming his own rival gang in order to increase his share of takings from gang activity. The Park Brigade and the Mooney Gang were fierce rival gangs from 1923-25, earning Sheffield the nickname 'Little Chicago'.

Lawrence & Wilfred Fowler (d.1925): Both hanged for the murder of war veteran William Plommer.

William Smedley: Last Sheffield resident to be executed for their crime (7th March 1947).

Bernard Hugh Walden: Last criminal given death penalty by Sheffield Assizes (executed 14th August 1959), in this case for a double murder in Rotherham.

Warming

Average monthly temperature in Sheffield since 1955 is shown below.

The data shows a large range of average temperatures in each month – for example January, February, March, April, November and December have all experienced an average temperature of 6°C. The data also seems to suggest that Sheffield hasn't escaped global warming.

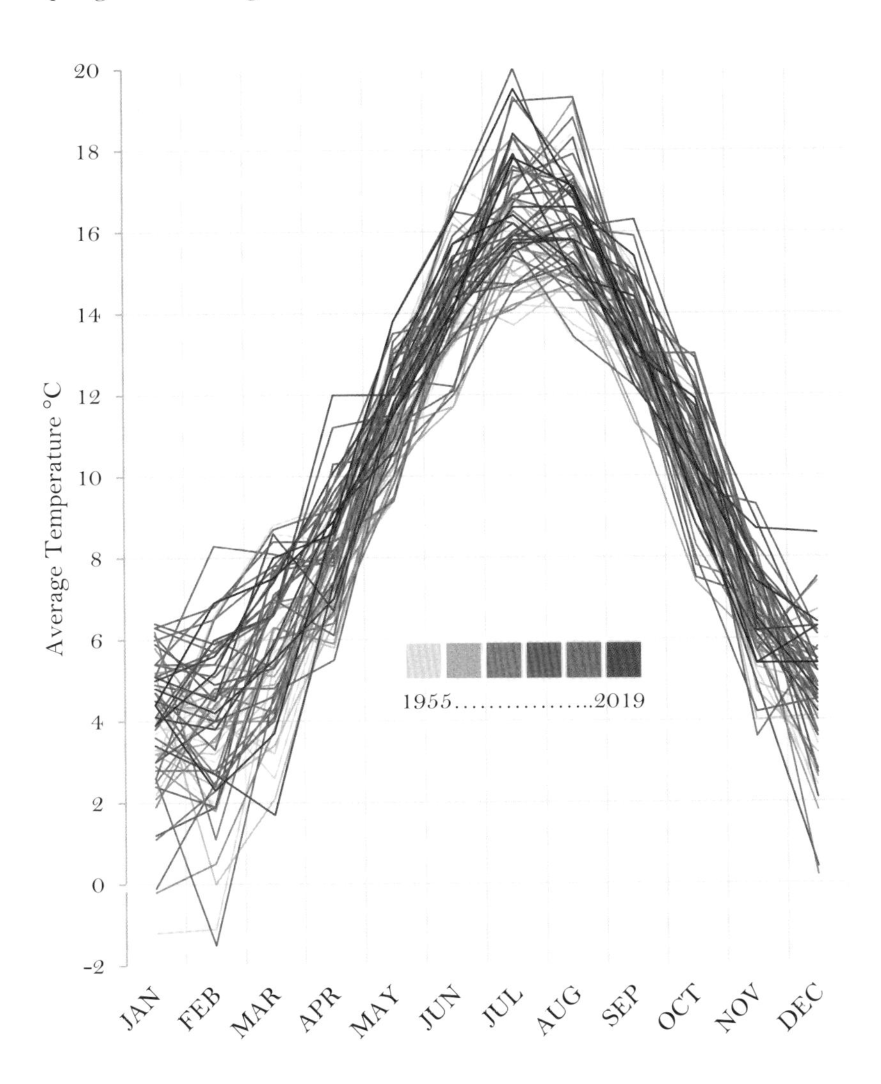

Waterpower

Sheffield's rise to an industrial powerhouse is due to a variety of factors, not least its abundance of steep, fast-flowing rivers that were able to provide power to a large number of industrial processes, from milling corn and paper, to grinding cutlery, to hammering and rolling metal.

The mills, forges, ponds, tilts and wheels of the Loxley, Porter, Rivelin and Sheaf are the best documented, but the Don and Car Brook also played their part powering Sheffield's industry. A walk of a just a couple of miles along pretty much any of Sheffield's rivers will take you past numerous remnants (still very visible) of this important aspect of Sheffield's industrial history.

River Loxley (Low Bradfield to confluence with the Don)

- Low Bradfield Corn Mill
- Damflask Corn Mill (submerged)
- Damflask Paper Mill (submerged)
- Stacey Wheel
- Storrs Bridge Forge & Wheel
- Loxley Old Wheel
- Rowell Bridge Wheel
- Olive Wheel/Olive Paper Mill
- Cliffe Wheel
- Low Matlock Wheel
- Lower Cliff Wheel
- Carr Wheel
- Green Wheel
- Glass Tilt
- Broadhead Wheel
- Scythe Wheel
- Wisewood Forge and Rolling Mill
- Malin Bridge Corn Mill
- Turner Wheel/La Plata Works
- Limbrick Wheels
- Upper Owlerton Wheel
- Nether Owlerton Wheel
- Owlerton Mill
- Birley Meadows Works
- Upper Slack Wheel
- Nether Slack Wheel

Porter Brook (Fulwood to confluence with the River Sheaf)

- Fulwood Cornmill
- Forge Dam
- Wiremill Dam
- Nether Wheel
- Shepherd Wheel
- Ibbotson's Wheel
- Nether Spurgear Wheel
- Second Endcliffe Wheel
- Holme Wheel
- First Endcliffe Wheel
- Upper Lescar Wheel
- Nether Lescar Wheel Dam
- Porter Works Dam
- Sharrow Mills
- Stalker Wheel
- Sharrow Forge
- Broomhall Cornmill
- Bennett's Wheel
- Leadmill Dam (Marriott's Wheel)
- Ponds Lane Dam

River Rivelin (Rivelin Dams to confluence with the River Loxley)

- Uppermost Mill
- Rivelin Corn Mill
- Upper Coppice Wheel
- Second Coppice Wheel
- Third Coppice Wheel
- Frank Wheel
- Wolf Wheel
- Swallow Wheel
- Plonk Wheel
- Hind Wheel
- Upper Cut Wheel
- Nether Cut Wheel
- Little London Wheel
- Holme Head Wheel
- Roscoe Wheel
- New Dam
- Spooners Wheel
- Hollins Bridge Mill
- Walkley Bank Tilt
- Mousehole Forge
- Grogram Wheel

River Sheaf and Tributaries

- Totley Forge
- Old Hay
- Upper Mill
- Nether Mill
- Totley Rolling Mill
- Upper Wheel
- Bradway Mill
- Walk Mill
- Whirlow Wheel (Limb Brook)
- Ryecroft Mill (Limb Brook)
- Abbeydale Works (Industrial Hamlet)
- Hutcliffe Wheel
- Bartin Wheel
- Ecclesall Mill
- Moscar Wheel
- Norton Hammer
- Smithy Wood
- Little London Wheel

Watery Street

Crookes Valley Stream ran as open waterway ran down the centre of Watery Lane until the 1850s, as part of the system of rivers and streams that ran from the network of reservoirs built on Crookesmoor down to the river Don. Today the stream is covered over. There is a manhole cover at the bottom of the Ponderosa where you can still hear the Crookes Valley Stream making its underground way downhill.

Weather Records

Sheffield's most extreme weather since 1st Jan 2003:

Highest temperature	35.2 °C	29th June 2019
Lowest temperature	-8.9 °C	21st December 2010
Lowest temperature with wind chill	-13.7 °C	28th February 2018
Highest minimum temperature	18.3 °C	24th July 2019
Lowest maximum temperature	-4.8 °C	28th November 2010
Maximum daily range	18.9 °C	24th June 2018
Minimum daily range	0.0 °C	14th October 2014
Highest rain rate	1646mm/hr	27th November 2010
Highest hourly rainfall	27mm	2nd July 2006
Highest daily rainfall*	79mm	7th November 2019
Highest monthly rainfall	245mm	June 2007
Longest wet period	36 days	Ending 2nd February 2014
Longest dry period	23 days	Ending 12th July 2018
Highest wind gust	83mph	20th January 2005
Highest daily wind speed average	55mph	13th September 2017
Highest recorded pressure	1051.98mb	16th February 2008
Lowest recorded pressure	962.96mb	15th February 2014

*Weston Park recorded a higher daily rainfall of 119mm on 15th July 1973.

Typical weather:

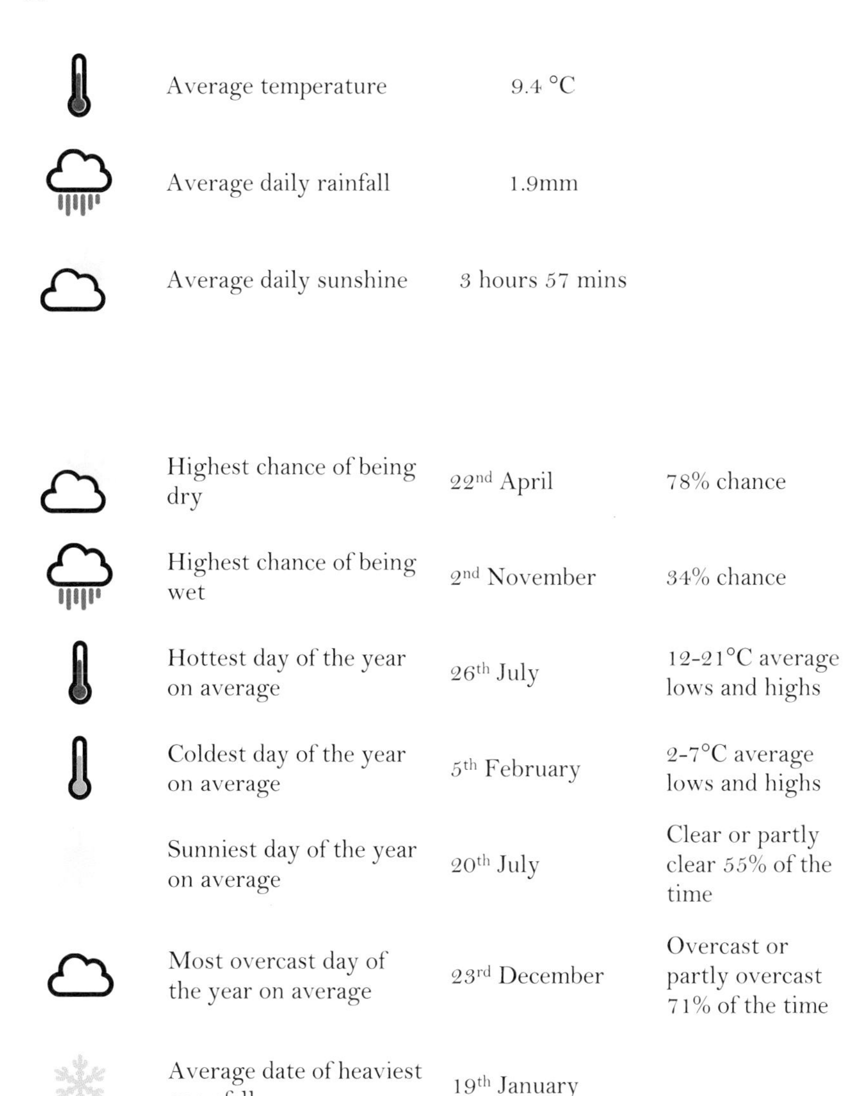

	Average temperature	9.4 °C	
	Average daily rainfall	1.9mm	
	Average daily sunshine	3 hours 57 mins	
	Highest chance of being dry	22nd April	78% chance
	Highest chance of being wet	2nd November	34% chance
	Hottest day of the year on average	26th July	12-21°C average lows and highs
	Coldest day of the year on average	5th February	2-7°C average lows and highs
	Sunniest day of the year on average	20th July	Clear or partly clear 55% of the time
	Most overcast day of the year on average	23rd December	Overcast or partly overcast 71% of the time
	Average date of heaviest snowfall	19th January	

What's in a Name

While the meanings of some of Sheffield's place names have been lost or can only be guessed at, the derivation of most can be attributed to either Anglo-Saxon or Norse origin. The Viking invasion and resulting period of Danelaw occurred after the Anglo-Saxon occupation of the area, and before the Norman invasion. All the place names translate as descriptions of the landscape or ownership.

Anglo Saxon

Arbourthorne	Shelter formed by trees
Attercliffe	Village by the cliff
Beighton	Farmstead by a stream
Birley	Cottage in the forest clearing
Brightside	Brik's ploughed land
Burngreave	A stream in a grove
Carbrook	A stream running through a water meadow
Carterknowle	Carter's hill
Darnall	Secluded piece of land
Dore	Door or gateway (into the Kingdom of Mercia)
Ecclesall	Witches hill
Endcliffe	Elf bank
Fulwood	Marshy woodland
Gleadless	Bright clearing/clearing frequented by kites
Grenoside	Quarried hillside
Handsworth	Enclosed homestead belonging to Hand
Hangingwater	Sloping field by the stream
Heeley	A high wood clearing
Longley	Long clearing
Loxley	Lynx glade
Meersbrook	Boundary brook (between Mercia & Northumbria)
Norton	North farmstead
Sheffield	Clearing by the Sheaf
Shirecliffe	Bright, steep hillside
Shiregreen	Bright meadowland
Stannington	Stoney farmstead
Tinsley	Field of Council
Totley	Watching or spying place
Wadsley	Wadde's forest clearing
Walkley	Walca's forest clearing
Wharncliffe	Quern (grinding stone) cliff
Woodseats	Fold in a wood

Norse

❦ Bell Hagg	Fire common
❦ Crookes	Nook, or corner of land
❦ Grimesthorpe	Grim's outlying farm
❦ Hackenthorpe	Hachen's outlying farm
❦ High Storrs	Brushwood area on a hill
❦ Jordanthorpe	Jordain's outlying farm
❦ Osgathorpe	Osga's outlying farm
❦ Ranmoor	Edge of the Moor
❦ Upperthorpe	Coopers (anglo saxon) outlying farm

Others

- Banner Cross – possibly 'cross of prayers.'
- Beauchief – beautiful headland, so named by the Norman monks who built the abbey.
- Frecheville – family name.
- Halfway – named after the Halfway House pub (since demolished)
- Hillsborough - named after Hillsborough House (now Hillsborough Library) that was built by Thomas Steade in 1779. Hillsborough House was named in honour of the Earl of Hillsborough who resided in County Down, Ireland. Hillsborough park, stadium and arena were all part of the estate.
- Stocksbridge – named after Thomas Stocks who built a bridge over the river in the 18th Century.

Anyone's guess

- Malin Bridge
    1. Bridge built by local resident Malin Stacie?
    2. Bridge by a mill?
    3. From the Old English *mellun* meaning worn, smooth stones on the bed of a river?

- Hallam
    1. 'On the rocks'?
    2. Derived from Norse *hallr* meaning hill, bank or slope?
    3. Derived from Old English *heall* meaning hall or manor?
    4. Derived from Old English *halgh* meaning land by a border?

White, Walter

What a beautiful place Sheffield would be, if Sheffield were not there!

A month in Yorkshire (1861).

Woods, Clinton

Born: 1st May 1972

Woods took part in amateur boxing until the age of 15 when he left school, quit boxing and spent a number of years as a brick layer, getting into trouble for fighting in the pubs at weekends. It was his mother's influence that got him back in the gym and he was quickly talent spotted and signed up as a professional. He fought 48 professional bouts between 1994 and 2009, winning 42, along with an enviable collection of titles. Exactly half of Woods' professional fights took place in a variety of venues in and around Sheffield.

Titles Held

Commonwealth Super - Middleweight	1997 – 98
British Light – Heavyweight	1999 – 00
European Light – Heavyweight	1999 – 01
Commonwealth Light – Heavyweight	1999 – 01
IBF Light - Heavyweight	2005 – 08

Clinton Woods was inducted into the Sheffield Walk of Fame in 2010. He has also been commemorated by one of three steel statues at a 'portrait bench' on the Trans-Pennine Trail. The bench concerned is between Halfway and Killamarsh. Today, Woods runs a boxing fitness gym in Westfield.

Woodland
New Hall Wood
Pot House Wood
Knoll Top
Fox Glen
Wharncliffe Woods
Westwood Country Park
Westwood Bottom
Thorncliffe Wood
Charlton Brook
Chapeltown Park Wood
Foxfield Spring
Hesley Wood
Smithy Wood
Stainery Clough
Oaken Bank
Ronksley Wood
Allas Wood
Allas Triangle
Rushey Wood
Yew Tree Wood
Sheffield District R'voir Woodlands
More Dam Hall
Wantley Dragon Wood
Bitholmes Wood
Greno Woods
Wigtwizzle Wood
Poggs Wood
Horse/ Foxhill
More Hall Plantation
Firth Wood
More Hall Wood
Dwarriden Lane
Raynor Clough
Peak Park
Glen Howe Wood
Wheata Woods
The Coppice
New Close Wood
Hey Bank
Catholes Wood
White Lee Moor Wood
Agden Side
Colley Park Wood
Woolley Wood
Eleven Acre Plantation
Windy Bank Wood
Rocher/ Oaking Bank
Birks Wood
Stubbing House Lane
Firth Park
Hinde Common
Wincobank
Thompson House Plantation
Scraith Wood
Doe House Wood
Mill Lea Wood
Ughill Wood
Banks Plantation
Busk Meadow
Roe Wood
Little Roe Wood
Wragg House Plantation
Hoyles Farm
Beacon Wood
Loxley Common
Parkwood Springs
Acorn Hill/ Little Matlock
Oaks Piece
Walkley Bank Wood
Rivelin Valley
Roscoe Plantation
Bole Hill Wood
Bole Hill Road Wood
Salmon Pastures
Tinsley Park
Bowden Housteads
Rivelin Glen 2
Crookesmoor Wood
Crookes Valley Park Wood
<1 hectare
Rivelin Glen 1
Millstone Edge Rough
Reaps Wood
Clough Fields
Clay Wood
Jervis Lum
Carbrook Ravine
1+ hectares
Rivelin Glen 3
Sunnybank
Fox Hagg
Blackbrook Wood
Porter Valley Woodlands
Buck Wood
Woodhouse Mill Woods
5+ hectares
Wyming Brook
Meersbrook Bank Wood
Brincliffe Edge
10+ hectares
Redmires Plantation
Brown Edge Plantation
Bole Hill Plantation
Hang Bank/Carr/ Coneygree Woods
Lee Hall Wood
Wickfield Plantation
Black Bank & Shirtcliffe Valley
20+ hectares
Barbers Field
Marriot Wood
Hutcliffe Wood
Rollestone Wood
Birley Spa Wood
Lady Cannings Plantation
Ecclesall Wood
Herdings Wood
Herdings Plantation
Westfield Plantation
50+ hectares
Lady Spring
Graves Park
Chancet Wood
Stonely Wood
Burbage Plantation
Park Bank Wood
Mosborough Old Plantation
100+ hectares
Bushey Wood
Poynton Wood
Gulleys Wood
Little Wood Bank
Parkwood Springs Wood
Akley Bank
Gillfield Wood
Clay Wood

World Records

World records broken in Sheffield (**S**), by a Sheffield individual (🚹) or by a Sheffield organisation (🚹🚹🚹) are listed below.

Category	Held by	Record	When	
Oldest football club	Sheffield FC	Founded 1857	1857	🚹🚹🚹
Oldest football ground	Sandygate (Hallam FC)	26 Dec 1860.	1860	🚹🚹🚹
Oldest Association Football trophy	Youdan Cup, which was awarded for Sheffield rules football	1867	1867	🚹🚹🚹
Heaviest goalkeeper (football)	Henry `Fatty' Foulke	141kg *22st 3lb*	1907	🚹
The fastest shot on goal during an English Premier League game	David Hirst (Sheff Weds)	183 km/h (114 mph)	1996	🚹
Fastest 147 break in snooker	Ronnie O'Sullivan	5 minutes 8 seconds	1997	**S**
Most UK airfields visited within 24 hours by helicopter	Richard Craske and Zoë Smith	102	2002	**S**
Fastest time to arrange a shuffled deck of cards	Zdenek Bradac	36.16s	2008	**S**
Fastest time to complete a skydive on 6 continents	Martin Downs	8 days 7 hours 30 minutes	2008	🚹
Fastest time to make a litre of ice cream	Andrew Ross	10.34s	2010	**S**
Furthest wall climbing dyno move	Skyler Weekes	2.85 m (9.35 ft)	2010	**S**
Largest spacehopper race	Yorkshire Cancer Research	771 participants	2010	**S**

Smallest trade union	Sheffield Wool Shear Workers Union	9 members	2011	
Most people tossing pancakes simultaneously	University of Sheffield	890	2012	
Most players to play in a continuous 5-a-side football exhibition match	BBC Radio Five Live and BBC Radio Sheffield	464	2012	S
Fastest 100 x100m swim relay	Swim4Leukemia	1 hour 29 minutes 3 seconds	2014	S
Farthest basketball slam dunk from a trampoline	Jordan Ramos	10.05m	2015	S
Most people motion-captured in real-time	B-Boy dance crews from Sheffield and Wolverhampton	19	2015	
Largest football shaped cake	Sheffield Wednesday	285kg	2017	
Most hula hoop rotations on the leg in the arabesque position in one minute	Ashlee Male	203	2017	
Most burpees in one minute (female)	Leigh Scott	40	2018	

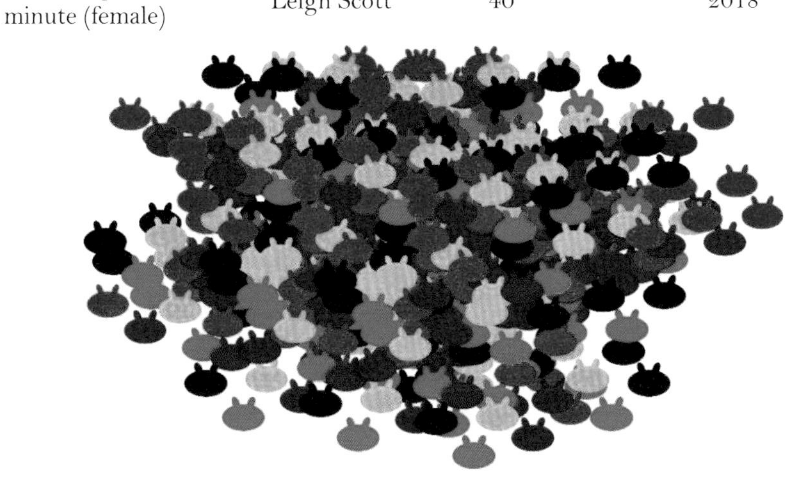

World War I

The Commonwealth War Graves Commission records 5754 men from Sheffield who lost their lives fighting in World War I. The true figure is undoubtedly higher, all lives taken too early, each one a tragedy for those left behind. Memorials across the city remember these sacrifices and Sheffield honours the contribution these and others have made for our country every Remembrance Sunday.

Each of these 5754 men are represented by a cross on the facing page. The first cross represents Engine Room Artificer 4th Class Ernest Fieldhouse who died on 6th August 1914. The final cross represents Private John Hayward who died of injuries sustained in the war on 31st August 1921.

The bloodiest day of the war was 1st July 2016, the first day of the Battle of the Somme. Sheffield lost 271 men on this day, most from the Sheffield 'Pals' Battalion – they are all listed below and represented by red crosses on the facing page.

To list all 5754 men would take 59 pages.

Abel, Samuel
Allemby, Harold
Alton, Walter
Andrews, John
Angus, G
Appleby, F O
Aspland, Sydney
Atkinson, Cyril
Atkinson, Freeman
Atkinson, Stanley
Bacon, Alfred
Bagshaw, William
Baines, Colin
Baldwin, Thomas
Barker, S
Barker, Willis
Barnlsey, Frank
Barrott, John
Barton, J A
Baxter, John
Beadle, G E
Beal, Arnold
Beaumont, Douglas
Bedford, Seaton
Bennet, Joseph
Biggin, Robert
Birley, Harry
Birtles, Henry
Black, Scott
Bradbury, William
Brader, Joseph
Braham, George
Brammer, Archie
Bratley, John
Briggs, Elijah
Briggs, Reuben
Broadhead, Charles
Brooke, John
Brouse, William
Brown, Frank
Brown, Frank
Brown, Stanley
Brunton, Harold
Bull, Albert
Burgon, John
Butcher, Herbert
Cain, Edward
Carding-Wells, John
Casey, Alpheaus
Cecil, James
Christian, A
Clark, William
Clifton, Edgar
Colley, Joseph
Colley, William
Cooper, John
Cooper, Randall
Copley, Frank
Copplest, John
Cowley, John
Culf, Frederick
Davenport, Laurence

†††††††† †††††††† †††††††† †††††††††††††††† †††††††††††††††† †††††††† †††††††† ††††††††
†††††††† †††††††† †††††††† †††††††††††††††† †††††††††††††††† †††††††† †††††††† ††††††††
†††††††† †††††††† †††††††† †††††††††††††††† †††††††††††††††† †††††††† †††††††† ††††††††
†††††††† †††††††† †††††††† †††††††††††††††† †††††††††††††††† †††††††† †††††††† ††††††††
†††††††† †††††††† †††††††† †††††††††††††††† †††††††††††††††† †††††††† †††††††† ††††††††
†††††††† †††††††† †††††††† †††††††††††††††† †††††††††††††††† †††††††† †††††††† ††††††††
†††††††† †††††††† †††††††† †††††††††††††††† †††††††††††††††† †††††††† †††††††† ††††††††
†††††††† †††††††† †††††††† †††††††††††††††† †††††††††††††††† †††††††† †††††††† ††††††††
†††††††† †††††††† †††††††† †††††††††††††††† †††††††††††††††† †††††††† †††††††† ††††††††
†††††††† †††††††† †††††††† †††††††††††††††† †††††††††††††††† †††††††† †††††††† ††††††††
†††††††† †††††††† †††††††† †††††††††††††††† †††††††††††††††† †††††††† †††††††† ††††††††
†††††††† †††††††† †††††††† †††††††††††††††† †††††††††††††††† †††††††† †††††††† ††††††††
†††††††† †††††††† †††††††† †††††††††††††††† †††††††††††††††† †††††††† †††††††† ††††††††
†††††††† †††††††† †††††††† †††††††††††††††† †††††††††††††††† †††††††† †††††††† ††††††††
†††††††† †††††††† †††††††† †††††††††††††††† †††††††††††††††† †††††††† †††††††† ††††††††
†††††††† †††††††† †††††††† †††††††††††††††† †††††††††††††††† †††††††† †††††††† ††††††††
†††††††† †††††††† †††††††† †††††††††††††††† †††††††††††††††† †††††††† †††††††† ††††††††
†††††††† †††††††† †††††††† †††††††††††††††† †††††††††††††††† †††††††† †††††††† ††††††††
†††††††† †††††††† †††††††† †††††††††††††††† †††††††††††††††† †††††††† †††††††† ††††††††
†††††††† †††††††† †††††††† †††††††††††††††† †††††††††††††††† †††††††† †††††††† ††††††††
†††††††† †††††††† †††††††† †††††††††††††††† †††††††††††††††† †††††††† †††††††† ††††††††
†††††††† †††††††† †††††††† †††††††††††††††† †††††††††††††††† †††††††† †††††††† ††††††††
†††††††† †††††††† †††††††† †††††††††††††††† †††††††††††††††† †††††††† †††††††† ††††††††
†††††††† †††††††† †††††††† †††††††††††††††† †††††††††††††††† †††††††† †††††††† ††††††††
†††††††† †††††††† †††††††† †††††††††††††††† †††††††††††††††† †††††††† †††††††† ††††††††
†††††††† †††††††† †††††††† †††††††††††††††† †††††††††††††††† †††††††† †††††††† ††††††††
†††††††† †††††††† †††††††† †††††††††††††††† †††††††††††††††† †††††††† †††††††† ††††††††
†††††††† †††††††† †††††††† †††††††††††††††† †††††††††††††††† †††††††† †††††††† ††††††††
†††††††† †††††††† †††††††† †††††††††††††††† †††††††††††††††† †††††††† †††††††† ††††††††
†††††††† †††††††† †††††††† †††††††††††††††† †††††††††††††††† †††††††† †††††††† ††††††††
†††††††† †††††††† †††††††† †††††††††††††††† †††††††††††††††† †††††††† †††††††† ††††††††
†††††††† †††††††† †††††††† †††††††††††††††† †††††††††††††††† †††††††† †††††††† ††††††††
†††††††† †††††††† †††††††† †††††††††††††††† †††††††††††††††† †††††††† †††††††† ††††††††
†††††††† †††††††† †††††††† †††††††††††††††† †††††††††††††††† †††††††† †††††††† ††††††††
†††††††† †††††††† †††††††† †††††††††††††††† †††††††††††††††† †††††††† †††††††† ††††††††
†††††††† †††††††† †††††††† †††††††††††††††† †††††††††††††††† †††††††† †††††††† ††††††††
†††††††† †††††††† †††††††† †††††††††††††††† †††††††††††††††† †††††††† †††††††† ††††††††
†††††††† †††††††† †††††††† †††††††††††††††† †††††††††††††††† †††††††† †††††††† ††††††††
†††††††† †††††††† †††††††† †††††††††††††††† †††††††††††††††† †††††††† †††††††† ††††††††
†††††††† †††††††† †††††††† †††††††††††††††† †††††††††††††††† †††††††† †††††††† ††††††††
†††††††† †††††††† †††††††† †††††††††††††††† †††††††††††††††† †††††††† †††††††† ††††††††
†††††††† †††††††† †††††††† †††††††††††††††† †††††††††††††††† †††††††† †††††††† ††††††††
†††††††† †††††††† †††††††† †††††††††††††††† †††††††††††††††† †††††††† †††††††† ††††††††
†††††††† †††††††† †††††††† †††††††††††††††† †††††††††††††††† †††††††† †††††††† ††††††††
†††††††† †††††††† †††††††† †††††††††††††††† †††††††††††††††† †††††††† †††††††† ††††††††
†††††††† †††††††† †††††††† †††††††††††††††† †††††††††††††††† †††††††† †††††††† ††††††††
†††††††† †††††††† †††††††† †††††††††††††††† †††††††††††††††† †††††††† †††††††† ††††††††
†††††††† †††††††† †††††††† †††††††††††††††† †††††††††††††††† †††††††† †††††††† ††††††††
†††††††† †††††††† †††††††† †††††††††††††††† †††††††††††††††† †††††††† †††††††† ††††††††
†††††††† †††††††† †††††††† †††††††††††††††† †††††††††††††††† †††††††† †††††††† ††††††††
†††††††† †††††††† †††††††† †††††††††††††††† †††††††††††††††† †††††††† †††††††† ††††††††
†††††††† †††††††† †††††††† †††††††††††††††† †††††††††††††††† †††††††† †††††††† ††††††††
†††††††† †††††††† †††††††† †††††††††††††††† †††††††††††††††† †††††††† †††††††† ††††††††
†††††††† †††††††† †††††††† †††††††††††††††† †††††††††††††††† †††††††† †††††††† ††††††††
†††††††† †††††††† †††††††† †††††††††††††††† †††††††††††††††† †††††††† †††††††† ††††††††
†††††††† †††††††† †††††††† †††††††††††††††† †††††††††††††††† †††††††† †††††††† ††††††††
†††††††† †††††††† †††††††† †††††††††††††††† †††††††††††††††† †††††††† †††††††† ††††††††
†††††††† †††††††† †††††††† †††††††††††††††† †††††††††††††††† †††††††† †††††††† ††††††††
†††††††† †††††††† †††††††† †††††††††††††††† †††††††††††††††† †††††††† †††††††† ††††††††
†††††††† †††††††† †††††††† †††††††††††††††† †††††††††††††††† †††††††† †††††††† ††††††††
†††††††† †††††††† †††††††† †††††††††††††††† †††††††††††††††† †††††††† †††††††† ††††††††
†††††††† †††††††† †††††††† †††††††††††††††† †††††††††††††††† †††††††† †††††††† ††††††††
†††††††† †††††††† †††††††† †††††††††††††††† †††††††††††††††† †††††††† †††††††† ††††††††
†††††††† †††††††† †††††††† †††††††††††††††† †††††††††††††††† †††††††† †††††††† ††††††††
†††††††† †††††††† †††††††† †††††††††††††††† †††††††††††††††† †††††††† †††††††† ††††††††
†††††††† †††††††† †††††††† †††††††††††††††† †††††††††††††††† †††††††† †††††††† ††††††††
†††††††† †††††††† †††††††† †††††††††††††††† †††††††††††††††† †††††††† †††††††† ††††††††
†††††††† †††††††† †††††††† †††††††††††††††† †††††††††††††††† †††††††† †††††††† ††††††††
†††††††† †††††††† †††††††† †††††††††††††††† †††††††††††††††† †††††††† †††††††† ††††††††
†††††††† †††††††† †††††††† †††††††††††††††† †††††††††††††††† †††††††† †††††††† ††††††††
†††††††† †††††††† †††††††† †††††††††††††††† †††††††††††††††† †††††††† †††††††† ††††††††
†††††††† †††††††† †††††††† †††††††††††††††† †††††††††††††††† †††††††† †††††††† ††

Davis, Harold
Deeks, Henry
Deighton, Percy
Dent, Thomas
Devey, Rodney
Doherty, Richard
Doman, Herbert
Drakett, James
Edwards, Dan
Elliott, James
Ellis, Hubert
Erratt, Harry
Exton, Joseph
Findlay, Fred
Fletcher, Arthur
Fletcher, Wilfred
Forsdike, Harold
Fox, Albert
Franks, Alexander
Froggatt, Cuthbert
Furniss, Edward
Gambles, Thomas
Garlick, William
Gill, John
Gill, W
Goddard, William
Goodlad, Alfred
Greensmith, Arthur
Greenwood, Matthias
Gregory, Ernest
Gregory, Frances
Grove, Arthur
Gunstone, Franks
Gunstone, William
Hackett, Robert
Hadfield, Alfred
Hague, Harold
Hampton, Fred
Handley, Robert
Hanson, Fred
Harrison, Thomas
Harrison, William
Hartley, Frank
Hastings, G C
Haycock, Isaac
Haywood, Harry
Hearson, G
Hibberd, Howard
Hill, Tom
Himsworth, Albert
Hinchcliffe, James
Hinchcliffe, Rowland
Hind, E
Hobson, Frederic
Hogg, Alfred
Hollingworth, Harold
Hollis, Arthur
Horsfield, Ronald
Houldsworth, Thomas
Howard, Arthur
Howson, Walter
Hudson, Albert
Hudson, Ernest
Hurst, Henry
Hutchinson, Bernard
Inman, E
Jackson, Alfred
Jane, William
Jones, David
Kelk, John
Kettell, Charles
Kidder, C
Kipling, George
Knighton, James
Langford, Reuben
Laycock, Lawrence
Ledger, Joseph
Lee, Henry
Lee, Willis
Levick, Harry
Levick, Thomas
Lewis, Ernest
Lewis, Tom
Lindley, W
Linley, John
Lister, Reginald
Little, Ernest
Longford, Joseph
Loxley, William
MacLaurin, Edgar
Maleham, Stewart
Marsden, Samuel
Martin, Andrew
Mason, Cecil
Mather, Frederick
McClarence, A
McIver, Leonard
Meeke, William
Millin, Edward
Mills, George
Mincher, Alfred
Moulds, Harry
Mountain, Arthur
Murphy, William
Mutlow, Alfred
Nadin, J A
Neesham, Harry
Neill, Harry
Nettleton, John
Nichols, Frank
Norrise, H
Owne, Geoffrey
Parker, J W
Parkin, Charles
Parkin, Horace
Parsons, William
Pashley, Arthur

Perkin, George
Pickersgill, Harold
Pickles, John
Pinney, Henry
Platts, Colin
Platts, Ernest
Potter, Albert
Potter, Edward
Priest , C W
Priestly, Harry
Rhodes, George
Rhodes, Thomas
Richmond, Joseph
Rippon, H
Roberts, Alexander
Robinson, John
Roebuck, H
Rogerson, Fred
Rose, Albert
Sadler, Gordon
Saunders, Walter
Scothern, Frederic
Sellars, Joseph
Sellers, Roger
Sharpe, John
Shaw, Tom
Sheffield, Roger
Shiell, Alexander
Shuttleworth, Ernest
Simpson, Henry
Slater, Tom
Smalley, Robert
Smith, George
Smith, Oswald
Smout, William
Staniforth, Thomas
Stansfield, Charles
Steane, Charles
Steeples, Harry
Stevenson, John
Stiles, E
Storey, George
Swift, James
Swinscoe, Thomas
Tagg, Reginald
Taylor, Henry
Teasdale, Willis
Thomas, Arthur
Thompson, G E
Thompson, Walter
Thorpe, John
Tomasson, Herbert
Tonge, William
Townley, William
Trickett, Andrew
Turner, William
Tyas, Fred
Uttley, F
Wainwright,
Edmond
Wales, Walter
Walker, F
Walker, Herbert
Walker, John
Wall, Walter
Wall, Walter
Wardill, Charles
Wardill, George
Waterfall, Nelson
Webster, Albert
Webster, John
Webster, Joseph
Webster, Walter
Webster, William
Westran, A
Wharton, Henry
White, Ronald
Whittaker, Joseph
Whitworth, B
Whyles, Frederick
Wilcock, Noel
Wilkinson, Benjamin
Wilkinson, Thomas
Williams, William
Willis, John
Witherow, Joseph
Wood, Harry
Wood, Joseph
Wragg, Herbert
Wright, Albert
Wright, Joseph
Wright, Joseph
Wrigley, Joseph

Year

JAN
Make a New Years resolution - do a parkrun.
Watch *Britain's Strongest Man Competition.*
Shop the sales at Meadowhall.
Take in some Comedy at the Leadmill or Last Laugh Comedy Club
FEB
Treat someone to a meal at Joro's, Sheffield's only Michelin restaurant.
Go climbing indoors at Awesome Walls.
Discover a new game at the Treehouse Board Game Cafe.
Watch some live football.
MAR
Run 13.1 miles at the Sheffield Half Marathon
Attend the *Sheffield Adventure Film Festival.*
Be stimulated at the *Festival of Debate.*
Test your mettle at the *Magnificent Seven* cycle event.
APR
Watch the *Snooker World Championships.*
Take advantage of gravity at *Peaty's Steel City Downhill.*
Enjoy the first bluebells - go for a walk in the woods.
Take in some industrial heritage at Kelham Island Museum.
MAY
Give your taste buds a treat at the *Sheffield Food Festival.*
Find out what the *Algo Mech Festival* is all about.
Walk the Five Weirs.
Shop at the Moor Market.
JUN
Take in *Sheffield Doc Fest.*
Have fun at the Fair.
Discover new bits of Sheffield in the Round Sheffield Run.
Walk around a reservoir.

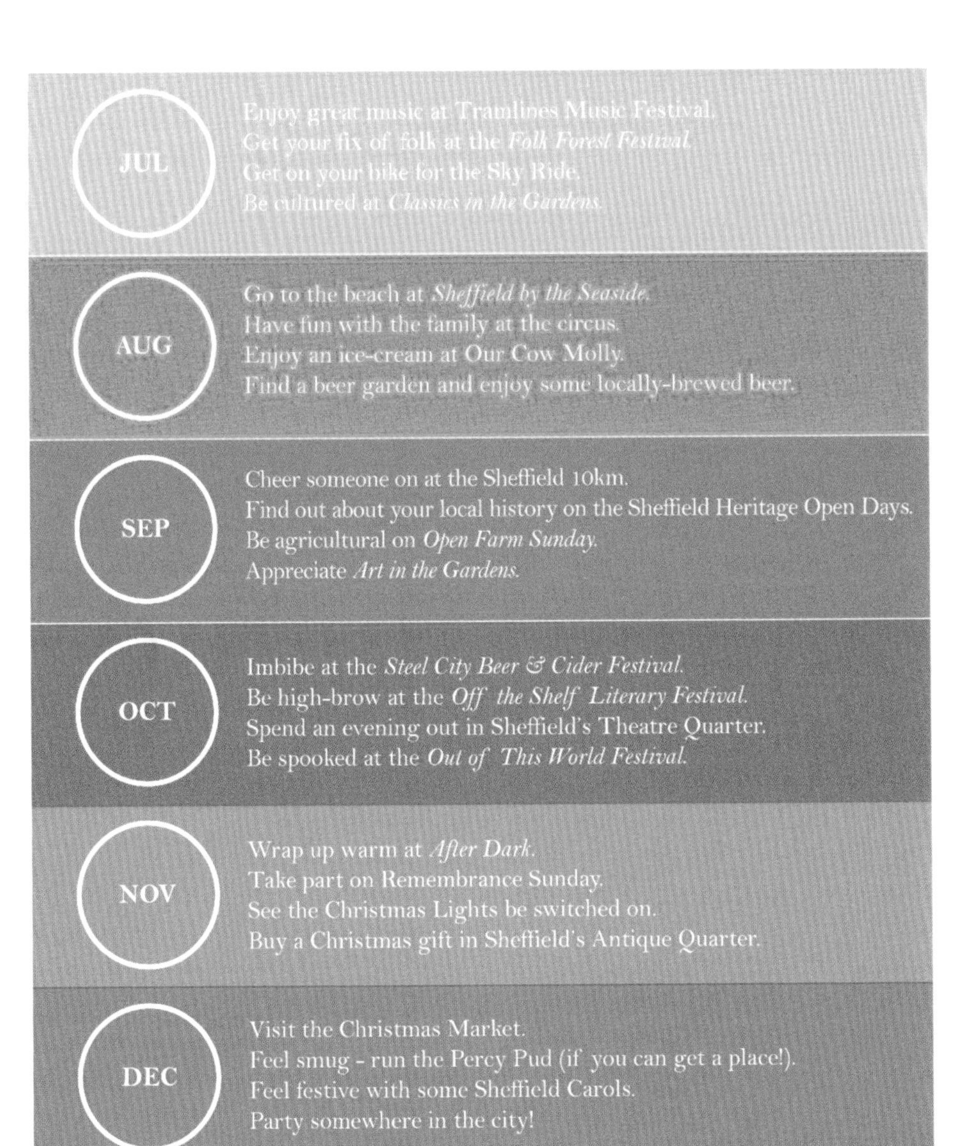
JUL
Enjoy great music at Tramlines Music Festival.
Get your fix of folk at the Folk Forest Festival.
Get on your bike for the Sky Ride.
Be cultured at Classics in the Gardens.
AUG
Go to the beach at Sheffield by the Seaside.
Have fun with the family at the circus.
Enjoy an ice-cream at Our Cow Molly.
Find a beer garden and enjoy some locally-brewed beer.
SEP
Cheer someone on at the Sheffield 10km.
Find out about your local history on the Sheffield Heritage Open Days.
Be agricultural on Open Farm Sunday.
Appreciate Art in the Gardens.
OCT
Imbibe at the Steel City Beer & Cider Festival.
Be high-brow at the Off the Shelf Literary Festival.
Spend an evening out in Sheffield's Theatre Quarter.
Be spooked at the Out of This World Festival.
NOV
Wrap up warm at After Dark.
Take part on Remembrance Sunday.
See the Christmas Lights be switched on.
Buy a Christmas gift in Sheffield's Antique Quarter.
DEC
Visit the Christmas Market.
Feel smug - run the Percy Pud (if you can get a place!).
Feel festive with some Sheffield Carols.
Party somewhere in the city!

Yellow Jersey

July 2014 saw the world's greatest bike race come to the world's greatest county when the Tour de France put on two spectacular days of racing on God's own roads and very definitely put Yorkshire on the global cycling map.

Stage 1 started in Leeds and, after an extensive detour around the Yorkshire Dales, finished in Harrogate.

Stage 2 started in York and, after covering 201km with 9 categorised climbs en route, finished in Sheffield. The sun shone and literally hundreds of thousands of spectators lined the roads to watch the peloton come through the Strines, High Bradfield, Oughtibridge and Grenoside before entering Sheffield and dealing with the infamous Cote de Jenkin Road, and then a final fast finish by Meadowhall. Drive the route today and you can still see messages for the riders (*va va Froome*) painted on the tarmac, yellow painted bicycles by the roads in improbable places and of course the Bank View Café sporting its fine polka dots.

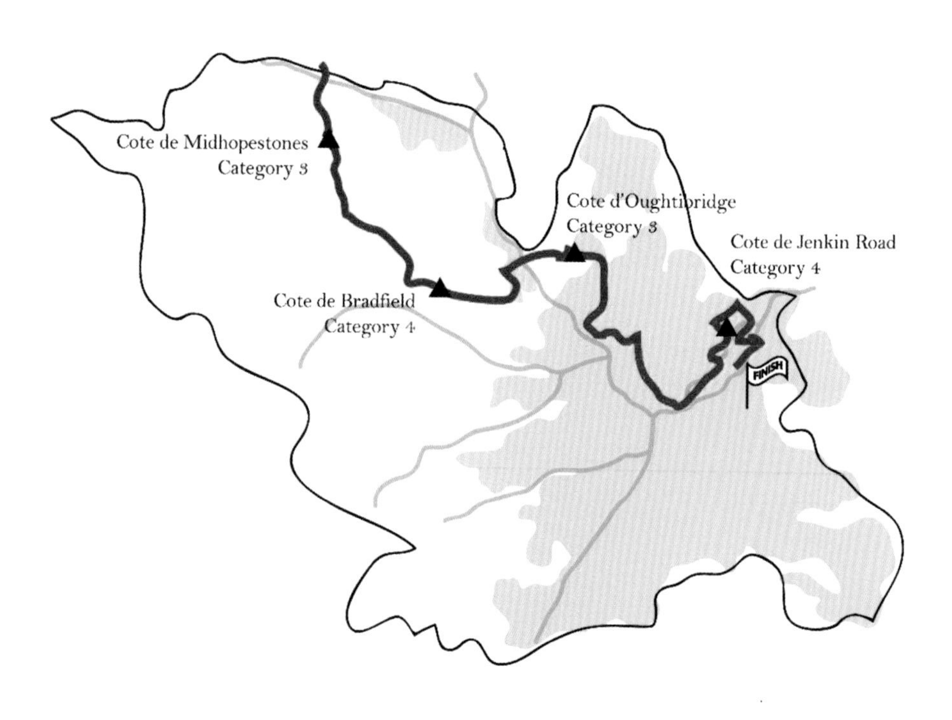

Stage 2 Results

Rider	Team	Time
Vincenzo Nibali	Astana	5h 08' 36"
Greg Van Avermaet	BMC	+2"
Michal Kwiatkowski	Omega Pharma	+2"
Peter Sagan	Cannondale	+2"
Tony Gallopin	Lotto-Belisol	+2"

General Classification after Stage 2

Rider	Team	Time
Vincenzo Nibali	Astana	9h 52' 43"
Peter Sagan	Cannondale	+2"
Greg Van Avermaet	BMC	+2"
Michael Albisini	Orica-GreenEDGE	+2"
Chris Froome	Sky	+2"

Yellow Jersey (Overall Lead)
Vincenzo Nibali Astana

Green Jersey (Sprint Points Leader)
Peter Sagan Cannondale

Polka Dot Jersey (King of the Mountains)
Cyril Lemoine Cofidis

White Jersey (Leader of the Young Rider Competition)
Romain Bardet A2GR

Zeppelin Raid

Air-raid sirens sounded 23 times in Sheffield during World War I. Fortunately 22 of these were false alarms with no loss of life or damage to property.

The exception was the night of 25th September 1916 when the sirens heralded the arrival of a single German Zeppelin arriving to the South East of the city. It circled clockwise and then moved towards the city centre over Fulwood and Ranmoor, before dropping a total of 36 bombs over Burngreave, Pitsmoor, Darnall and Tinsley and then heading back out over the North Sea. The Zeppelin was an enormous craft, 585 feet long with a top speed of 60mph. Bombs were dropped by hand, therefore explaining their general lack of accuracy – none of the bombs that fell on Sheffield hit their industrial targets.

Cloud cover restricted the ability of the city's air defences to respond. Defensive efforts were further hampered as the military officials in the city were all at a tea dance at the time. In fact, there were only two shots fired at the Zeppelin from an anti-aircraft gun at Shiregreen.

Almost all of the 29 victims were buried in Burngreave Cemetery. A plaque can be seen on Effingham Street by the former Baltic Works with the inscription *'Lest we Forget' on September 26th 1916 nine men, ten women and ten children were killed by a German air raid on Sheffield. One of the bombs fell close to this spot'.*

In September 1917, another Zeppelin craft dropped bombs (harmlessly as it turned out) near Rotherham. The explosions were heard in Sheffield.

Damage

29 killed, 19 injured

89 houses badly damaged, 150 with minor damage